MANIFEST YOUR POTENTIAL

in the

BAHÁ'Í FAITH

QUOTATIONS

A selection of passages from the
Bahá'í holy writings and other materials

THE WHYUNITE? SERIES
BOOKS AND VIDEOS

MANY PATHS TO THE BAHÁ'Í FAITH
How people from different faith experiences discover fulfillment in the Bahá'í Faith

QUOTATIONS FOR MANY PATHS TO THE BAHÁ'Í FAITH
Selected passages from the Bahá'í holy writings and other materials

FIRESIDE TALK FOR MANY PATHS TO THE BAHÁ'Í FAITH
A video presentation about the Bahá'í Faith by the author, Nathan Thomas

MANIFEST YOUR POTENTIAL IN THE BAHÁ'Í FAITH
How the beliefs, practices, and vision of the Bahá'í Faith can change your life

QUOTATIONS FOR MANIFESTING YOUR POTENTIAL IN THE BAHÁ'Í FAITH
Selected passages from the Bahá'í holy writings and other materials

FIRESIDE TALK FOR MANIFESTING YOUR POTENTIAL IN THE BAHÁ'Í FAITH
A video presentation about the Bahá'í Faith by the author, Nathan Thomas

MAKING A BETTER WORLD WITH THE BAHÁ'Í FAITH
How Bahá'ís are transforming our world into a more unified, prosperous, and spiritual home for all mankind

QUOTATIONS FOR MAKING A BETTER WORLD WITH THE BAHÁ'Í FAITH
Selected passages from the Bahá'í holy writings and other materials

FIRESIDE TALK FOR MAKING A BETTER WORLD WITH THE BAHÁ'Í FAITH
A video presentation about the Bahá'í Faith by the author, Nathan Thomas

PATHS TO THE BAHÁ'Í FAITH
A nine-part collection of video interviews of Bahá'ís from a variety of backgrounds

Learn more at http://www.whyunite.com

TABLE OF CONTENTS

PREFACE TO THE WHYUNITE? SERIES

A NEW WORLD RELIGION DEDICATED TO TRANSFORMING HUMANITY

The Bahá'í Faith is a world religion that brings teachings designed to help all of mankind while renewing the spiritual capacities of the human race. Founded by Bahá'u'lláh (meaning "the Glory of God" in Arabic) in the mid-nineteenth century, the goal of the Bahá'í Faith is to bring out the best in humanity. As Bahá'u'lláh wrote, through the teachings of this worldwide faith "every man will advance and develop until he attaineth the station at which he can manifest all the potential forces with which his inmost true self hath been endowed." (*Gleanings from the Writings of Bahá'u'lláh,* no. 27.5).

With practical teachings, a diverse global community, acceptance for of all the world's religions, and a message specifically designed to solve humanity's most pressing needs, the Bahá'í Faith brings a contemporary approach to religion that is unique among all the world's faiths. Bahá'u'lláh writes, "My object is none other than the betterment of the world and the tranquility of its peoples." (*Gleanings from the Writings of Bahá'u'lláh,* no. 131.2).

Today millions of people from every background have found this Faith through the individual investigation of truth. For them, it offers a compelling and fulfilling foundation for their spiritual experience. As

'Abdu'l-Bahá, the son and successor of Bahá'u'lláh said, "Man must walk in many paths and be subjected to various processes in his evolution upward." (*Promulgation of Universal Peace,* p. 295). Throughout all these paths we take in our lives, every person must judge for him or herself what is good and true for their own spiritual journey. For many, that process leads to the Bahá'í Faith.

AN INVITATION TO LEARN MORE WITH THE WHYUNITE? SERIES

The WhyUnite? Series is an individual initiative begun to produce compelling, unique, and practical content about the Bahá'í Faith. Our goal is to develop materials that educate, empower, and inspire people to follow their own path to the truth, to manifest their own potential as spiritual beings, and to make this world a better place in the process. To that end, we are dedicated to the continuous development of books, compilations, videos, and more to help people discover the spiritual richness, endless diversity, and wondrous wisdom offered to humanity through the Bahá'í Faith. Learn more about our work and get involved at www.whyunite.com.

INTRODUCTION TO QUOTATIONS FOR MANIFESTING YOUR POTENTIAL IN THE BAHÁ'Í FAITH

This book is designed to be a companion to the book *Manifest Your Potential in the Bahá'í Faith*, which provides an introduction to the Bahá'í Faith focused on its capacity to transform us into truly spiritual beings. Divided into three sections, the book discusses the beliefs that sustain us, the practices that empower us, and vision that inspires us in our faith. It covers:

- How people can find their own place in creating a better world
- The Bahá'í concept of God, religion, and spiritual development
- The Bahá'í path to fulfillment, happiness, and contentment
- How Bahá'ís deal with sins, forgiveness, tests, and difficulties in life
- How Bahá'í prayers, meditation, fasting, and laws help people grow spiritually
- How people can align their marriages and careers to serve mankind while they fulfill their destinies
- What the vision of Bahá'u'lláh is for the world and how it can inspire people to do more with their lives

ABOUT THE QUOTATIONS IN THIS BOOK

This book of quotations is intended to offer more direct insight into what the Bahá'í Faith directly says on the subjects covered in its companion book, *Manifest Your Potential in the Bahá'í Faith*. It includes many quotations from a wide variety of sources. Many of these sources are authentic documents written by the Founder of the Bahá'í Faith Himself, Bahá'u'lláh, which were often sealed with His personal seal. To that end, any quotations in this book attributed to Bahá'u'lláh are from approved translations of His works. It might be noted that Bahá'ís believe that Bahá'u'lláh revealed the Word of God for this age. Therefore His works are very important to the Bahá'í community. Any reader of His words, though, will soon notice that He revealed His works in many styles. At some times He revealed them as a "lawgiver," at other times He revealed them as a "mystic" or spiritual guide, and at other times as a counselor to His followers. He even revealed works in the voice of God Himself. The reality is, for many people, reading the words of Bahá'u'lláh can take some getting used to. But once people get used to the different tone and language of the Holy Writings, many Bahá'ís spend their entire lives exploring the endless meanings and implications of the words revealed by the Founder of this faith.

In addition this book includes many quotations from Bahá'u'lláh's son and successor, 'Abdu'l-Bahá. While 'Abdu'l-Bahá did write many books and letters that can be considered authentic, he also gave many talks throughout his long career as a Central Figure of this Faith. The reader should realize, therefore, that many of the quotations that were gathered from such lectures and forums were written down by observers. Thus some of these passages are not considered authoritative, but can be used for personal edification and spiritual discovery. To that end, the reader should recognize that some of the materials from such works should be balanced with everything else in the Bahá'í Writings that is considered authoritative.

After the Writings of Bahá'u'lláh and 'Abdu'l-Bahá, this book also includes quotations from the grandson of 'Abdu'l-Bahá, the appointed Guardian of the Bahá'í Faith, Shoghi Effendi. These writings include materials, letters, and books that the Guardian wrote to the Bahá'í world, and to individual believers. Sometimes he wrote these letters himself, in other cases they were recorded by his secretaries. The Guardian's writings are considered an authoritative source for guidance and interpretation of the Word of God. And while this material is considered a critical source for understanding the teachings, concepts, and ideas of the Bahá'í Faith, they must also be approached with care when taken from letters to individuals. That is, in some cases direction may have been given to one person that would not necessarily fit the whole of humanity. Therefore, again, Bahá'ís are encouraged to weigh and judge for themselves in these matters with respect to all the other authoritative content we have available to us.

In addition, this book includes writings of the Universal House of Justice, the authoritative word of the supreme governing body of the worldwide Bahá'í community. It also includes works from other sources such as the Bahá'í International Community, which is an agency of the Universal House of Justice that works with non-governmental organizations around the world. These works, while not authoritative, shed insight into the inner workings of the Faith and offer a global perspective on how things should be carried out in the Bahá'í world and beyond.

SUGGESTIONS FOR READING THE QUOTATIONS

It is strongly suggested that the reader explore the book that inspired this collection of quotations, *Manifest Your Potential in the Bahá'í Faith,* before diving fully into the quotes in this book. The fact is, the Bahá'í Faith is rich and nuanced. Many of these quotations are better understood when their context and perspective is considered. In addition, it can also be helpful to read and study these books in book clubs or study classes with other people, including and especially other Bahá'ís. It can be very useful to explore spiritual topics with others, to hear their ideas, their interpretations, and their questions and concerns when one is making his or her own decisions in spiritual development.

Lastly, it is encouraged that new believers take their time when it comes to studying the Bahá'í Writings. This is because it takes patience for many to learn the language of these works, to gain confidence with the terms, to acquire a taste for the grammatical and stylistic approaches, and to build up a solid foundation of understanding that can then be used as a lens to discover, interpret, and cultivate spiritual truths in our lives.

CHAPTER 1:

INTRODUCTION TO MANIFEST YOUR POTENTIAL

FROM THE WRITINGS
OF BAHÁ'U'LLÁH

1.1   Through the Teachings of this Day Star of Truth every man will advance and develop until he attaineth the station at which he can manifest all the potential forces with which his inmost true self hath been endowed.

1.2   From the exalted source, and out of the essence of His favor and bounty He hath entrusted every created thing with a sign of His knowledge, so that none of His creatures may be deprived of its share in expressing, each according to its capacity and rank, this knowledge. This sign is the mirror of His beauty in the world of creation. The greater the effort exerted for the refinement of this sublime and noble mirror, the more faithfully will it be made to reflect the glory of the names and attributes of God, and reveal the wonders of His signs and knowledge. Every created thing will be enabled (so great is this reflecting power) to reveal the potentialities of its pre-ordained station, will recognize its capacity and limitations, and will testify to the truth that "He, verily, is God; there is none other God besides Him."...

1.3   Wert thou to attain to but a dewdrop of the crystal waters of divine knowledge, thou wouldst readily realize that true life is not the life of the flesh but the life of the spirit. For the life of the flesh is common to both men and animals, whereas the life of the spirit is possessed only by the pure in heart who have quaffed from the ocean of faith and partaken of the fruit of certitude. This life knoweth no death, and this existence is crowned by immortality.

1.4   My eternity is My creation, I have created it for thee. Make it the garment of thy temple. My unity is My handiwork; I have wrought it for thee; clothe thyself therewith, that thou mayest be to all eternity the revelation of My everlasting being.

1.5   The purpose underlying the revelation of every heavenly Book, nay, of every divinely-revealed verse, is to endue all men with righteousness and understanding, so that peace and tranquillity

may be firmly established amongst them. Whatsoever instilleth assurance into the hearts of men, whatsoever exalteth their
station or promoteth their contentment, is acceptable in the
sight of God. How lofty is the station which man, if he but
choose to fulfill his high destiny, can attain! To what depths
of degradation he can sink, depths which the meanest of creatures have never reached! Seize, O friends, the chance which
this Day offereth you, and deprive not yourselves of the liberal
effusions of His grace. I beseech God that He may graciously
enable every one of you to adorn himself, in this blessed Day,
with the ornament of pure and holy deeds. He, verily, doeth
whatsoever He willeth.

1.6   Give a hearing ear, O people, to that which I, in truth, say
unto you. The one true God, exalted be His glory, hath ever
regarded, and will continue to regard, the hearts of men as His
own, His exclusive possession.

FROM THE WRITINGS AND UTTERANCES OF 'ABDU'L-BAHÁ

1.7   It is my hope that because of these high ideals, these noble intimations of the heart, and these tidings of heaven, thou shalt
become so luminous that down all the ages the light of thy love
for God will shed its glory.

1.8   O Thou Provider! Assist Thou these noble friends to win Thy
good pleasure, and make them well-wishers of stranger and
friend alike. Bring them into the world that abideth forever;
grant them a portion of heavenly grace; cause them to be true
Bahá'ís, sincerely of God; save them from outward semblances,
and establish them firmly in the truth. Make them signs and
tokens of the Kingdom, luminous stars above the horizons of
this nether life. Make them to be a comfort and a solace to
humankind and servants to the peace of the world. Exhilarate
them with the wine of Thy counsel, and grant that all of them
may tread the path of Thy commandments.

1.9　Man is in the highest degree of materiality, and at the beginning of spirituality—that is to say, he is the end of imperfection and the beginning of perfection. He is at the last degree of darkness, and at the beginning of light; that is why it has been said that the condition of man is the end of the night and the beginning of day, meaning that he is the sum of all the degrees of imperfection, and that he possesses the degrees of perfection. He has the animal side as well as the angelic side, and the aim of an educator is to so train human souls that their angelic aspect may overcome their animal side. Then if the divine power in man, which is his essential perfection, overcomes the satanic power, which is absolute imperfection, he becomes the most excellent among the creatures; but if the satanic power overcomes the divine power, he becomes the lowest of the creatures. That is why he is the end of imperfection and the beginning of perfection. Not in any other of the species in the world of existence is there such a difference, contrast, contradiction and opposition as in the species of man. Thus the reflection of the Divine Light was in man, as in Christ, and see how loved and honored He is! At the same time we see man worshiping a stone, a clod of earth or a tree. How vile he is, in that his object of worship should be the lowest existence—that is, a stone or clay, without spirit; a mountain, a forest or a tree. What shame is greater for man than to worship the lowest existences? In the same way, knowledge is a quality of man, and so is ignorance; truthfulness is a quality of man; so is falsehood; trustworthiness and treachery, justice and injustice, are qualities of man, and so forth. Briefly, all the perfections and virtues, and all the vices, are qualities of man.

1.10　Man has two aspects: the physical, which is subject to nature, and the merciful or divine, which is connected with God. If the physical or natural disposition in him should overcome the heavenly and merciful, he is, then, the most degraded of animal beings; and if the divine and spiritual should triumph over the human and natural, he is, verily, an angel. The Prophets come into the world to guide and educate humanity so that the animal nature of man may disappear and the divinity of his powers become awakened. The divine aspect or spiritual nature consists of the breaths of the

Holy Spirit. The second birth of which Jesus has spoken refers to the appearance of this heavenly nature in man. It is expressed in the baptism of the Holy Spirit, and he who is baptized by the Holy Spirit is a veritable manifestation of divine mercy to mankind. Then he becomes just and kind to all humanity; he entertains prejudice and ill will toward none; he shuns no nation or people.

I.II   In this present age the world of humanity is afflicted with severe sicknesses and grave disorders which threaten death. Therefore, Bahá'u'lláh has appeared. He is the real Physician, bringing divine remedy and healing to the world of man. He has brought teachings for all ailments—the Hidden Words, Ishraqat, Tarazat, Tajalliyat, Words of Paradise, Glad Tidings, etc. These Holy Words and teachings are the remedy for the body politic, the divine prescription and real cure for the disorders which afflict the world. Therefore, we must accept and partake of this healing remedy in order that complete recovery may be assured. Every soul who lives according to the teachings of Bahá'u'lláh is free from the ailments and indispositions which prevail throughout the world of humanity; otherwise, selfish disorders, intellectual maladies, spiritual sicknesses, imperfections and vices will surround him, and he will not receive the life-giving bounties of God.

Bahá'u'lláh is the real Physician. He has diagnosed human conditions and indicated the necessary treatment. The essential principles of His healing remedies are the knowledge and love of God, severance from all else save God, turning our faces in sincerity toward the Kingdom of God, implicit faith, firmness and fidelity, loving-kindness toward all creatures and the acquisition of the divine virtues indicated for the human world. These are the fundamental principles of progress, civilization, international peace and the unity of mankind. These are the essentials of Bahá'u'lláh's teachings, the secret of everlasting health, the remedy and healing for man.

It is my hope that you may assist in healing the sick body of the world through these teachings so that eternal radiance may illumine all the nations of mankind.

FROM THE WRITINGS AND LETTERS WRITTEN BY, OR ON BEHALF OF, SHOGHI EFFENDI

1.12   The need is very great, everywhere in the world, in and outside the Faith, for a true spiritual awareness to pervade and motivate peoples' lives. No amount of administrative procedure or adherence to rules can take the place of this soul-characteristic, this spirituality which is the essence of Man. He is very glad to see you are stressing this and aiding the friends to realize its supreme importance.

1.13   When a person becomes a Bahá'í, actually what takes place is that the seed of the spirit starts to grow in the human soul. This seed must be watered by the outpourings of the Holy Spirit. These gifts of the spirit are received through prayer, meditation, study of the Holy Utterances and service to the Cause of God. The fact of the matter is that service in the Cause is like the plough which ploughs the physical soil when seeds are sown. It is necessary that the soil be ploughed up, so that it can be enriched, and thus cause a stronger growth of the seed. In exactly the same way the evolution of the spirit takes place through ploughing up the soil of the heart so that it is a constant reflection of the Holy Spirit. In this way the human spirit grows and develops by leaps and bounds.

    Naturally there will be periods of distress and difficulty, and even severe test.; but if that person turns firmly towards the Divine Manifestation, studies carefully His Spiritual teachings and receives the blessings of the Holy Spirit, he will find that in reality these tests and difficulties have been the gifts of God to enable him to grow and develop.

FROM THE WRITINGS AND LETTERS WRITTEN BY, OR ON BEHALF OF, THE UNIVERSAL HOUSE OF JUSTICE

1.14   People everywhere have customs which must be abandoned so as to clear the path along which their societies must evolve towards that glorious, new civilization which is to be the fruit of Bahá'u'lláh's stupendous Revelation. Indeed, in no society on earth can there be found practices which adequately mirror the standards of His Cause. His own truth-bearing Words clarify the matter: "The summons and the message which We gave were never intended to reach or to benefit one land or one people only. Mankind in its entirety must firmly adhere to whatsoever hath been revealed and vouchsafed unto it. Then and only then will it attain unto true liberty. The whole earth is illuminated with the resplendent glory of God's Revelation.

1.15   A responsibility, at once weighty and inescapable, must rest on the communities which occupy so privileged a position in so vast and turbulent an area of the globe. However great the distance that separates them; however much they differ in race, language, custom, and religion; however active the political forces which tend to keep them apart and foster racial and political antagonisms, the close and continued association of these communities in their common, their peculiar and paramount task of raising up and of consolidating the embryonic World Order of Bahá'u'lláh in those regions of the globe, is a matter of vital and urgent importance, which should receive on the part of the elected representatives of their communities, a most earnest and prayerful consideration

1.16   Most particularly, it is in the glorification of material pursuits, at once the progenitor and common feature of all such ideologies, that we find the roots which nourish the falsehood that human beings are incorrigibly selfish and aggressive. It is here that the ground must be cleared for the building of a new world fit for our descendants.

That materialistic ideals have, in the light of experience, failed to satisfy the needs of mankind calls for an honest acknowledgement that a fresh effort must now be made to find the solutions to the agonizing problems of the planet. The intolerable conditions pervading society bespeak a common failure of all, a circumstance which tends to incite rather than relieve the entrenchment on every side. Clearly, a common remedial effort is urgently required. It is primarily a matter of attitude. Will humanity continue in its waywardness, holding to outworn concepts and unworkable assumptions? Or will its leaders, regardless of ideology, step forth and, with a resolute will, consult together in a united search for appropriate solutions?

Those who care for the future of the human race may well ponder this advice. "If long-cherished ideals and time-honoured institutions, if certain social assumptions and religious formulae have ceased to promote the welfare of the generality of mankind, if they no longer minister to the needs of a continually evolving humanity, let them be swept away and relegated to the limbo of obsolescent and forgotten doctrines. Why should these, in a world subject to the immutable law of change and decay, be exempt from the deterioration that must needs overtake every human institution? For legal standards, political and economic theories are solely designed to safeguard the interests of humanity as a whole, and not humanity to be crucified for the preservation of the integrity of any particular law or doctrine."

CHAPTER 2.

WHAT IS THE BAHÁ'Í FAITH?

FROM THE WRITINGS OF BAHÁ'U'LLÁH

2.1   Great indeed is this Day! The allusions made to it in all the sacred Scriptures as the Day of God attest its greatness. The soul of every Prophet of God, of every Divine Messenger, hath thirsted for this wondrous Day. All the diverse kindreds of the earth have, likewise, yearned to attain it. No sooner, however, had the Day Star of His Revelation manifested itself in the heaven of God's Will, than all, except those whom the Almighty was pleased to guide, were found dumbfounded and heedless.

2.2   We desire but the good of the world and the happiness of the nations; yet they deem Us a stirrer up of strife and sedition worthy of bondage and banishment.... That all nations should become one in faith and all men as brothers; that the bonds of affection and unity between the sons of men should be strengthened; that diversity of religion should cease, and differences of race be annulled—what harm is there in this?... Yet so it shall be; these fruitless strifes, these ruinous wars shall pass away, and the 'Most Great Peace' shall come.... Yet do We see your kings and rulers lavishing their treasures more freely on means for the destruction of the human race than on that which would conduce to the happiness of mankind.... These strifes and this bloodshed and discord must cease, and all men be as one kindred and one family.... Let not a man glory in this, that he loves his country; let him rather glory in this, that he loves his kind...

2.3   We, verily, have come to unite and weld together all that dwell on earth.

2.4   Give ear unto the verses of God which He Who is the sacred Lote-Tree reciteth unto you. They are assuredly the infallible balance, established by God, the Lord of this world and the next. Through them the soul of man is caused to wing its flight towards the Dayspring of Revelation, and the heart of every true believer is suffused with light. Such are the laws which God hath enjoined upon you, such His commandments prescribed unto you in His Holy Tablet; obey them with joy and gladness, for this is best for you, did ye but know.

2.5   I was but a man like others, asleep upon My couch, when lo, the
      breezes of the All-Glorious were wafted over Me, and taught
      Me the knowledge of all that hath been. This thing is not from
      Me, but from One Who is Almighty and All-Knowing. And He
      bade Me lift up My voice between earth and heaven, and for
      this there befell Me what hath caused the tears of every man
      of understanding to flow. The learning current amongst men I
      studied not; their schools I entered not. Ask of the city wherein
      I dwelt, that thou mayest be well assured that I am not of them
      who speak falsely. This is but a leaf which the winds of the will
      of thy Lord, the Almighty, the All-Praised, have stirred. Can it
      be still when the tempestuous winds are blowing? Nay, by Him
      Who is the Lord of all Names and Attributes! They move it
      as they list. The evanescent is as nothing before Him Who is
      the Ever-Abiding. His all-compelling summons hath reached
      Me, and caused Me to speak His praise amidst all people. I was
      indeed as one dead when His behest was uttered. The hand of
      the will of thy Lord, the Compassionate, the Merciful, trans-
      formed Me.

2.6   While engulfed in tribulations I heard a most wondrous, a
      most sweet voice, calling above My head. Turning My face, I
      beheld a Maiden—the embodiment of the remembrance of the
      name of My Lord—suspended in the air before Me. So rejoiced
      was she in her very soul that her countenance shone with the
      ornament of the good pleasure of God, and her cheeks glowed
      with the brightness of the All-Merciful. Betwixt earth and
      heaven she was raising a call which captivated the hearts and
      minds of men. She was imparting to both My inward and outer
      being tidings which rejoiced My soul, and the souls of God's
      honoured servants.
           Pointing with her finger unto My head, she addressed all
      who are in heaven and all who are on earth, saying: By God!
      This is the Best-Beloved of the worlds, and yet ye comprehend
      not. This is the Beauty of God amongst you, and the power of
      His sovereignty within you, could ye but understand. This is
      the Mystery of God and His Treasure, the Cause of God and
      His glory unto all who are in the kingdoms of Revelation and
      of creation, if ye be of them that perceive. This is He Whose

Presence is the ardent desire of the denizens of the Realm of eternity, and of them that dwell within the Tabernacle of glory, and yet from His Beauty do ye turn aside.

FROM THE WRITINGS AND UTTERANCES OF 'ABDU'L-BAHÁ

2.7   When delivering the glad tidings, speak out and say: the Promised One of all the world's peoples hath now been made manifest. For each and every people, and every religion, await a Promised One, and Bahá'u'lláh is that One Who is awaited by all; and therefore the Cause of Bahá'u'lláh will bring about the oneness of mankind, and the tabernacle of unity will be upraised on the heights of the world, and the banners of the universality of all humankind will be unfurled on the peaks of the earth. When thou dost loose thy tongue to deliver this great good news, this will become the means of teaching the people.

2.8   Unless these Teachings are effectively spread among the people, until the old ways, the old concepts, are gone and forgotten, this world of being will find no peace, nor will it reflect the perfections of the Heavenly Kingdom. Strive ye with all your hearts to make the heedless conscious, to waken those who sleep, to bring knowledge to the ignorant, to make the blind to see, the deaf to hear, and restore the dead to life.

2.9   Throughout the world generally war and dissension prevailed. At this time Bahá'u'lláh appeared in Persia and began devoting Himself to the uplift and education of the people. He united divergent sects and creeds, removed religious, racial, patriotic and political prejudices and established a strong bond of unity and reconciliation among varying degrees and classes of mankind. The enmity then existing among the people was so bitter and intense that even ordinary association was out of the question. They would not meet and consult with each other at all. Through the power of the teachings of Bahá'u'lláh the most wonderful results were witnessed. He removed the prejudices and hatred from human hearts and wrought such transformation in their attitudes toward each other that today in Persia there is perfect accord among hitherto bigoted religionists, varying sects and divergent classes. This was not an easy accomplishment, for Bahá'u'lláh underwent severe trials, great difficulties and violent persecution. He was imprisoned, tortures were inflicted upon Him, and finally He was banished from His native land. He bore every ordeal and infliction cheerfully. In His successive exiles from country to country up to the time of His ascension from this world, He was enabled to promulgate His teachings, even from prison. Wherever His oppressors sent Him, He hoisted the standard of the oneness of the world of humanity and promulgated the principles of the unity of mankind. Some of these principles are as follows. First, it is incumbent upon all mankind to investigate truth. If such investigation be made, all should agree and be united, for truth or reality is not multiple; it is not divisible. The different religions have one truth underlying them; therefore, their reality is one.

2.10   From time immemorial the divine teachings have been successively revealed, and the bounties of the Holy Spirit have ever been emanating. All the teachings are one reality, for reality is single and does not admit multiplicity. Therefore, the divine Prophets are one, inasmuch as They reveal the one reality, the Word of God. Abraham announced teachings founded upon reality, Moses proclaimed reality, Christ established reality and Bahá'u'lláh was the Messenger and Herald of reality. But humanity, having forsaken the one essential and fundamental reality which underlies the religion of God, and holding blindly to imitations of ancestral forms and interpretations of belief, is separated and divided in the strife, contention and bigotry of various sects and religious factions. If all should be true to the original reality of the Prophet and His teaching, the peoples and nations of the world would become unified, and these differences which cause separation would be lost sight of. To accomplish this great and needful unity in reality, Bahá'u'lláh appeared in the Orient and renewed the foundations of the divine teachings. His revelation of the Word embodies completely the teachings of all the Prophets, expressed in principles and precepts applicable to the needs and conditions of the modern world, amplified and adapted to present-day questions and critical human problems. That is to

say, the words of Bahá'u'lláh are the essences of the words of the
Prophets of the past. They are the very spirit of the age and the
cause of the unity and illumination of the East and the West. The
followers of His teachings are in conformity with the precepts and
commands of all the former heavenly Messengers. Differences
and dissensions, which destroy the foundations of the world of
humanity and are contrary to the will and good pleasure of God,
disappear completely in the light of the revelation of Bahá'u'lláh;
difficult problems are solved, unity and love are established. For the
good pleasure of God is the effulgence of love and the establishment of unity and fellowship in the human world, whereas discord,
contention, warfare and strife are satanic outcomes and contrary
to the will of the Merciful. In order that human souls, minds and
spirits may attain advancement, tranquillity and vision in broader
horizons of unity and knowledge, Bahá'u'lláh proclaimed certain
principles or teachings, some of which I will mention.

2.11   Briefly, the Blessed Perfection bore all these ordeals and
calamities in order that our hearts might become enkindled
and radiant, our spirits be glorified, our faults become virtues,
our ignorance be transformed into knowledge; in order that we
might attain the real fruits of humanity and acquire heavenly
graces; in order that, although pilgrims upon earth, we should
travel the road of the heavenly Kingdom, and, although needy
and poor, we might receive the treasures of eternal life. For this
has He borne these difficulties and sorrows.

FROM THE WRITINGS AND LETTERS WRITTEN BY, OR ON BEHALF OF, SHOGHI EFFENDI

2.12   The Bahá'í Faith upholds the unity of God, recognizes the unity
of His Prophets, and inculcates the principle of the oneness and
wholeness of the entire human race. it proclaims the necessity
and the inevitability of the unification of mankind, asserts
that it is gradually approaching, and claims that nothing short
of the transmuting spirit of God, working through His chosen

Mouthpiece in this day, can ultimately succeed in bringing it about. It, moreover, enjoins upon its followers the primary duty of an unfettered search after truth, condemns all manner of prejudice and superstition, declares the purpose of religion to be the promotion of amity and concord, proclaims its essential harmony with science, and recognizes it as the foremost agency for the pacification and the orderly progress of human society. It unequivocally maintains the principle of equal rights, opportunities and privileges for men and women, insists on compulsory education, eliminates extremes of poverty and wealth, abolishes the institution of priesthood, prohibits slavery, asceticism, mendicancy and monasticism, prescribes monogamy, discourages divorce, emphasizes the necessity of strict obedience to one's government, exalts any work performed in the spirit of service to the level of worship, urges either the creation or selection of an auxiliary international language, and delineates the outlines of those institutions that must establish and perpetuate the general peace of mankind.

2.13 The independent search after truth, unfettered by superstition or tradition; the oneness of the entire human race, the pivotal principle and fundamental doctrine of the Faith; the basic unity of all religions; the condemnation of all forms of prejudice, whether religious, racial, class or national; the harmony which must exist between religion and science; the equality of men and women, the two wings on which the bird of human kind is able to soar; the introduction of compulsory education; the adoption of a universal auxiliary language; the abolition of the extremes of wealth and poverty; the institution of a world tribunal for the adjudication of disputes between nations; the exaltation of work, performed in the spirit of service, to the rank of worship; the glorification of justice as the ruling principle in human society, and of religion as a bulwark for the protection of all peoples and nations; and the establishment of a permanent and universal peace as the supreme goal of all mankind—these stand out as the essential elements of that Divine polity which He proclaimed to leaders of public thought as well as to the masses at large in the course of these missionary journeys.

FROM THE WRITINGS AND LETTERS WRITTEN BY, OR ON BEHALF OF, THE UNIVERSAL HOUSE OF JUSTICE

2.14 The Bahá'í Faith regards the current world confusion and calamitous condition in human affairs as a natural phase in an organic process leading ultimately and irresistibly to the unification of the human race in a single social order whose boundaries are those of the planet. The human race, as a distinct, organic unit, has passed through evolutionary stages analogous to the stages of infancy and childhood in the lives of its individual members, and is now in the culminating period of its turbulent adolescence approaching its long-awaited coming of age.

2.15 …Whatever suffering and turmoil the years immediately ahead may hold, however dark the immediate circumstances, the Bahá'í community believes that humanity can confront this supreme trial with confidence in its ultimate outcome. Far from signalizing the end of civilization, the convulsive changes towards which humanity is being ever more rapidly impelled will serve to release the "potentialities inherent in the station of man" and reveal "the full measure of his destiny on earth, the innate excellence of his reality".

PART I: BELIEFS

CHAPTER 3:

ACCEPTING A PRACTICAL CONCEPT OF GOD

FROM THE WRITINGS OF BAHÁ'U'LLÁH

3.1 I loved thy creation, hence I created thee. Wherefore, do thou love Me, that I may name thy name and fill thy soul with the spirit of life.

3.2 Out of the wastes of nothingness, with the clay of My command I made thee to appear, and have ordained for thy training every atom in existence and the essence of all created things

3.3 The vitality of men's belief in God is dying out in every land; nothing short of His wholesome medicine can ever restore it. The corrosion of ungodliness is eating into the vitals of human society; what else but the Elixir of His potent Revelation can cleanse and revive it?

3.4 As to thy question concerning the origin of creation. Know assuredly that God's creation hath existed from eternity, and will continue to exist forever. Its beginning hath had no beginning, and its end knoweth no end. His name, the Creator, presupposeth a creation, even as His title, the Lord of Men, must involve the existence of a servant.

3.5 O SON OF MAN! Wert thou to speed through the immensity of space and traverse the expanse of heaven, yet thou wouldst find no rest save in submission to Our command and humbleness before Our Face.

3.6 Thou art even as a finely tempered sword concealed in the darkness of its sheath and its value hidden from the artificer's knowledge. Wherefore come forth from the sheath of self and desire that thy worth may be made resplendent and manifest unto all the world.

3.7 Lauded and glorified art Thou, O Lord, my God! How can I make mention of Thee, assured as I am that no tongue, however deep its wisdom, can befittingly magnify Thy name, nor can the bird of the human heart, however great its longing, ever hope to ascend into the heaven of Thy majesty and knowledge.

If I describe Thee, O my God, as Him Who is the All-Perceiving, I find myself compelled to admit that They Who are the highest Embodiments of perception have been created by virtue of Thy behest. And if I extol Thee as Him Who is the All-Wise, I, likewise, am forced to recognize that the Well Springs of wisdom have themselves been generated through the operation of Thy Will. And if I proclaim Thee as the Incomparable One, I soon discover that they Who are the inmost essence of oneness have been sent down by Thee and are but the evidences of Thine handiwork. And if I acclaim Thee as the Knower of all things, I must confess that they Who are the Quintessence of knowledge are but the creation and instruments of Thy Purpose.

Exalted, immeasurably exalted, art Thou above the strivings of mortal man to unravel Thy mystery, to describe Thy glory, or even to hint at the nature of Thine Essence. For whatever such strivings may accomplish, they never can hope to transcend the limitations imposed upon Thy creatures, inasmuch as these efforts are actuated by Thy decree, and are begotten of Thine invention. The loftiest sentiments which the holiest of saints can express in praise of Thee, and the deepest wisdom which the most learned of men can utter in their attempts to comprehend Thy nature, all revolve around that Center Which is wholly subjected to Thy sovereignty, Which adoreth Thy Beauty, and is propelled through the movement of Thy Pen.

3.8 The door of the knowledge of the Ancient Being hath ever been, and will continue for ever to be, closed in the face of men. No man's understanding shall ever gain access unto His holy court. As a token of His mercy, however, and as a proof of His loving-kindness, He hath manifested unto men the Day Stars of His divine guidance, the Symbols of His divine unity, and hath ordained the knowledge of these sanctified Beings to be identical with the knowledge of His own Self. Whoso recognizeth them hath recognized God. Whoso hearkeneth to their call, hath hearkened to the Voice of God, and whoso testifieth to the truth of their Revelation, hath testified to the truth of God Himself. Whoso turneth away from them, hath turned away from God, and whoso disbelieveth in them, hath disbelieved in God. Every one of them is the Way of God that connecteth this world with the realms above, and the Standard of His Truth unto every one in the kingdoms of earth and heaven. They are the Manifestations of God amidst men, the evidences of His Truth, and the signs of His glory.

3.9 These sanctified Mirrors, these Day Springs of ancient glory, are, one and all, the Exponents on earth of Him Who is the central Orb of the universe, its Essence and ultimate Purpose. From Him proceed their knowledge and power; from Him is derived their sovereignty. The beauty of their countenance is but a reflection of His image, and their revelation a sign of His deathless glory. They are the Treasuries of Divine knowledge, and the Repositories of celestial wisdom. Through them is transmitted a grace that is infinite, and by them is revealed the Light that can never fade.... These Tabernacles of Holiness, these Primal Mirrors which reflect the light of unfading glory, are but expressions of Him Who is the Invisible of the Invisibles. By the revelation of these Gems of Divine virtue all the names and attributes of God, such as knowledge and power, sovereignty and dominion, mercy and wisdom, glory, bounty, and grace, are made manifest.

3.10 The Prophets of God should be regarded as physicians whose task is to foster the well-being of the world and its peoples, that, through the spirit of oneness, they may heal the sickness of a divided humanity. To none is given the right to question their words or disparage their conduct, for they are the only ones who can claim to have understood the patient and to have correctly diagnosed its ailments. No man, however acute his perception, can ever hope to reach the heights which the wisdom and understanding of the Divine Physician have attained. Little wonder, then, if the treatment prescribed by the physician in this day should not be found to be identical with that which he prescribed before. How could it be otherwise when the ills affecting the sufferer necessitate at every stage of his sickness a special remedy? In like manner, every time the Prophets of God have illumined the world with the resplendent radiance of the Day Star of Divine knowledge, they have invariably summoned its peoples to embrace the light of God through such means as best befitted the exigencies of the age in which they appeared. They were thus able to scatter the darkness of ignorance, and to shed upon the world the glory of their own knowledge. It is towards the inmost essence of these Prophets, therefore, that the eye of every man of discernment must be directed, inasmuch as their one and only purpose hath always been to guide the erring, and give peace to the afflicted.... These are not days of prosperity and triumph. The whole of mankind is in the grip of manifold ills. Strive, therefore, to save its life through the wholesome medicine which the almighty hand of the unerring Physician hath prepared.

FROM THE WRITINGS AND UTTERANCES OF 'ABDU'L-BAHÁ

3.11   One of the proofs and demonstrations of the existence of God is the fact that man did not create himself: nay, his creator and designer is another than himself.

3.12   The contingent world is the source of imperfections: God is the origin of perfections. The imperfections of the contingent world are in themselves a proof of the perfections of God.

For example, when you look at man, you see that he is weak. This very weakness of the creature is a proof of the power of the Eternal Almighty One, because, if there were no power, weakness could not be imagined. Then the weakness of the creature is a proof of the power of God; for if there were no power, there could be no weakness; so from this weakness it becomes evident that there is power in the world. Again, in the contingent world there is poverty; then necessarily wealth exists, since poverty is apparent in the world. In the contingent world there is ignorance; necessarily knowledge exists, because ignorance is found; for if there were no knowledge, neither would there be ignorance. Ignorance is the nonexistence of knowledge, and if there were no existence, nonexistence could not be realized.

3.13   It is certain that the whole contingent world is subjected to a law and rule which it can never disobey; even man is forced to submit to death, to sleep and to other conditions—that is to say, man in certain particulars is governed, and necessarily this state of being governed implies the existence of a governor. Because a characteristic of contingent beings is dependency, and this dependency is an essential necessity, therefore, there must be an independent being whose independence is essential.

3.14 These obvious arguments are adduced for weak souls; but if the inner perception be open, a hundred thousand clear proofs become visible. Thus, when man feels the indwelling spirit, he is in no need of arguments for its existence; but for those who are deprived of the bounty of the spirit, it is necessary to establish external arguments

3.15 When we consider existence, we see that the mineral, vegetable, animal and human worlds are all in need of an educator.

If the earth is not cultivated, it becomes a jungle where useless weeds grow; but if a cultivator comes and tills the ground, it produces crops which nourish living creatures. It is evident, therefore, that the soil needs the cultivation of the farmer. Consider the trees: if they remain without a cultivator, they will be fruitless, and without fruit they are useless; but if they receive the care of a gardener, these same barren trees become fruitful, and through cultivation, fertilization and engrafting the trees which had bitter fruits yield sweet fruits. These are rational proofs; in this age the peoples of the world need the arguments of reason.

The same is true with respect to animals: notice that when the animal is trained it becomes domestic, and also that man, if he is left without education, becomes bestial, and, moreover, if left under the rule of nature, becomes lower than an animal, whereas if he is educated he becomes an angel. For the greater number of animals do not devour their own kind, but men, in the Sudan, in the central regions of Africa, kill and eat each other.

Now reflect that it is education that brings the East and the West under the authority of man; it is education that produces wonderful industries; it is education that spreads great sciences and arts; it is education that makes manifest new discoveries and institutions. If there were no educator, there would be no such things as comforts, civilization, or humanity.

If a man be left alone in a wilderness where he sees none of his own kind, he will undoubtedly become a mere brute; it is then clear that an educator is needed.

3.16 But education is of three kinds: material, human and spiritual. Material education is concerned with the progress and development of the body, through gaining its sustenance, its material comfort and ease. This education is common to animals and man.

Human education signifies civilization and progress—that is to say, government, administration, charitable works, trades, arts and handicrafts, sciences, great inventions and discoveries and elaborate institutions, which are the activities essential to man as distinguished from the animal.

Divine education is that of the Kingdom of God: it consists in acquiring divine perfections, and this is true education; for in this state man becomes the focus of divine blessings, the manifestation of the words, "Let Us make man in Our image, and after Our likeness."[1] This is the goal of the world of humanity. [1 Cf. Gen. 1:26.]

3.17 Now we need an educator who will be at the same time a material, human and spiritual educator, and whose authority will be effective in all conditions. So if anyone should say, "I possess perfect comprehension and intelligence, and I have no need of such an educator," he would be denying that which is clear and evident, as though a child should say, "I have no need of education; I will act according to my reason and intelligence, and so I shall attain the perfections of existence"; or as though the blind should say, "I am in no need of sight, because many other blind people exist without difficulty."

Then it is plain and evident that man needs an educator, and this educator must be unquestionably and indubitably perfect in all respects and distinguished above all men. Otherwise, if he should be like the rest of humanity, he could not be their educator, more particularly because he must be at the same time their material and human as well as their spiritual educator—that is to say, he must teach men to organize and carry out physical matters, and to form a social order in order to establish cooperation and mutual aid in living so that material affairs may be organized and regulated for any circumstances that may occur. In the same way he must establish human education—that is to say, he must educate intelligence and thought in such a way that they may attain complete development, so that knowledge and science may increase, and the reality of things, the mysteries of beings and the properties of existence may be discovered; that, day by day, instructions, inventions and institutions may be improved; and from things perceptible to the senses conclusions as to intellectual things may be deduced.

He must also impart spiritual education, so that intelligence and comprehension may penetrate the metaphysical world, and may receive benefit from the sanctifying breeze of the Holy Spirit, and may enter into relationship with the Supreme Concourse. He must so educate the human reality that it may become the center of the divine appearance, to such a degree that the attributes and the names of God shall be resplendent in the mirror of the reality of man, and the holy verse "We will make man in Our image and likeness" shall be realized. [1]
[1 Cf. Gen. 1:26.]

It is clear that human power is not able to fill such a great office, and that reason alone could not undertake the responsibility of so great a mission. How can one solitary person without help and without support lay the foundations of such a noble construction? He must depend on the help of the spiritual and divine power to be able to undertake this mission. One Holy Soul gives life to the world of humanity, changes the aspect of the terrestrial globe, causes intelligence to progress, vivifies souls, lays the basis of a new life, establishes new foundations, organizes the world, brings nations and religions under the shadow of one standard, delivers man from the world of imperfections and vices, and inspires him with the desire and need of natural and acquired perfections. Certainly nothing short of a divine power could accomplish so great a work. We ought to consider this with justice, for this is the office of justice

3.18   Therefore, the Universal Educator must be at the same time a physical, human and spiritual educator; and He must possess a supernatural power, so that He may hold the position of a divine teacher. If He does not show forth such a holy power, He will not be able to educate, for if He be imperfect, how can He give a perfect education? If He be ignorant, how can He make others wise? If He be unjust, how can He make others just? If He be earthly, how can He make others heavenly?

3.19   I do not wish to mention the miracles of Bahá'u'lláh, for it may perhaps be said that these are traditions, liable both to truth and to error, like the accounts of the miracles of Christ in the Gospel, which come to us from the apostles, and not from anyone else, and are denied by the Jews. Though if I wish to mention the supernatural acts of Bahá'u'lláh, they are numerous; they are acknowledged in the Orient, and even by some non-Bahá'ís. But these narratives are not decisive proofs and evidences to all; the hearer might perhaps say that this account may not be in accordance with what occurred, for it is known that other sects recount miracles performed by their founders. For instance, the followers of Brahmanism relate miracles. From what evidence may we know that those are false and that these are true? If these are fables, the others also are fables; if these are generally accepted, so also the others are generally accepted. Consequently, these accounts are not satisfactory proofs. Yes, miracles are proofs for the eyewitness only, and even he may regard them not as a miracle but as an enchantment. Extraordinary feats have also been related of some conjurors.

3.20   Strange indeed that after twenty years training in colleges and universities man should reach such a station wherein he will deny the existence of the ideal or that which is not perceptible to the senses. Have you ever stopped to think that the animal already has graduated from such a university? Have you ever realized that the cow is already a professor emeritus of that university? For the cow without hard labor and study is already a philosopher of the superlative degree in the school of nature. The cow denies everything that is not tangible, saying, "I can see! I can eat! Therefore, I believe only in that which is tangible!"

    Then why should we go to the colleges? Let us go to the cow.

FROM THE WRITINGS AND LETTERS WRITTEN BY, OR ON BEHALF OF, SHOGHI EFFENDI

3.21 In a Tablet Bahá'u'lláh says that even though absolute being can be attributed only to God we cannot say that other objects have no being. A table has an existence even though its existence compared with the existence of the carpenter who is its maker is almost nothing. Compared to God nothing has existence but this does not mean that even stones do not have being. It is speaking relatively. Moreover, God reveals Himself in all things in the sense that He is the source of their being and the Cause of their existence. Without Him all things will shrink down into nothing. This however does not mean that all things are parts of God as the pantheist believes. The pantheist says that only god exists, objects are mere modes of His attributes. Bahá'u'lláh however says that objects have a separate reality that is created by God. The Master explains these things in the 'Some Answered Questions', especially in one of the last chapters. There are also many *tablets of Bahá'u'lláh* explaining these matters. Most of them, however, have not yet been translated into English. Let us hope that some day this work will be done and the friends will appreciate how Bahá'u'lláh has solved their problems.

FROM THE WRITINGS AND LETTERS WRITTEN BY, OR ON BEHALF OF, THE UNIVERSAL HOUSE OF JUSTICE

3.22 The Bahá'í Faith confesses the unity of God and the justice of the divine Essence. It recognizes that Almighty God is an exalted, unknowable and concealed entity, sanctified from ascent and descent, from egress and regress, and from assuming a physical body. The Bahá'í Faith, which professes the existence of the invisible God, the One, the Single, the Eternal, the Peerless, bows before the loftiness of His Threshold, believes in all divine Manifestations, considers all the Prophets from Adam to the Seal of the Prophets as true divine Messengers Who are the Manifestations of Truth in the world of creation, accepts Their Books as having come from God, believes in the continuation of the divine out-pourings, emphatically believes in reward and punishment and, uniquely among existing revealed religions outside Islam, accepts the Prophet Muhammad as a true Prophet and the Qur'án as the Word of God.

CHAPTER 4:

RENEWING THE ROLE OF RELIGION IN MODERN LIFE

.

FROM THE WRITINGS OF BAHÁ'U'LLÁH

4.1   The purpose of religion as revealed from the heaven of God's holy Will is to establish unity and concord amongst the peoples of the world; make it not the cause of dissension and strife. The religion of God and His divine law are the most potent instruments and the surest of all means for the dawning of the light of unity amongst men. The progress of the world, the development of nations, the tranquillity of peoples, and the peace of all who dwell on earth are among the principles and ordinances of God. Religion bestoweth upon man the most precious of all gifts, offereth the cup of prosperity, imparteth eternal life, and showereth imperishable benefits upon mankind. It behoveth the chiefs and rulers of the world, and in particular the Trustees of God's House of Justice, to endeavour to the utmost of their power to safeguard its position, promote its interests and exalt its station in the eyes of the world. In like manner it is incumbent upon them to enquire into the conditions of their subjects and to acquaint themselves with the affairs and activities of the divers communities in their dominions. We call upon the manifestations of the power of God—the sovereigns and rulers on earth—to bestir themselves and do all in their power that haply they may banish discord from this world and illumine it with the light of concord.

4.2   When the Day-Star of Wisdom rose above the horizon of God's Holy Dispensation it voiced this all-glorious utterance: They that are possessed of wealth and invested with authority and power must show the profoundest regard for religion. In truth, religion is a radiant light and an impregnable stronghold for the protection and welfare of the peoples of the world, for the fear of God impelleth man to hold fast to that which is good, and shun all evil. Should the lamp of religion be obscured, chaos and confusion will ensue, and the lights of fairness and justice, of tranquillity and peace cease to shine. Unto this will bear witness every man of true understanding.

4.3   And now concerning thy question regarding the nature of religion. Know thou that they who are truly wise have likened the world unto the human temple. As the body of man needeth a garment to clothe it, so the body of mankind must needs be adorned with the mantle of justice and wisdom. Its robe is the Revelation vouchsafed unto it by God. Whenever this robe hath fulfilled its purpose, the Almighty will assuredly renew it. For every age requireth a fresh measure of the light of God. Every Divine Revelation hath been sent down in a manner that befitted the circumstances of the age in which it hath appeared.

4.4 The essence of religion is to testify unto that which the Lord hath revealed, and follow that which He hath ordained in His mighty Book.

4.5 The Great Being saith: O ye children of men! The fundamental purpose animating the Faith of God and His Religion is to safeguard the interests and promote the unity of the human race, and to foster the spirit of love and fellowship amongst men. Suffer it not to become a source of dissension and discord, of hate and enmity. This is the straight Path, the fixed and immovable foundation. Whatsoever is raised on this foundation, the changes and chances of the world can never impair its strength, nor will the revolution of countless centuries undermine its structure. Our hope is that the world's religious leaders and the rulers thereof will unitedly arise for the reformation of this age and the rehabilitation of its fortunes. Let them, after meditating on its needs, take counsel together and, through anxious and full deliberation, administer to a diseased and sorely-afflicted world the remedy it requireth.

4.6 O ye that dwell on earth! The religion of God is for love and unity; make it not the cause of enmity or dissension. In the eyes of men of insight and the beholders of the Most Sublime Vision, whatsoever are the effective means for safeguarding and promoting the happiness and welfare of the children of men have already been revealed by the Pen of Glory. But the foolish ones of the earth, being nurtured in evil passions and desires, have remained heedless of the consummate wisdom of Him Who is, in truth, the All-Wise, while their words and deeds are prompted by idle fancies and vain imaginings.

4.7 ... School must first train the children in the principles of religion, so that the promise and the Threat recorded in the Books of God may prevent them from the things forbidden and adorn them with the mantle of the commandments; but this in such a measure that it may not injure the children by resulting in ignorant fanaticism and bigotry.

FROM THE WRITINGS AND UTTERANCES OF 'ABDU'L-BAHÁ

4.8   Our purpose is to show how true religion promotes the civilization and honor, the prosperity and prestige, the learning and advancement of a people once abject, enslaved and ignorant, and how, when it falls into the hands of religious leaders who are foolish and fanatical, it is diverted to the wrong ends, until this greatest of splendors turns into blackest night.

4.9   Likewise the divine religions of the holy Manifestations of God are in reality one though in name and nomenclature they differ. Man must be a lover of the light no matter from what day-spring it may appear. He must be a lover of the rose no matter in what soil it may be growing. He must be a seeker of the truth no matter from what source it come. Attachment to the lantern is not loving the light. Attachment to the earth is not befitting but enjoyment of the rose which develops from the soil is worthy. Devotion to the tree is profitless but partaking of the fruit is beneficial. Luscious fruits no matter upon what tree they grow or where they may be found must be enjoyed. The word of truth no matter which tongue utters it must be sanctioned. Absolute verities no matter in what book they be recorded must be accepted. If we harbor prejudice it will be the cause of deprivation and ignorance. The strife between religions, nations and races arises from misunderstanding. If we investigate the religions to discover the principles underlying their foundations we will find they agree, for the fundamental reality of them is one and not multiple. By this means the religionists of the world will reach their point of unity and reconciliation. They will ascertain the truth that the purpose of religion is the acquisition of praiseworthy virtues, betterment of morals, spiritual development of mankind, the real life and divine bestowals.

4.10   Universal benefits derive from the grace of the Divine religions, for they lead their true followers to sincerity of intent, to high purpose, to purity and spotless honor, to surpassing kindness and compassion, to the keeping of their covenants when they have covenanted, to concern for the rights of others, to liberality, to justice in every aspect of life, to humanity and philanthropy, to valor and to unflagging efforts in the service of mankind. It is religion, to sum up, which produces all human virtues, and it is these virtues which are the bright candles of civilization. If a man is not characterized by these excellent qualities, it is certain that he has never attained to so much as a drop out of the fathomless river of the waters of life that flows through the teachings of the Holy Books, nor caught the faintest breath of the fragrant breezes that blow from the gardens of God; for nothing on earth can be demonstrated by words alone, and every level of existence is known by its signs and symbols, and every degree in man's development has its identifying mark.

The purpose of these statements is to make it abundantly clear that the Divine religions, the holy precepts, the heavenly teachings, are the unassailable basis of human happiness, and that the peoples of the world can hope for no real relief or deliverance without this one great remedy. This panacea must, however, be administered by a wise and skilled physician, for in the hands of an incompetent all the cures that the Lord of men has ever created to heal men's ills could produce no health, and would on the contrary only destroy the helpless and burden the hearts of the already afflicted.

4.11   Religion is the light of the world, and the progress, achievement, and happiness of man result from obedience to the laws set down in the holy Books.

4.12   ... religion must be conducive to love and unity among mankind; for if it be the cause of enmity and strife, the absence of religion is preferable. When Moses appeared, the tribes of Israel were in a state of disunion as captives of the Pharaohs. Moses gathered them together, and the divine law established fellowship among them. They became as one people, united, consolidated, after which they were rescued from bondage. They passed into the promised land, advanced in all degrees, developed sciences and arts, progressed in material affairs, increased in divine or spiritual civilization until their nation rose to its zenith in the sovereignty of Solomon. It is evident, therefore, that religion is the cause of unity, fellowship and progress among mankind. The function of a shepherd is to gather the sheep together and not to scatter them. Then Christ appeared. He united varying and divergent creeds and warring people of His time. He brought together Greeks and Romans, reconciled Egyptians and Assyrians, Chaldeans and Phoenicians. Christ established unity and agreement among people of these hostile and warring nations. Therefore, it is again evident that the purpose of religion is peace and concord. Likewise, Muhammad appeared at a time when the peoples and tribes of Arabia were divergent and in a state of continual warfare. They killed each other, pillaged and took captive wives and children. Muhammad united these fierce tribes, established a foundation of fellowship among them so that they gave up warring against each other absolutely and established communities. The result was that the Arabian tribes freed themselves from the Persian yoke and Roman control, established an independent sovereignty which rose to a high degree of civilization, advanced in sciences and arts, extended the Saracen dominion as far west as Spain and Andalusia and became famous throughout the world. Therefore, it is proved once more that the religion of God is intended to be the cause of advancement and solidarity and not of enmity and dissolution. If it becomes the cause of hatred and strife, its absence is preferable. Its purpose is unity, and its foundations are one.

4.13   Religion has two main parts:
(1) The Spiritual.
(2) The Practical.

      The spiritual part never changes. All the Manifestations of God and His Prophets have taught the same truths and given the same spiritual law. They all teach the one code of morality. There is no division in the truth. The Sun has sent forth many rays to illumine human intelligence, the light is always the same.

      The practical part of religion deals with exterior forms and ceremonies, and with modes of punishment for certain offences. This is the material side of the law, and guides the customs and manners of the people.

4.14   The foundations of the divine religions are one. If we investigate
these foundations, we discover much ground for agreement, but if
we consider the imitations of forms and ancestral beliefs, we find
points of disagreement and division; for these imitations differ,
while the sources and foundations are one and the same. That is
to say, the fundamentals are conducive to unity, but imitations are
the cause of disunion and dismemberment. Whosoever is lacking
in love for humanity or manifests hatred and bigotry toward any
part of it violates the foundation and source of his own belief and
is holding to forms and imitations. Jesus Christ declares that the
sun rises upon the evil and the good, and the rain descends upon
the just and the unjust—upon all humanity alike. Christ was a
divine mercy which shone upon all mankind, the medium for the
descent of the bounty of God, and the bounty of God is transcendent, unrestricted, universal.

4.15   The material world is subject to change and transformation. The
Cause of the Kingdom is eternal; therefore, it is the most important.
But, alas, day by day the power of the Kingdom in human hearts is
weakened, and material forces gain the ascendancy. The divine signs
are becoming less and less, and human evidences grow stronger.
They have reached such a degree that materialists are advancing and
aggressive while divine forces are waning and vanishing. Irreligion
has conquered religion. The cause of the chaotic condition lies in the
differences among the religions and finds its origin in the animosity
and hatred existing between sects and denominations. The materialists have availed themselves of this dissension amongst the religions
and are constantly attacking them, intending to uproot the tree of
divine planting. Owing to strife and contention among themselves,
the religions are being weakened and vanquished. If a commander is
at variance with his army in the execution of military tactics, there is
no doubt he will be defeated by the enemy. Today the religions are at
variance; enmity, strife and recrimination prevail among them; they
refuse to associate; nay, rather, if necessary they shed each other's
blood. Read history and record to see what dreadful events have
happened in the name of religion. For instance, the Hebrew prophets were sent to announce Christ, but unfortunately the Talmud and
its superstitions veiled Him so completely that they crucified their
promised Messiah. Had they renounced the talmudic traditions and

investigated the reality of the religion of Moses, they would have become believers in Christ. Blind adherence to forms and imitations of ancestral beliefs deprived them of their messianic bounty. They were not refreshed by the downpouring rain of mercy, nor were they illumined by the rays of the Sun of Truth.

Imitation destroys the foundation of religion, extinguishes the spirituality of the human world, transforms heavenly illumination into darkness and deprives man of the knowledge of God. It is the cause of the victory of materialism and infidelity over religion; it is the denial of Divinity and the law of revelation; it refuses Prophethood and rejects the Kingdom of God. When materialists subject imitations to the intellectual analysis of reason, they find them to be mere superstitions; therefore, they deny religion. For instance, the Jews have ideas as to the purity and impurity of religion, but when you subject these ideas to scientific scrutiny, they are found to be without foundation.

4.16 Still another cause of disagreement and dissension has been the formation of religious sects and denominations. Bahá'u'lláh said that God has sent religion for the purpose of establishing fellowship among humankind and not to create strife and discord, for all religion is founded upon the love of humanity. Abraham promulgated this principle, Moses summoned all to its recognition, Christ established it, and Muhammad directed mankind to its standard. This is the reality of religion. If we abandon hearsay and investigate the reality and inner significance of the heavenly teachings, we will find the same divine foundation of love for humanity. The purport is that religion is intended to be the cause of unity, love and fellowship and not discord, enmity and estrangement. Man has forsaken the foundation of divine religion and adhered to blind imitations. Each nation has clung to its own imitations, and because these are at variance, warfare, bloodshed and destruction of the foundation of humanity have resulted. True religion is based upon love and agreement. Bahá'u'lláh has said, "If religion and faith are the causes of enmity and sedition, it is far better to be nonreligious, and the absence of religion would be preferable; for we desire religion to be the cause of amity and fellowship. If enmity and hatred exist, irreligion is preferable." Therefore, the removal of this dissension has been specialized in Bahá'u'lláh, for religion is the divine remedy for human antagonism and discord. But when we make the remedy the cause of the disease, it would be better to do without the remedy.

FROM THE WRITINGS AND LETTERS WRITTEN BY, OR ON BEHALF OF, SHOGHI EFFENDI

4.17   The fundamental principle enunciated by Bahá'u'lláh ... is that religious truth is not absolute but relative, that Divine Revelation is a continuous and progressive process, that all the great religions of the world are divine in origin, that their basic principles are in complete harmony, that their aims and purposes are one and the same, that their teachings are but facets of one truth, that their functions are complementary, that they differ only in the nonessential aspects of their doctrines, and that their missions represent successive stages in the spiritual evolution of human society....

... His mission is to proclaim that the ages of the infancy and of the childhood of the human race are past, that the convulsions associated with the present stage of its adolescence are slowly and painfully preparing it to attain the stage of manhood, and are heralding the approach of that Age of Ages when swords will be beaten into plowshares, when the Kingdom promised by Jesus Christ will have been established, and the peace of the planet definitely and permanently ensured. Nor does Bahá'u'lláh claim finality for His own Revelation, but rather stipulates that a fuller measure of the truth He has been commissioned by the Almighty to vouchsafe to humanity, at so critical a juncture in its fortunes, must needs be disclosed at future stages in the constant and limitless evolution of mankind."

4.18   That the forces of irreligion, of a purely materialistic philosophy, of unconcealed paganism have been unloosed, are now spreading, and, by consolidating themselves, are beginning to invade some of the most powerful Christian institutions of the western world, no unbiased observer can fail to admit. That these institutions are becoming increasingly restive, that a few among them are already dimly aware of the pervasive influence of the Cause of Bahá'u'lláh, that they will, as their inherent strength deteriorates and their discipline relaxes, regard with deepening dismay the rise of His New 181 World Order, and will gradually determine to assail it, that such an opposition will in turn accelerate their decline, few, if any, among those who are attentively watching the progress of His Faith would be inclined to question.

4.19   ... the condition that the world is in is bringing many issues to a head. It would be perhaps impossible to find a nation or people not in a state of crisis today. The materialism, the lack of true religion and the consequent baser forces in human nature which are being released, have brought the whole world to the brink of probably the greatest crisis it has ever faced or will have to face. The Bahá'ís are a part of the world. They too feel the great pressures which are brought to bear upon all people today, whoever and wherever they may be. On the other hand, the Divine Plan, which is the direct method of working towards the establishment of peace and World Order, has perforce reached an important and challenging point in its unfoldment; because of the desperate needs of the world, the Bahá'ís find themselves, even though so limited in numbers, in financial strength and in prestige, called upon to fulfill a great responsibility.

4.20   Indeed, the chief reason for the evils now rampant in society is the lack of spirituality. The materialistic civilization of our age has so much absorbed the energy and interest of mankind that people in general do no longer feel the necessity of raising themselves above the forces and conditions of their daily material existence. There is not sufficient demand for things that we should call spiritual to differentiate them from the needs and requirements of our physical existence.

The universal crisis affecting mankind is, therefore, essentially spiritual in its causes. The spirit of the age, taken on the whole, is irreligious. Man's outlook on life is too crude and materialistic to enable him to elevate himself into the higher realms of the spirit.

It is this condition, so sadly morbid, into which society has fallen, that religion seeks to improve and transform...

FROM THE WRITINGS AND LETTERS WRITTEN BY, OR ON BEHALF OF, THE UNIVERSAL HOUSE OF JUSTICE

4.21   As you quite correctly appreciate, the fundamental purpose of all religion is the spiritual development of the souls of human beings.

4.22   ... the Bahá'í Faith upholds the freedom of conscience which permits a person to follow his chosen religion: no one may be compelled to become a Bahá'í, or to remain a Bahá'í if he conscientiously wishes to leave the Faith.

4.23   It has become customary in the West to think of science and religion as occupying two distinct—and even opposed—areas of human thought and activity. This dichotomy can be characterized in the pairs of antitheses: faith and reason; value and fact. It is a dichotomy which is foreign to Bahá'í thought and should, we feel, be regarded with suspicion by Bahá'í scholars in every field. The principle of the harmony of science and religion means not only that religious teachings should be studied with the light of reason and evidence as well as of faith and inspiration, but also that everything in this creation, all aspects of human life and knowledge, should be studied in the light of revelation as well as in that of purely rational investigation. In other words, a Bahá'í scholar, when studying a subject, should not lock out of his mind any aspect of truth that is known to him.

4.24   It is, therefore, an inadequate recognition of the unique station of Moses, Buddha, Zoroaster, Jesus, Muhammad-or of the succession of Avatars who inspired the Hindu scriptures-to depict their work as the founding of distinct religions. Rather are they appreciated when acknowledged as the spiritual Educators of history, as the animating forces in the rise of the civilizations through which consciousness has flowered...

CHAPTER 5:

FINDING HAPPINESS THAT ENDURES

FROM THE WRITINGS OF BAHÁ'U'LLÁH

5.1   We desire but the good of the world and the happiness of the nations...

5.2   Behold, how the divers peoples and kindreds of the earth have been waiting for the coming of the Promised One. No sooner had He, Who is the Sun of Truth, been made manifest, than, lo, all turned away from Him, except them whom God was pleased to guide. We dare not, in this Day, lift the veil that concealeth the exalted station which every true believer can attain, for the joy which such a revelation must provoke might well cause a few to faint away and die.

5.3   O My friends that dwell upon the dust! Haste forth unto your celestial habitation. Announce unto yourselves the joyful tidings: "He Who is the Best-Beloved is come! He hath crowned Himself with the glory of God's Revelation, and hath unlocked to the face of men the doors of His ancient Paradise." Let all eyes rejoice, and let every ear be gladdened, for now is the time to gaze on His beauty, now is the fit time to hearken to His voice. Proclaim unto every longing lover: "Behold, your Well-Beloved hath come among men!" and to the messengers of the Monarch of love impart the tidings: "Lo, the Adored One hath appeared arrayed in the fullness of His glory!" O lovers of His beauty! Turn the anguish of your separation from Him into the joy of an everlasting reunion, and let the sweetness of His presence dissolve the bitterness of your remoteness from His court.

5.4   Whoso hath searched the depths of the oceans that lie hid within these exalted words, and fathomed their import, can be said to have discovered a glimmer of the unspeakable glory with which this mighty, this sublime, and most holy Revelation hath been endowed. From the excellence of so great a Revelation the honor with which its faithful followers must needs be invested can be well imagined. By the righteousness of the one true God! The very breath of these souls is in itself richer than all the treasures of the earth. Happy is the man that hath attained thereunto, and woe betide the heedless.

5.5 All these stainless hearts and sanctified souls have, with absolute resignation, responded to the summons of His decree. Instead of complaining, they rendered thanks unto God, and amidst the darkness of their anguish they revealed naught but radiant acquiescence to His will.

5.6 Happy is the man that pondereth in his heart that which hath been revealed in the Books of God, the Help in Peril, the Self-Subsisting.

FROM THE WRITINGS AND UTTERANCES OF 'ABDU'L-BAHÁ

5.7 Know ye, verily, that the happiness of mankind lieth in the unity and the harmony of the human race, and that spiritual and material developments are conditioned upon love and amity among all men.

5.8 The other is the soul-stirring call of God, Whose spiritual teachings are safeguards of the everlasting glory, the eternal happiness and illumination of the world of humanity, and cause attributes of mercy to be revealed in the human world and the life beyond.

5.9 ... Is any larger bounty conceivable than this that an individual, looking within himself, should find that by the confirming grace of God he has become the cause of peace and well being, of happiness and advantage to his fellowmen. No, by the one true God, there is no greater bliss, no more complete delight.

5.10 ... for human happiness is founded upon spiritual behaviour.

5.11 Speak thou no word of politics; thy task concerneth the life of the soul, for this verily leadeth to man's joy in the world of God. Except to speak well of them, make thou no mention of the earth's kings, and the worldly governments thereof. Rather, confine thine utterance to spreading the blissful tidings of the Kingdom of God, and demonstrating the influence of the Word of God, and the holiness of the Cause of God. Tell thou of abiding joy and spiritual delights, and godlike qualities, and of how the Sun of Truth hath risen above the earth's horizons: tell of the blowing of the spirit of life into the body of the world.

5.12   In this world we are influenced by two sentiments, Joy and Pain.

    Joy gives us wings! In times of joy our strength is more vital, our intellect keener, and our understanding less clouded. We seem better able to cope with the world and to find our sphere of usefulness. But when sadness visits us we become weak, our strength leaves us, our comprehension is dim and our intelligence veiled. The actualities of life seem to elude our grasp, the eyes of our spirits fail to discover the sacred mysteries, and we become even as dead beings.

    There is no human being untouched by these two influences; but all the sorrow and the grief that exist come from the world of matter—the spiritual world bestows only the joy!

    If we suffer it is the outcome of material things, and all the trials and troubles come from this world of illusion.

5.13   Man is, in reality, a spiritual being, and only when he lives in the spirit is he truly happy.

5.14   You must manifest complete love and affection toward all mankind. Do not exalt yourselves above others, but consider all as your equals, recognizing them as the servants of one God. Know that God is compassionate toward all; therefore, love all from the depths of your hearts, prefer all religionists before yourselves, be filled with love for every race, and be kind toward the people of all nationalities. Never speak disparagingly of others, but praise without distinction. Pollute not your tongues by speaking evil of another. Recognize your enemies as friends, and consider those who wish you evil as the wishers of good. You must not see evil as evil and then compromise with your opinion, for to treat in a smooth, kindly way one whom you consider evil or an enemy is hypocrisy, and this is not worthy or allowable. You must consider your enemies as your friends, look upon your evil-wishers as your well-wishers and treat them accordingly. Act in such a way that your heart may be free from hatred. Let not your heart be offended with anyone. If some one commits an error and wrong toward you, you must instantly forgive him. Do not complain of others. Refrain from reprimanding them, and if you wish to give admonition or advice, let it be offered in such a way that it will not burden the bearer. Turn all your thoughts toward bringing joy to hearts. Beware! Beware! lest ye offend any heart. Assist the world of humanity as much as possible. Be the source of consolation to every sad one, assist every weak one, be helpful to every indigent one, care for every sick one, be the cause of glorification to every lowly one, and shelter those who are overshadowed by fear.

In brief, let each one of you be as a lamp shining forth with the light of the virtues of the world of humanity. Be trustworthy, sincere, affectionate and replete with chastity. Be illumined, be spiritual, be divine, be glorious, be quickened of God, be a Bahá'í.

5.15   We should all visit the sick. When they are in sorrow and suffering, it is a real help and benefit to have a friend come. Happiness is a great healer to those who are ill. In the East it is the custom to call upon the patient often and meet him individually. The people in the East show the utmost kindness and compassion to the sick and suffering. This has greater effect than the remedy itself. You must always have this thought of love and affection when you visit the ailing and affected.

5.16   When a man turns his face to God he finds sunshine everywhere.

5.17   Your utmost desire must be to confer happiness upon each other. Each one must be the servant of the others, thoughtful of their comfort and welfare. In the path of God one must forget himself entirely. He must not consider his own pleasure but seek the pleasure of others. He must not desire glory nor gifts of bounty for himself but seek these gifts and blessings for his brothers and sisters. It is my hope that you may become like this, that you may attain to the supreme bestowal and be imbued with such spiritual qualities as to forget yourselves entirely and with heart and soul offer yourselves as sacrifices for the Blessed Perfection. You should have neither will nor desire of your own but seek everything for the beloved of God and live together in complete love and fellowship. May the favors of Bahá'u'lláh surround you from all directions. This is the greatest bestowal and supreme bounty. These are the infinite favors of God

5.18 If you do not smile now, for what time will you await and what greater happiness could you expect? This is the springtime of manifestation. The vernal shower has descended from the cloud of divine mercy; the life-giving breeze of the Holy Spirit is wafting the perfume of blossoms. From field and meadow rises a fragrant breath of thanksgiving like pure incense ascending to the throne of God. The world has become a new world; souls are quickened, spirits renewed, refreshed. Truly it is a time for happiness.

FROM THE WRITINGS AND LETTERS WRITTEN BY, OR ON BEHALF OF, SHOGHI EFFENDI

5.19 If people only realized it, the inner life of the spirit is that which counts, but they are so blinded by desires and so misled that they have brought upon themselves all the suffering we see at present in the world. The Bahá'ís seek to lead people back to a knowledge of their true selves and the purpose for which they were created, and thus to their greatest happiness and highest good.

5.20 Do not grieve, dear brother, for being poor, for you are rich instead in faith and in spirit. This is a divine wealth for which the richest of the world will crave for in vain. True we must work hard, earn money and keep our family in happiness and prosperity, but we must always realize that our lives must be devoted to things higher and more sublime. We must remember what great souls, whose lives still inspire hundreds and thousands, were of the poorest in the world.

5.21   We do not know what form the immediate future will take, any-where. Because the passions of mankind are so unregenerate, and it is so deaf to the voice of Bahá'u'lláh, no doubt great suffering will be experienced. What we do know however, is that we are Bahá'ís and that our salvation lies in this God-sent Faith.

As we give to God, as we serve Him and love Him, so will He vouchsafe to us His Mercy, Guidance and Protection. We must, at all times, put the Faith first and our personal desires and comfort second. Having this Faith we have eternal security and happiness which nothing can take away from us ever, no matter what afflictions may befall a faithless world. The Cause of God is our security, and confidence in Bahá'u'lláh our pro-tection.

5.22   The great thing is to 'Live the Life'—to have our lives so satu-rated with the Divine teaching and the Bahá'í Spirit that people cannot fail to see a joy, a power, a love, a purity, a radiance, an efficiency in our character and work that will distinguish us from worldly-minded people and make people wonder what is the secret of this new life in us. We must become entirely self-less and devoted to God so that every day and every moment we seek to do only what God would have us do and in the way He would have us do it. If we do this sincerely then we shall have perfect unity & harmony with each other. Where there is want of harmony there is lack of the true Bahá'í Spirit. Unless we can show this transformation in our lives, this new power, this mutual love and harmony, then the Bahá'í teachings are but a name to us.

5.23   He was very sorry to hear of the condition of your dear sister. He would advise her to turn her thoughts determinedly and intelligently—by that I mean unemotionally—to God, realis-ing that He is forgiving, that in one moment He can, through His Blessed Mercy, take away our sense of failure and help us to do better in the future—if we sincerely wish to; to turn to Him in prayer and seek to draw closer to Him; and to accept His Will and submit her own desires and opinions to His Wish and plan for her. There is a tremendous darkness in the world today, the darkness caused by mankind's going against the Laws of God and giving way to the animal side of human nature. People must recognize this fact, and consciously struggle against pessimism and depression.

FROM THE WRITINGS AND LETTERS WRITTEN BY, OR ON BEHALF OF, THE UNIVERSAL HOUSE OF JUSTICE

5.24 The Manifestation of God describes the reality which is conducive to the happiness, health and development of mankind. His Teachings serve as a compass to help us find our way in the new world. They outline not only what is good for mankind but also the steps to be taken to secure individual freedom and well-being. Within this framework it is important to understand the statements in the Writing about evil spirits and psychic phenomena.

CHAPTER 6:

ACHIEVING CONTENTMENT THROUGH DETACHMENT

FROM THE WRITINGS OF BAHÁ'U'LLÁH

6.1 O SON OF MAN! Thou dost wish for gold and I desire thy freedom from it. Thou thinkest thyself rich in its possession, and I recognize thy wealth in thy sanctity therefrom...

6.2 If ye meet the abased or the down-trodden, turn not away disdainfully from them, for the King of Glory ever watcheth over them and surroundeth them with such tenderness as none can fathom except them that have suffered their wishes and desires to be merged in the Will of your Lord, the Gracious, the All-Wise. O ye rich ones of the earth! Flee not from the face of the poor that lieth in the dust, nay rather befriend him and suffer him to recount the tale of the woes with which God's inscrutable Decree hath caused him to be afflicted.

6.3 The friends of God shall win and profit under all conditions, and shall attain true wealth. In fire they remain cold, and from water they emerge dry. Their affairs are at variance with the affairs of men. Gain is their lot, whatever the deal.

6.4 The purpose underlying the revelation of every heavenly Book, nay, of every divinely-revealed verse, is to endue all men with righteousness and understanding, so that peace and tranquillity may be firmly established amongst them. Whatsoever instilleth assurance into the hearts of men, whatsoever exalteth their station or promoteth their contentment, is acceptable in the sight of God. How lofty is the station which man, if he but choose to fulfill his high destiny, can attain! To what depths of degradation he can sink, depths which the meanest of creatures have never reached! Seize, O friends, the chance which this Day offereth you, and deprive not yourselves of the liberal effusions of His grace. I beseech God that He may graciously enable every one of you to adorn himself, in this blessed Day, with the ornament of pure and holy deeds. He, verily, doeth whatsoever He willeth.

6.5 O MY SERVANT! Free thyself from the fetters of this world, and loose thy soul from the prison of self. Seize thy chance, for it will come to thee no more.

6.6   That hour is now come. The world is illumined with the
      effulgent glory of His countenance. And yet, behold how far
      its peoples have strayed from His path! None have believed
      in Him except them who, through the power of the Lord of
      Names, have shattered the idols of their vain imaginings and
      corrupt desires and entered the city of certitude.

6.7   Say: Deliver your souls, O people, from the bondage of self,
      and purify them from all attachment to anything besides Me.
      Remembrance of Me cleanseth all things from defilement,
      could ye but perceive it.

6.8   Rejoicest thou in that thou rulest a span of earth, when the
      whole world, in the estimation of the people of Baha, is worth
      as much as the black in the eye of a dead ant? Abandon it unto
      such as have set their affections upon it, and turn thou unto
      Him Who is the Desire of the world. Whither are gone the
      proud and their palaces? Gaze thou into their tombs, that thou
      mayest profit by this example, inasmuch as We made it a lesson
      unto every beholder. Were the breezes of Revelation to seize
      thee, thou wouldst flee the world, and turn unto the Kingdom,
      and wouldst expend all thou possessest, that thou mayest draw
      nigh unto this sublime Vision.

FROM THE WRITINGS AND
UTTERANCES OF 'ABDU'L-BAHÁ

6.9   How long shall we drift on the wings of passion and vain desire;
      how long shall we spend our days like barbarians in the depths
      of ignorance and abomination? God has given us eyes, that we
      may look about us at the world, and lay hold of whatsoever
      will further civilization and the arts of living. He has given us
      ears, that we may hear and profit by the wisdom of scholars
      and philosophers and arise to promote and practice it. Senses
      and faculties have been bestowed upon us, to be devoted to the
      service of the general good; so that we, distinguished above all
      other forms of life for perceptiveness and reason, should labor

at all times and along all lines, whether the occasion be great or small, ordinary or extraordinary, until all mankind are safely gathered into the impregnable stronghold of knowledge.

6.10   Let nothing grieve thee, and be thou angered at none. It behoveth thee to be content with the Will of God, and a true and loving and trusted friend to all the peoples of the earth, without any exceptions whatever. This is the quality of the sincere, the way of the saints, the emblem of those who believe in the unity of God, and the raiment of the people of Baha.

6.11   O ye lovers of God! Do not dwell on what is coming to pass in this holy place, and be ye in no wise alarmed. Whatsoever may happen is for the best, because affliction is but the essence of bounty, and sorrow and toil are mercy unalloyed, and anguish is peace of mind, and to make a sacrifice is to receive a gift, and whatsoever may come to pass hath issued from God's grace.

6.12   O thou believer in the oneness of God! Know thou that nothing profiteth a soul save the love of the All-Merciful, nothing lighteth up a heart save the splendour that shineth from the realm of the Lord.

Forsake thou every other concern, let oblivion overtake the memory of all else. Confine thy thoughts to whatever will lift up the human soul to the Paradise of heavenly grace, and make every bird of the Kingdom wing its way unto the Supreme Horizon, the central point of everlasting honour in this contingent world.

6.13   Rely upon God. Trust in Him. Praise Him, and call Him continually to mind. He verily turneth trouble into ease, and sorrow into solace, and toil into utter peace. He verily hath dominion over all things.

If thou wouldst hearken to my words, release thyself from the fetters of whatsoever cometh to pass. Nay rather, under all conditions thank thou thy loving Lord, and yield up thine affairs unto His Will that worketh as He pleaseth. This verily is better for thee than all else, in either world.

6.14   Consequently, one must close his eyes wholly to these thoughts, long for eternal life, the sublimity of the world of humanity, the celestial developments, the Holy Spirit, the promotion of the Word of God, the guidance of the inhabitants of the globe, the promulgation of universal peace and the proclamation of the oneness of the world of humanity! This is the work! Otherwise like unto other animals and birds one must occupy himself with the requirements of this physical life, the satisfaction of which is the highest aspiration of the animal kingdom, and one must stalk across the earth like unto the quadrupeds.

Consider ye! No matter how much man gains wealth, riches and opulence in this world, he will not become as independent as a cow. For these fattened cows roam freely over the vast tableland. All the prairies and meadows are theirs for grazing, and all the springs and rivers are theirs for drinking! No matter how much they graze, the fields will not be exhausted! It is evident that they have earned these material bounties with the utmost facility.

Still more ideal than this life is the life of the bird. A bird, on the summit of a mountain, on the high, waving branches, has built for itself a nest more beautiful than the palaces of the kings! The air is in the utmost purity, the water cool and clear as crystal, the panorama charming and enchanting. In such glorious surroundings, he expends his numbered days. All the harvests of the plain are his possessions, having earned all this wealth without the least labor. Hence, no matter how much man may advance in this world, he shall not attain to the station of this bird! Thus it becomes evident that in the matters of this world, however much man may strive and work to the point of death, he will be unable to earn the abundance, the freedom and the independent life of a small bird. This proves and establishes the fact that man is not created for the life of this ephemeral world—nay, rather, is he created for the acquirement of infinite perfections, for the attainment to the sublimity of the world of humanity, to be drawn nigh unto the divine threshold, and to sit on the throne of everlasting sovereignty!

6.15   Now is the time for you to divest yourselves of the garment of attachment to this world that perisheth, to be wholly severed from the physical world, become heavenly angels, and travel to these countries. I swear by Him, besides Whom there is none other God, that each one of you will become an Israfil of Life, and will blow the Breath of Life into the souls of others.

6.16 Consequently, rest ye not, seek ye no composure, attach not yourselves to the luxuries of this ephemeral world, free yourselves from every attachment, and strive with heart and soul to become fully established in the Kingdom of God.

6.17 The mind and spirit of man advance when he is tried by suffering. The more the ground is ploughed the better the seed will grow, the better the harvest will be. Just as the plough furrows the earth deeply, purifying it of weeds and thistles, so suffering and tribulation free man from the petty affairs of this worldly life until he arrives at a state of complete detachment. His attitude in this world will be that of divine happiness. Man is, so to speak, unripe: the heat of the fire of suffering will mature him. Look back to the times past and you will find that the greatest men have suffered most.'

6.18 You see all round you proofs of the inadequacy of material things—how joy, comfort, peace and consolation are not to be found in the transitory things of the world. Is it not then foolishness to refuse to seek these treasures where they may be found? The doors of the spiritual Kingdom are open to all, and without is absolute darkness.

6.19 What are the fruits of the human world? They are the spiritual attributes which appear in man. If man is bereft of those attributes, he is like a fruitless tree. One whose aspiration is lofty and who has developed self-reliance will not be content with a mere animal existence. He will seek the divine Kingdom; he will long to be in heaven although he still walks the earth in his material body, and though his outer visage be physical, his face of inner reflection will become spiritual and heavenly. Until this station is attained by man, his life will be utterly devoid of real outcomes. The span of his existence will pass away in eating, drinking and sleeping, without eternal fruits, heavenly traces or illumination—without spiritual potency, everlasting life or the lofty attainments intended for him during his pilgrimage through the human world.

6.20 We must look higher than all earthly thoughts; detach ourselves from every material idea, crave for the things of the spirit; fix our eyes on the everlasting bountiful Mercy of the Almighty, who will fill our souls with the gladness of joyful service to His command 'Love One Another

FROM THE WRITINGS AND LETTERS WRITTEN BY, OR ON BEHALF OF, SHOGHI EFFENDI

6.21 The gross materialism that engulfs the entire nation at the present hour; the attachment to worldly things that enshrouds the souls of men; the fear and anxieties that distract their minds; the pleasure and dissipations that fill their time, the prejudices and animosities that darken their outlook, the apathy and lethargy that paralyze their spiritual faculties—these are among the formidable obstacles that stand in the path of every world-be warrior in the service of Bahá'u'lláh, obstacles which he must battle against the surmount in his crusade for the redemption of his own countrymen.

6.22 ... Peace of mind is gained by the centering of the spiritual consciousness on the Prophet of God; therefore you should study the spiritual Teachings, and receive the Water of Life from the Holy Utterances. Then by translating these high ideals into action, your entire character will be changed, and your mind will not only find peace, but your entire being will find joy and enthusiasm.

FROM THE WRITINGS AND LETTERS WRITTEN BY, OR ON BEHALF OF, THE UNIVERSAL HOUSE OF JUSTICE

6.23 You ask about 'spiritual indigestion': Bahá'ís should seek to be many-sided, normal and well-balanced, mentally and spiritually. We must not give the impression of being fanatics but at the same time we must live up to our principles.

CHAPTER 7:

APPRECIATING THE ROLE OF SINS AND FORGIVENESS IN FAITH

FROM THE WRITINGS OF BAHÁ'U'LLÁH

7.1   By My beauty! All your doings hath My pen graven with open characters upon tablets of chrysolite.

7.2   Should anyone be afflicted by a sin, it behoveth him to repent thereof and return unto his Lord. He, verily, granteth forgiveness unto whomsoever He willeth, and none may question that which it pleaseth Him to ordain.

7.3   The beginning of all things is the knowledge of God, and the end of all things is strict observance of whatsoever hath been sent down from the empyrean of the Divine Will that pervadeth all that is in the heavens and all that is on the earth.

7.4   Wherefore, hearken ye unto My speech, and return ye to God and repent, that He, through His grace, may have mercy upon you, may wash away your sins, and forgive your trespasses. The greatness of His mercy surpasseth the fury of His wrath, and His grace encompasseth all who have been called into being and been clothed with the robe of life, be they of the past or of the future.

7.5   ... man's knowledge of God cannot develop fully and adequately save by observing whatever hath been ordained by Him and is set forth in His heavenly Book.

7.6   Will not the dread of Divine displeasure, the fear of Him Who hath no peer or equal, arouse you?

7.7   Alas! How strange and pitiful; for a mere cupful, they have turned away from the billowing seas of the Most High, and remained far from the most effulgent horizon.

7.8   One gleam from the splendors of Thy Name, the All-Merciful, sufficeth to banish and blot out every trace of sinfulness from the world, and a single breath from the breezes of the Day of Thy Revelation is enough to adorn all mankind with a fresh attire.

7.9 O Lord! Thou seest this essence of sinfulness turning unto the ocean
of Thy favour and this feeble one seeking the kingdom of Thy divine
power and this poor creature inclining himself towards the day-star
of Thy wealth. By Thy mercy and Thy grace, disappoint him not, O
Lord, nor debar him from the revelations of Thy bounty in Thy days,
nor cast him away from Thy door which Thou hast opened wide to
all that dwell in Thy heaven and on Thine earth.

Alas! Alas! My sins have prevented me from approaching
the Court of Thy holiness and my trespasses have caused me to
stray far from the Tabernacle of Thy majesty. I have committed
that which Thou didst forbid me to do and have put away what
Thou didst order me to observe.

I pray Thee by Him Who is the sovereign Lord of Names
to write down for me with the Pen of Thy bounty that which will
enable me to draw nigh unto Thee and will purge me from my
trespasses which have intervened between me and Thy forgiveness and Thy pardon.

7.10 Live then the days of thy life, that are less than a fleeting
moment, with thy mind stainless, thy heart unsullied, thy
thoughts pure, and thy nature sanctified, so that, free and
content, thou mayest put away this mortal frame, and repair
unto the mystic paradise and abide in the eternal kingdom for
evermore.

7.11 O MOVING FORM OF DUST! I desire communion with thee,
but thou wouldst put no trust in Me. The sword of thy rebellion
hath felled the tree of thy hope. At all times I am near unto thee,
but thou art ever far from Me. Imperishable glory I have chosen
for thee, yet boundless shame thou hast chosen for thyself. While
there is yet time, return, and lose not thy chance.

7.12 Say: Commit not, O people, that which will bring shame upon you
or dishonor the Cause of God in the eyes of men, and be not of
the mischief-makers. Approach not the things which your minds
condemn. Eschew all manner of wickedness, for such things are
forbidden unto you in the Book which none touch except such
as God hath cleansed from every taint of guilt, and numbered
among the purified.

7.13 Blessed are the learned that pride not themselves on their attainments; and well is it with the righteous that mock not the sinful, but rather conceal their misdeeds, so that their own shortcomings may remain veiled to men's eyes.

7.14 Indeed, there existeth in man a faculty which deterreth him from, and guardeth him against, whatever is unworthy and unseemly, and which is known as his sense of shame. This, however, is confined to but a few; all have not possessed, and do not possess, it. It is incumbent upon the kings and the spiritual leaders of the world to lay fast hold on religion, inasmuch as through it the fear of God is instilled in all else but Him.

7.15 Know ye that the world and its vanities and its embellishments shall pass away. Nothing will endure except God's Kingdom which pertaineth to none but Him, the Sovereign Lord of all, the Help in Peril, the All-Glorious, the Almighty. The days of your life shall roll away, and all the things with which ye are occupied and of which ye boast yourselves shall perish, and ye shall, most certainly, be summoned by a company of His angels to appear at the spot where the limbs of the entire creation shall be made to tremble, and the flesh of every oppressor to creep. Ye shall be asked of the things your hands have wrought in this, your vain life, and shall be repaid for your doings. This is the day that shall inevitably come upon you, the hour that none can put back. To this the Tongue of Him that speaketh the truth and is the Knower of all things hath testified.

7.16 My God, my God! If none be found to stray from Thy path, how, then, can the ensign of Thy mercy be unfurled, or the banner of Thy bountiful favor be hoisted? And if iniquity be not committed, what is it that can proclaim Thee to be the Concealer of men's sins, the Ever-Forgiving, the Omniscient, the All-Wise? May my soul be a sacrifice to the trespasses of them that trespass against Thee, for upon such trespasses are wafted the sweet savors of the tender mercies of Thy Name, the Compassionate, the All-Merciful. May my life be laid down for the transgressions of such as transgress against Thee, for through them the breath of Thy grace and the fragrance of Thy loving-kindness are made known and diffused amongst men. May my inmost being be offered up for the sins of them that have sinned against Thee, for it is as a result of such sins that the Day Star of Thy manifold favors revealeth itself above the horizon of Thy bounty, and the clouds of Thy never-failing providence rain down their gifts upon the realities of all created things.

FROM THE WRITINGS AND UTTERANCES OF 'ABDU'L-BAHÁ

7.17   As to the difference between that material civilization now pre-vailing, and the divine civilization which will be one of the benefits to derive from the House of Justice, it is this: material civilization, through the power of punitive and retaliatory laws, restraineth the people from criminal acts; and notwithstanding this, while laws to retaliate against and punish a man are continually proliferating, as ye can see, no laws exist to reward him. In all the cities of Europe and America, vast buildings have been erected to serve as jails for the criminals.

      Divine civilization, however, so traineth every member of society that no one, with the exception of a negligible few, will undertake to commit a crime. There is thus a great difference between the prevention of crime through measures that are violent and retaliatory, and so training the people, and enlight-ening them, and spiritualizing them, that without any fear of punishment or vengeance to come, they will shun all criminal acts. They will, indeed, look upon the very commission of a crime as a great disgrace and in itself the harshest of punish-ments. They will become enamoured of human perfections, and will consecrate their lives to whatever will bring light to the world and will further those qualities which are acceptable at the Holy Threshold of God.

7.18   For just as the effects and the fruitage of the uterine life are not to be found in that dark and narrow place, and only when the child is transferred to this wide earth do the benefits and uses of growth and development in that previous world become revealed—so likewise reward and punishment, heaven and hell, requital and retribution for actions done in this present life, will stand revealed in that other world beyond. And just as, if human life in the womb were limited to that uterine world, existence there would be non-sensical, irrelevant—so too if the life of this world, the deeds here done and their fruitage, did not come forth in the world beyond, the whole process would be irrational and foolish.

7.19   The immortality of the spirit is mentioned in the Holy Books; it is the fundamental basis of the divine religions. Now punishments and rewards are said to be of two kinds: first, the rewards and punishments of this life; second, those of the other world. But the paradise and hell of existence are found in all the worlds of God, whether in this world or in the spiritual heavenly worlds. Gaining these rewards is the gaining of eternal life. That is why Christ said, "Act in such a way that you may find eternal life, and that you may be born of water and the spirit, so that you may enter into the Kingdom."[1]
        [1 Cf. John 3:5.]
        The rewards of this life are the virtues and perfections which adorn the reality of man. For example, he was dark and becomes luminous; he was ignorant and becomes wise; he was neglectful and becomes vigilant; he was asleep and becomes awakened; he was dead and becomes living; he was blind and becomes a seer; he was deaf and becomes a hearer; he was earthly and becomes heavenly; he was material and becomes spiritual. Through these rewards he gains spiritual birth and becomes a new creature. He becomes the manifestation of the verse in the Gospel where it is said of the disciples that they "were born, not of blood, nor of the will of the flesh, nor of the will of man, but of God"[1]—that is to say, they were delivered from the animal characteristics and qualities which are the characteristics of human nature, and they became qualified with the divine characteristics, which are the bounty of God. This is the meaning of the second birth. For such people there is no greater torture than being veiled from God, and no more severe punishment than sensual vices, dark qualities, lowness of nature, engrossment in carnal desires. When they are delivered through the light of faith from the darkness of these vices,

and become illuminated with the radiance of the sun of reality, and ennobled with all the virtues, they esteem this the greatest reward, and they know it to be the true paradise. In the same way they consider that the spiritual punishment—that is to say, the torture and punishment of existence—is to be subjected to the world of nature; to be veiled from God; to be brutal and ignorant; to fall into carnal lusts; to be absorbed in animal frailties; to be characterized with dark qualities, such as falsehood, tyranny, cruelty, attachment to the affairs of the world, and being immersed in satanic ideas. For them, these are the greatest punishments and tortures.
[1 John 1:13.]

Likewise, the rewards of the other world are the eternal life which is clearly mentioned in all the Holy Books, the divine perfections, the eternal bounties and everlasting felicity. The rewards of the other world are the perfections and the peace obtained in the spiritual worlds after leaving this world, while the rewards of this life are the real luminous perfections which are realized in this world, and which are the cause of eternal life, for they are the very progress of existence. It is like the man who passes from the embryonic world to the state of maturity and becomes the manifestation of these words: "Blessed, therefore, be God, the most excellent of Makers."[1] The rewards of the other world are peace, the spiritual graces, the various spiritual gifts in the Kingdom of God, the gaining of the desires of the heart and the soul, and the meeting of God in the world of eternity. In the same way the punishments of the other world—that is to say, the torments of the other world—consist in being deprived of the special divine blessings and the absolute bounties, and falling into the lowest degrees of existence. He who is deprived of these divine favors, although he continues after death, is considered as dead by the people of truth.
[1 Qur'án 23:14.]

7.20 As forgiveness is one of the attributes of the Merciful One, so also justice is one of the attributes of the Lord. The tent of existence is upheld upon the pillar of justice and not upon forgiveness. The continuance of mankind depends upon justice and not upon forgiveness. So if, at present, the law of pardon were practiced in all countries, in a short time the world would be disordered, and the foundations of human life would crumble. For example, if the governments of Europe had not withstood the notorious Attila, he would not have left a single living man.

7.21 O Thou forgiving Lord! Thou art the shelter of all these Thy servants. Thou knowest the secrets and art aware of all things. We are all helpless, and Thou art the Mighty, the Omnipotent. We are all sinners, and Thou art the Forgiver of sins, the Merciful, the Compassionate. O Lord! Look not at our shortcomings. Deal with us according to Thy grace and bounty. Our shortcomings are many, but the ocean of Thy forgiveness is boundless. Our weakness is grievous, but the evidences of Thine aid and assistance are clear. Therefore, confirm and strengthen us. Enable us to do that which is worthy of Thy holy Threshold. Illumine our hearts, grant us discerning eyes and attentive ears. Resuscitate the dead and heal the sick. Bestow wealth upon the poor and give peace and security to the fearful. Accept us in Thy kingdom and illumine us with the light of guidance. Thou art the Powerful and the Omnipotent. Thou art the Generous. Thou art the Clement. Thou art the Kind.

7.22 O kind Father! Confer Thy blessings. Consider not our shortcomings. Shelter us under Thy protection. Remember not our sins. Heal us with Thy mercy. We are weak; Thou art mighty. We are poor; Thou art rich. We are sick; Thou art the Physician. We are needy; Thou art most generous.

7.23 The divine bounties are flowing. Each one of you has been given the opportunity of becoming a tree yielding abundant fruits. This is the springtime of Bahá'u'lláh. The verdure and foliage of spiritual growth are appearing in great abundance in the gardens of human hearts. Know ye the value of these passing days and vanishing nights. Strive to attain a station of absolute love one toward another. By the absence of love, enmity increases. By the exercise of love, love strengthens and enmities dwindle away.

7.24 God is great! God is kind! He does not behold human short-comings; He does not regard human weaknesses. Man is a creature of His mercy, and to His mercy He summons all. Why then should we despise or detest His creatures because this one is a Jew, another a Buddhist or Zoroastrian and so on? This is ignorance, for the oneness of humanity as servants of God is an assured and certain fact.

7.25 In the highest prayer, men pray only for the love of God, not because they fear Him or Hell, or hope for bounty or heaven... When a man falls in love with a human being, it is impossible for him to keep from mentioning the name of his beloved. How much more difficult is it to keep from mentioning the Name of God when he has come to love Him... The spiritual man finds no delight in anything save in commemoration of God.

FROM THE WRITINGS AND LETTERS WRITTEN BY, OR ON BEHALF OF, SHOGHI EFFENDI

7.26 In explaining the fear of God to children, there is no objection to teaching it as 'Abdu'l-Bahá so often taught everything, in the form of parables. Also the child should be made to understand that we don't fear God because He is cruel, but we fear Him because He is just, and, if we do wrong and deserve to be punished, then in His justice He may see fit to punish us. We must both love God and fear Him.

7.27 The deprivation of a person's voting rights should only be resorted to when absolutely necessary, and a National Spiritual Assembly should always feel reluctant to impose this very heavy sanction which is a severe punishment. Of course sometimes, to protect the Cause, it must be done, but he feels that if the believer so deprived makes an effort to mend his ways, rectifies his mistakes, or sincerely seeks forgiveness, every effort should be made to help him and enable him to re-establish himself in the Community as a member in good standing.

7.28 The Guardian does not feel that, if a person has approached this Cause and desires to become a Bahá'í, and is determined to change his way of life, his past should be held against him. Where would forgiveness be if every prospective Bahá'í was judged by his past! But once a Bahá'í, a change of life is expected and hoped for, and the friend must help the people to change.

7.29 You ask him about the fear of God: perhaps the friends do not realize that the majority of human beings need the element of fear in order to discipline their conduct? Only a relatively very highly evolved soul would always be disciplined by love alone. Fear of punishment, fear of the anger of God if we do evil, are needed to keep people's feet on the right path. Of course we should love God—but we must fear Him in the sense of a child fearing the righteous anger and chastisement of a parent; not cringe before Him as before a tyrant, but know His mercy exceeds His justice!

FROM THE WRITINGS AND LETTERS WRITTEN BY, OR ON BEHALF OF, THE UNIVERSAL HOUSE OF JUSTICE

7.30 On the subject of Confession the Guardian's secretary wrote on his behalf to an individual believer: 'We are forbidden to confess to any person, as do the Catholics to their priests, our sins and shortcomings, or to do so in public, as some religious sects do. However, if we spontaneously desire to acknowledge we have been wrong in something, or that we have some fault of character, and ask another person's forgiveness or pardon, we are quite free to do so. The Guardian wants to point out, however, that we are not obliged to do so. It rests entirely with the individual'.

CHAPTER 8:

OVERCOMING TESTS AND DIFFICULTIES

FROM THE WRITINGS OF BAHÁ'U'LLÁH

8.1   Know ye that trials and tribulations have, from time immemorial, been the lot of the chosen Ones of God and His beloved, and such of His servants as are detached from all else but Him, they whom neither merchandise nor traffic beguile from the remembrance of the Almighty, they that speak not till He hath spoken, and act according to His commandment. Such is God's method carried into effect of old, and such will it remain in the future. Blessed are the steadfastly enduring, they that are patient under ills and hardships, who lament not over anything that befalleth them, and who tread the path of resignation....

8.2   O SON OF MAN! For everything there is a sign. The sign of love is fortitude under My decree and patience under My trials.

8.3   He Who is your Lord, the All-Merciful, cherisheth in His heart the desire of beholding the entire human race as one soul and one body.

8.4   O SON OF MAN! The true lover yearneth for tribulation even as doth the rebel for forgiveness and the sinful for mercy.

8.5   O SON OF MAN! If adversity befall thee not in My path, how canst thou walk in the ways of them that are content with My pleasure? If trials afflict thee not in thy longing to meet Me, how wilt thou attain the light in thy love for My beauty?

8.6   O SON OF MAN! My calamity is My providence, outwardly it is fire and vengeance, but inwardly it is light and mercy. Hasten thereunto that thou mayest become an eternal light and an immortal spirit. This is My command unto thee, do thou observe it.

8.7   Well is it with him whom the changes and chances of this world have failed to deter from recognizing the Day Spring of the Unity of God, who hath quaffed, with unswerving resolve, and in the name of the Self-Subsisting, the sealed wine of His Revelation.

8.8   Build ye for yourselves such houses as the rain and floods can never destroy, which shall protect you from the changes and chances of this life.

8.9   Meditate profoundly, that the secret of things unseen may be revealed unto you, that you may inhale the sweetness of a spiritual and imperishable fragrance, and that you may acknowledge the truth that from time immemorial even unto eternity the Almighty hath tried, and will continue to try, His servants, so that light may be distinguished from darkness, truth from falsehood, right from wrong, guidance from error, happiness from misery, and roses from thorns. Even as He hath revealed: "Do men think when they say 'We believe' they shall be let alone and not be put to proof?"[1] [1 Qur'án 29:2.]

8.10   If tribulation touch thee for My sake, call thou to mind My ills and troubles, and remember My banishment and imprison-ment. Thus do We devolve on thee what hath descended upon Us from Him Who is the All-Glorious, the All-Wise.

8.11   Say: Tribulation is a horizon unto My Revelation. The day star of grace shineth above it, and sheddeth a light which neither the clouds of men's idle fancy nor the vain imaginations of the aggressor can obscure.

8.12   He is indeed a captive who hath not recognized the Supreme Redeemer, but hath suffered his soul to be bound, distressed and helpless, in the fetters of his desires.

8.13   Suffer not yourselves to be wrapt in the dense veils of your selfish desires, inasmuch as I have perfected in every one of you My creation, so that the excellence of My handiwork may be fully revealed unto men. It follows, therefore, that every man hath been, and will continue to be, able of himself to appreciate the Beauty of God, the Glorified. Had he not been endowed with such a capacity, how could he be called to account for his failure?

8.14   If ye believe, to your own behoof will ye believe; and if ye believe not, ye yourselves will suffer.

8.15 Help Thou Thy loved ones, O my Lord, them that have forsaken their all, that they may obtain the things Thou dost possess, whom trials and tribulations have encompassed for having renounced the world and set their affections on Thy realm of glory. Shield them, I entreat Thee, O my Lord, from the assaults of their evil passions and desires, and aid them to obtain the things that shall profit them in this present world and in the next.

8.16 The virtues and attributes pertaining unto God are all evident and manifest, and have been mentioned and described in all the heavenly Books. Among them are trustworthiness, truthfulness, purity of heart while communing with God, forbearance, resignation to whatever the Almighty hath decreed, contentment with the things His Will hath provided, patience, nay, thankfulness in the midst of tribulation, and complete reliance, in all circumstances, upon Him. These rank, according to the estimate of God, among the highest and most laudable of all acts. All other acts are, and will ever remain, secondary and subordinate unto them....

8.17 Thy glory is my witness! At each daybreak they who love Thee wake to find the cup of woe set before their faces, because they have believed in Thee and acknowledged Thy signs. Though I firmly believe that Thou hast a greater compassion on them than they have on their own selves, though I recognize that Thou hast afflicted them for no other purpose except to proclaim Thy Cause, and to enable them to ascend into the heaven of Thine eternity and the precincts of Thy court, yet Thou knowest full well the frailty of some of them, and art aware of their impatience in their sufferings.

FROM THE WRITINGS AND UTTERANCES OF 'ABDU'L-BAHÁ

8.18 ... the tests and trials of God take place in this world, not in the world of the Kingdom.

8.19 These trials cause the feeble souls to waver while those who are firm are not affected.

8.20 It is clear, then, that tests and trials are, for sanctified souls, but God's bounty and grace, while to the weak, they are a calamity, unexpected and sudden.

These tests, even as thou didst write, do but cleanse the spotting of self from off the mirror of the heart, till the Sun of Truth can cast its rays thereon; for there is no veil more obstructive than the self, and however tenuous that veil may be, at the last it will completely shut a person out, and deprive him of his portion of eternal grace.

8.21 Lord! Turn the distressing cares of Thy holy ones into ease, their hardship into comfort, their abasement into glory, their sorrow into blissful joy, O Thou that holdest in Thy grasp the reins of all mankind!

8.22 In short, the day is approaching when the gay trappings of this earthly life will have been rolled up and the sorry plight and adversity of the people of iniquity will have waxed more grievous than those experienced by the oppressed. The inmates of palaces will have been subjected to the confinement of graves. and such as occupy the seats of honour will have fallen upon the dust of misery and abasement.

However, those who have offered up their lives as martyrs will shine resplendent even as a candle, and the effulgent glory of the friends of God will shed its radiance from the horizon of eternity like unto a brilliant star. Behold how wondrous is the bounty whereunto ye have attained. Ye have followed the example set by Him Whom the world hath wronged. Like unto the Day-Star of the world ye have outwardly suffered an eclipse by reason of the injustice the people of malice have wrought. However, far from an eclipse, this is naught but splendour; far from concealment, this is naught but the defeat of the legions. Ere long ye shall behold the shining light of the one true God shedding its radiance upon the whole world, while the heedless ones find themselves in the darkness of extinction.

In the estimation of the loved ones of God abasement is exaltation itself, and affliction leadeth to faithfulness. Earthly glory and comfort are but a mirage of illusion, while in the realm of the spirit heavenly gifts are everlasting and imperishable. The lights in the nether world may be bright, but they are put out at the break of dawn. whereas the stars that shine in the heaven of the love of God will sparkle continually throughout ages and centuries. Such is everlasting glory; such is infinite bounty; such is life eternal; and such is boundless grace. And upon you rest salutation and praise.

8.23 O spiritual friends and loved ones of the All-Merciful! In every Age believers are many but the tested are few. Render ye praise unto God that ye are tested believers, that ye have been subjected to every kind of trial and ordeal in the path of the supreme Lord. In the fire of ordeals your faces have flushed aglow like unto pure gold, and amidst the flames of cruelty and oppression which the wicked had kindled, ye suffered yourselves to be consumed while remaining all the time patient. Thus ye have initiated every believer into the ways of steadfastness and fortitude. You showed them the meaning of forbearance, of constancy, and of sacrifice, and what leadeth to dismay and distress. This indeed is a token of the gracious providence of God and a sign of the infinite favours vouchsafed by the Abha Beauty Who hath singled out the friends of that region to bear grievous sufferings in the path of His love. Outwardly they are fire, but inwardly light and an evidence of His glory. Ye have been examples of the verse: 'Let them that are men of action follow in their footsteps.' 'And to this let those aspire who aspire unto bliss.'

8.24 To attain eternal happiness one must suffer. He who has reached the state of self-sacrifice has true joy. Temporal joy will vanish

8.25 If we suffer it is the outcome of material things, and all the trials and troubles come from this world of illusion.

For instance, a merchant may lose his trade and depression ensues. A workman is dismissed and starvation stares him in the face. A farmer has a bad harvest, anxiety fills his mind. A man builds a house which is burnt to the ground and he is straightway homeless, ruined, and in despair.

All these examples are to show you that the trials which beset our every step, all our sorrow, pain, shame and grief, are born in the world of matter; whereas the spiritual Kingdom never causes sadness. A man living with his thoughts in this Kingdom knows perpetual joy. The ills all flesh is heir to do not pass him by, but they only touch the surface of his life, the depths are calm and serene.

Today, humanity is bowed down with trouble, sorrow and grief, no one escapes; the world is wet with tears; but, thank God, the remedy is at our doors. Let us turn our hearts away from the world of matter and live in the spiritual world! It alone can give us freedom! If we are hemmed in by difficulties we have only to call upon God, and by His great Mercy we shall be helped.

If sorrow and adversity visit us, let us turn our faces to the Kingdom and heavenly consolation will be outpoured.

If we are sick and in distress let us implore God's healing, and He will answer our prayer.

When our thoughts are filled with the bitterness of this world, let us turn our eyes to the sweetness of God's compassion and He will send us heavenly calm! If we are imprisoned in the material world, our spirit can soar into the Heavens and we shall be free indeed!

FROM THE WRITINGS AND LETTERS WRITTEN BY, OR ON BEHALF OF, SHOGHI EFFENDI

8.26 No matter what happens, nothing is as important as our feeling of trust in God, our inner peacefulness and faith that all, in the end, in spite of the severity of the ordeals we may pass through will come out as Bahá'u'lláh has promised. "He urges you to put these dark thoughts from your mind, and remember that God, the Creator of all men, can bear to see them suffer so, it is not for us to question His wisdom. He can compensate the innocent, in His own way, for the afflictions they bear.

8.27 No doubt to the degree we Bahá'ís the would over—strive to spread the Cause and live up to its teachings, there will be some mitigation to the suffering of the peoples of the world. But it seems apparent that the great failure to respond to Bahá'u'lláh's instructions, appeals and warnings issued in the 19th Century, has now sent the world along a path, and released forces, which must culminate in a still more violent upheaval and agony. The thing is out of hand, so to speak, and it is too late to avert catastrophic trials.

8.28 We must always look ahead and seek to accomplish in the future what we may have failed to do in the past. Failures, tests, and trials, if we use them correctly, can become the means of purifying our spirit, strengthening our characters, and enable us to rise to greater heights of service.

8.29 You should not consider yourself unfeeling because you see in this world agony the birth of a new and better world. This is just what the Bahá'ís should teach to others. However much pity and sympathy we may have for humanity, we nevertheless realize that people today are suffering for their own sins of omission and commission. We must help them to see this and to turn their thoughts and acts into the channels Divinely prescribed by Bahá'u'lláh.

8.30 We do not know what form the immediate future will take, anywhere. Because the passions of mankind are so unregenerate, and it is so deaf to the voice of Bahá'u'lláh, no doubt great suffering will be experienced. What we do know however, is that we are Bahá'ís and that our salvation lies in this God-sent Faith.

As we give to God, as we serve Him and love Him, so will He vouchsafe to us His Mercy, Guidance and Protection. We must, at all times, put the Faith first and our personal desires and comfort second. Having this Faith we have eternal security and happiness which nothing can take away from us ever, no matter what afflictions may befall a faithless world. The Cause of God is our security, and confidence in Bahá'u'lláh our protection.

8.31 Naturally there will be periods of distress and difficulty, and even severe test.; but if that person turns firmly towards the Divine Manifestation, studies carefully His Spiritual teachings and receives the blessings of the Holy Spirit, he will find that in reality these tests and difficulties have been the gifts of God to enable him to grow and develop.

8.32　Life is a constant struggle, not only against forces around us, but above all against our own 'ego'. We can never afford to rest on our oars, for if we do, we soon see ourselves carried down stream again. Many of those who drift away from the Cause do so for the reason that they had ceased to go on developing. They became complacent, or indifferent, and consequently ceased to draw the spiritual strength and vitality from the Cause which they should have. Sometimes, of course, people fail because of a test they just do not meet, and often our severest tests come from each other. Certainly the believers should try to avert such things, and if they happen, remedy them through love. Generally speaking nine-tenths of the friends' troubles are because they don't do the Bahá'í thing, in relation to each other, to the administrative bodies or in their personal lives.

8.33　And yet, how often we seem to forget the clear and repeated warning of our beloved Master, who in particular during the concluding years of His Mission on earth, laid stress on the severe mental tests that would inevitably sweep over His loved ones of the West... tests that would purge, purify and prepare them for their noble mission in life.

　　　　Ours then is the duty and privilege to labour, by day, by night, amidst the storm and stress of these troublous days, that we may quicken the zeal of our fellow-man, rekindle their hopes, stimulate their interests, open their eyes to the true Faith of God and enlist their active support in the carrying out of our common task for the peace and regeneration of the world.

8.34　We must always remember that in the cesspool of materialism, which is what modern civilization has to a certain extent become, Bahá'ís—that is some of them—are still to a certain extent affected by the society from which they have sprung. In other words, they have recognized the Manifestation of God, but they have not been believers long enough, or perhaps not tried hard enough, to become 'a new Creation'. He feels that, if you close your eyes to the failings of others, and fix your love and prayers upon Bahá'u'lláh, you will have the strength to weather this storm, and will be much better for it in the end, spiritually. Although you suffer, you will gain a maturity that will enable you to be of greater help to both your fellow-Bahá'ís and your children.

8.35 Perhaps the greatest test Bahá'ís are ever subjected to is from each other; but for the sake of the Master they should be ever ready to overlook each other's mistakes, apologize for harsh words they have uttered, forgive and forget. He strongly recommends to you this course of action.

8.36 We must never take one sentence in the Teachings and isolate it from the rest: it does not mean we must not love, but we must reach a spiritual plane where God comes first and great human passions are unable to turn us away from Him. All the time we see people who either through the force of hate or the passionate attachment they have to another person, sacrifice principle or bar themselves from the Path of God.

We know absence of light is darkness, but no one would assert darkness was not a fact. It exists even though it is only the absence of something else. So evil exists too, and we cannot close our eyes to it, even though it is a negative existence. We must seek to supplant it by good, and if we see an evil person is not influenceable by us, then we should shun his company for it is unhealthy.

We must love God, and in this state, a general love for all men becomes possible. We cannot love each human being for himself but our feeling towards humanity should be motivated by our love for the Father who created all men.

The Bahá'í Faith teaches man was always potentially man, even when passing through lower stages of evolution. Because he has more powers, and subtler powers than the animal, when he turns towards evil he becomes more vicious than an animal because of these very powers.

8.37 He was very sorry to hear that you have had so many tests in your Bahá'í life. There is no doubt that many of them are due to our own nature. In other words, if we are very sensitive, or if we are in some way brought up in a different environment from the Bahá'ís amongst whom we live, we naturally see things differently and may feel them more acutely; and the other side of it is that the imperfections of our fellow-Bahá'ís can be a great trial to us.

FROM THE WRITINGS AND LETTERS WRITTEN BY, OR ON BEHALF OF, THE UNIVERSAL HOUSE OF JUSTICE

8.38 Obedience to the Laws of Bahá'u'lláh will necessarily impose hardships in individual cases. No one should expect, upon becoming a Bahá'í, that faith will not be tested, and to our finite understanding of such matters these tests may occasionally seem unbearable. But we are aware of the assurance which Bahá'u'lláh Himself has given the believers that they will never be called upon to meet a test greater than their capacity to endure.

8.39 Even though you feel that the conflict between sensuality and spirituality is more than you can bear, your affirmation—'I do know I am a Bahá'í' is a positive factor in the battle you must wage. Every believer needs to remember that an essential characteristic of this physical world is that we are constantly faced with trials, tribulations, hardships and sufferings and that by overcoming them we achieve our moral and spiritual development; that we must seek to accomplish in the future what we may have failed to do in the past; that this is the way God tests His servants and we should look upon every failure or shortcoming as an opportunity to try again and to acquire a fuller consciousness of the Divine Will and purpose.

8.40 Certainly the problem confronting you is a difficult one. However, its solution lies within your power, for Bahá'u'lláh has assured us that God 'will never deal unjustly with anyone, neither will He task a soul a beyond its power'.[1] And again, 'Whensoever he hath fulfilled the conditions implied in the verse: 'Whoso maketh efforts for Us,' he shall enjoy the blessings conferred by the words: 'In Our Way shall we assuredly guide him.' You can be confident that with the help of doctors, by prayer and meditation, by self-abnegation and by giving as much time as possible to serving the Cause in your community you can eventually succeed in overcoming your problem."

[1 Bahá'u'lláh: *Gleanings from the Writings of Bahá'u'lláh*, p.106 1982 U.S. edition]

8.41 We are instructed to say that although there is every reason to expect that the world will experience travails and testing as never before, we do not know that what form these upheavals will take, when exactly they will come, how severe they will be, nor how long they will last. "The Faith itself as it emerges from obscurity will suffer severe trials. Sensitive souls such as yourself are particularly aware of these impending developments. However, Bahá'u'lláh has given us the Administrative Order which is the channel through which the spirit and guidance flow to the Bahá'ís and to mankind. The beloved Guardian spent his entire lifetime unfolding and explaining the pattern, and it is this administrative machinery that we should seek to support and strengthen. As weak and fragile as it is in these formative years of the Faith, it is still the haven and protection of the Bahá'ís and of the world. You are therefore encouraged to expend your energies and your many-faceted talents in teaching and consolidating the Bahá'í communities under the direction of the National Spiritual Assembly and its agencies.

8.42 You make reference to calamities and request specific answers if there are any as to when they may occur and with what magnitude. The House of Justice noted your comments that you have read what Bahá'u'lláh had to say about the collapse of the old world order and the coming of the new, and that in recent times friends returning from their pilgrimages spoke of meeting with Hands of the Cause and members of the House of Justice in which the coming of great world upheavals was related to a time 'around the end of the Five Year Plan and afterwards'. The House of Justice points out that calamities have been and are occurring and will continue to happen until mankind has been chastened sufficiently to accept the Manifestation for this day. 'Abdu'l-Bahá anticipated that the Lesser Peace could be established before the end of the twentieth century. However, Bahá'ís should not be diverted from the work of the Cause by the fear of catastrophes but should try to understand why they occur. The beloved Guardian, in innumerable places, has explained the reasons for these occurrences, and since they happen from time to time as explained above we should not be concerned as to when they occur.

8.43 In considering the effect of obedience to the laws on individual lives, one must remember that the purpose of this life is to prepare the soul for the next. Here one must learn to control and direct one's animal impulses, not to be a slave to them. Life in this world is a succession of tests and achievements, of falling short and of making new spiritual advances. Sometimes the course may seem very hard, but one can witness, again and again, that the soul who steadfastly obeys the Law of Bahá'u'lláh, however hard it may seem, grows spiritually, while the one who compromises with the law for the sake of his own apparent happiness is seen to have been following a chimera: he does not attain the happiness he sought, he retards his spiritual advance and often brings new problems upon himself.

CHAPTER 9:

LEARNING ABOUT LIFE THROUGH DEATH

FROM THE WRITINGS OF
BAHÁ'U'LLÁH

9.1   I came forth from God, and return unto Him, detached from all save Him, holding fast to His Name, the Merciful, the Compassionate.

9.2   O SON OF BEING! Bring thyself to account each day ere thou art summoned to a reckoning; for death, unheralded, shall come upon thee and thou shalt be called to give account for thy deeds.

9.3   O SON OF THE SUPREME! I have made death a messenger of joy to thee. Wherefore dost thou grieve? I made the light to shed on thee its splendor. Why dost thou veil thyself therefrom?

9.4   O SON OF SPIRIT! With the joyful tidings of light I hail thee: rejoice! To the court of holiness I summon thee; abide therein that thou mayest live in peace for evermore.

9.5   O SON OF MAN! Sorrow not save that thou art far from Us. Rejoice not save that thou art drawing near and returning unto Us.

9.6   Know thou that every hearing ear, if kept pure and undefiled, must, at all times and from every direction, hearken to the voice that uttereth these holy words: "Verily, we are God's, and to Him shall we return." The mysteries of man's physical death and of his return have not been divulged, and still remain unread. By the righteousness of God! Were they to be revealed, they would evoke such fear and sorrow that some would perish, while others would be so filled with gladness as to wish for death, and beseech, with unceasing longing, the one true God—exalted be His glory—to hasten their end.

Death proffereth unto every confident believer the cup that is life indeed. It bestoweth joy, and is the bearer of gladness. It conferreth the gift of everlasting life.

As to those that have tasted of the fruit of man's earthly existence, which is the recognition of the one true God, exalted be His glory, their life hereafter is such as We are unable to describe. The knowledge thereof is with God, alone, the Lord of all worlds.

9.7   In several of Our Tablets We have referred to this theme, and have set forth the various stages in the development of the soul. Verily I say, the human soul is exalted above all egress and regress. It is still, and yet it soareth; it moveth, and yet it is still. It is, in itself, a testimony that beareth witness to the existence of a world that is contingent, as well as to the reality of a world that hath neither beginning nor end. Behold how the dream thou hast dreamed is, after the lapse of many years, re-enacted before thine eyes. Consider how strange is the mystery of the world that appeareth to thee in thy dream. Ponder in thine heart upon the unsearchable wisdom of God, and meditate on its manifold revelations....

9.8   And now concerning thy question whether human souls continue to be conscious one of another after their separation from the body. Know thou that the souls of the people of Baha, who have entered and been established within the Crimson Ark, shall associate and commune intimately one with another, and shall be so closely associated in their lives, their aspirations, their aims and strivings as to be even as one soul. They are indeed the ones who are well-informed, who are keen-sighted, and who are endued with understanding. Thus hath it been decreed by Him Who is the All-Knowing, the All-Wise.

        The people of Bahá, who are the inmates of the Ark of God, are, one and all, well aware of one another's state and condition, and are united in the bonds of intimacy and fellowship. Such a state, however, must depend upon their faith and their conduct. They that are of the same grade and station are fully aware of one another's capacity, character, accomplishments and merits. They that are of a lower grade, however, are incapable of comprehending adequately the station, or of estimating the merits, of those that rank above them. Each shall receive his share from thy Lord. Blessed is the man that hath turned his face towards God, and walked steadfastly in His love, until his soul hath winged its flight unto God, the Sovereign Lord of all, the Most Powerful, the Ever-Forgiving, the All-Merciful.

        The souls of the infidels, however, shall—and to this I bear witness—when breathing their last be made aware of the good things that have escaped them, and shall bemoan their plight, and shall humble themselves before God. They shall continue doing so after the separation of their souls from their bodies.

It is clear and evident that all men shall, after their physical death, estimate the worth of their deeds, and realize all that their hands have wrought. I swear by the Day Star that shineth above the horizon of Divine power! They that are the followers of the one true God shall, the moment they depart out of this life, experience such joy and gladness as would be impossible to describe, while they that live in error shall be seized with such fear and trembling, and shall be filled with such consternation, as nothing can exceed. Well is it with him that hath quaffed the choice and incorruptible wine of faith through the gracious favor and the manifold bounties of Him Who is the Lord of all Faiths....

9.9　The world beyond is as different from this world as this world is different from that of the child while still in the womb of its mother.

9.10　The Prophets and Messengers of God have been sent down for the sole purpose of guiding mankind to the straight Path of Truth. The purpose underlying Their revelation hath been to educate all men, that they may, at the hour of death, ascend, in the utmost purity and sanctity and with absolute detachment, to the throne of the Most High. The light which these souls radiate is responsible for the progress of the world and the advancement of its peoples. They are like unto leaven which leaveneth the world of being, and constitute the animating force through which the arts and wonders of the world are made manifest. Through them the clouds rain their bounty upon men, and the earth bringeth forth its fruits. All things must needs have a cause, a motive power, an animating principle. These souls and symbols of detachment have provided, and will continue to provide, the supreme moving impulse in the world of being. The world beyond is as different from this world as this world is different from that of the child while still in the womb of its mother. When the soul attaineth the Presence of God, it will assume the form that best befitteth its immortality and is worthy of its celestial habitation.

9.11　The light which these souls radiate is responsible for the progress of the world and the advancement of its peoples. They are like unto leaven which leaveneth the world of being, and constitute the animating force through which the arts and wonders of the world are made manifest. Through them the clouds rain their bounty upon men, and the earth bringeth forth its fruits. All things must needs have a cause, a motive power, an animating principle. These souls and symbols of detachment have provided, and will continue to provide, the supreme moving impulse in the world of being.

9.12 The mysteries of man's physical death and of his return have not been divulged, and still remain unread. By the righteousness of God! Were they to be revealed, they would evoke such fear and sorrow that some would perish, while others would be so filled with gladness as to wish for death, and beseech, with unceasing longing, the one true God—exalted be His glory—to hasten their end.

9.13 I beseech Thee, however, O Thou Who art the Enlightener of the world and the Lord of the nations, at this very moment when, with the hands of hope, I have clung to the hem of the raiment of Thy mercy and Thy bounty, to forgive Thy servants who have soared in the atmosphere of Thy nearness, and set their faces towards the splendors of the light of Thy countenance, and turned unto the horizon of Thy good pleasure, and approached the ocean of Thy mercy, and all their lives long have spoken forth Thy praise, and have been inflamed with the fire of their love for Thee. Do Thou ordain for them, O Lord my God, both before and after their death, what becometh the loftiness of Thy bounty and the excellence of Thy loving-kindness.

9.14 Grant, O my Lord, that they who have ascended unto Thee may repair unto Him Who is the most exalted Companion, and abide beneath the shadow of the Tabernacle of Thy majesty and the Sanctuary of Thy glory. Sprinkle, O my Lord, upon them from the ocean of Thy forgiveness what will make them worthy to abide, so long as Thine own sovereignty endureth, within Thy most exalted kingdom and Thine all-highest dominion. Potent art Thou to do what pleaseth Thee.

FROM THE WRITINGS AND UTTERANCES OF 'ABDU'L-BAHÁ

9.15   As 'Abdu'l-Bahá wrote to a grieving mother who had lost her son, "That beloved child addresseth thee from the hidden world: 'O thou kind Mother, thank divine Providence that I have been freed from a small and gloomy cage and, like the birds of the meadows, have soared to the divine world—a world which is spacious, illumined, and ever gay and jubilant. Therefore, lament not, O Mother, and be not grieved; I am not of the lost, nor have I been obliterated and destroyed. I have shaken off the mortal form and have raised my banner in this spiritual world. Following this separation is everlasting companionship. Thou shalt find me in the heaven of the Lord, immersed in an ocean of light.'

9.16   As to thy question regarding discoveries made by the soul after it hath put off its human form: certainly, that world is a world of perceptions and discoveries, for the interposed veil will be lifted away and the human spirit will gaze upon souls that are above, below, and on a par with itself. It is similar to the condition of a human being in the womb, where his eyes are veiled, and all things are hidden away from him. Once he is born out of the uterine world and entereth this life, he findeth it, with relation to that of the womb, to be a place of perceptions and discoveries, and he observeth all things through his outer eye. In the same way, once he hath departed this life, he will behold, in that world whatsoever was hidden from him here: but there he will look upon and comprehend all things with his inner eye. There will he gaze on his fellows and his peers, and those in the ranks above him, and those below. As for what is meant by the equality of souls in the all-highest realm, it is this: the souls of the believers, at the time when they first become manifest in the world of the body, are equal, and each is sanctified and pure. In this world, however, they will begin to differ one from another, some achieving the highest station, some a middle one, others remaining at the lowest stage of being. Their equal status is at the beginning of their existence; the differentiation followeth their passing away.

9.17 Love is the one means that ensureth true felicity both in this world and the next.

9.18 When the human soul soareth out of this transient heap of dust and riseth into the world of God, then veils will fall away, and verities will come to light, and all things unknown before will be made clear, and hidden truths be understood... Consider how a being, in the world of the womb, was deaf of ear and blind of eye, and mute of tongue; how he was bereft of any perceptions at all. But once, out of that world of darkness, he passed into this world of light, then his eye saw, his ear heard, his tongue spoke. In the same way, once he hath hastened away from this mortal place into the Kingdom of God, then he will be born in the spirit; then the eye of his perception will open, the ear of his soul will hearken, and all the truths of which he was ignorant before will be made plain and clear.

9.19 Know then that the Lord God possesseth invisible realms which the human intellect can never hope to fathom nor the mind of man conceive. When once thou hast cleansed the channel of thy spiritual sense from the pollution of this worldly life, then wilt thou breathe in the sweet scents of holiness that blow from the blissful bowers of that heavenly land.

9.20 O ye two patient souls! Your letter was received. The death of that beloved youth and his separation from you have caused the utmost sorrow and grief; for he winged his flight in the flower of his age and the bloom of his youth to the heavenly nest. But he hath been freed from this sorrow-stricken shelter and hath turned his face toward the everlasting nest of the Kingdom, and, being delivered from a dark and narrow world, hath hastened to the sanctified realm of light; therein lieth the consolation of our hearts.

   The inscrutable divine wisdom underlieth such heart-rending occurrences. It is as if a kind gardener transferreth a fresh and tender shrub from a confined place to a wide open area. This transfer is not the cause of the withering, the lessening or the destruction of that shrub; nay, on the contrary, it maketh it to grow and thrive, acquire freshness and delicacy, become green and bear fruit. This hidden secret is well known to the gardener, but those souls who are unaware of this bounty suppose that the gardener, in his anger and wrath, hath uprooted the shrub. Yet to those who are aware, this concealed fact is manifest, and this predestined decree is considered a bounty. Do not feel grieved or disconsolate, therefore, at the ascension of that bird of faithfulness; nay, under all circumstances pray for that youth, supplicating for him forgiveness and the elevation of his station.

I hope that ye will attain the utmost patience, composure and resignation, and I entreat and implore at the Threshold of Oneness, begging for forgiveness and pardon. My hope from the infinite bounties of God is that He may shelter this dove of the garden of faith, and cause him to abide on the branch of the Supreme Concourse, that he may sing in the best of melodies the praise and glorification of the Lord of Names and Attributes.

9.21   To consider that after the death of the body the sprit perishes is like imagining that a bird in a cage will be destroyed if the cage is broken, though the bird has nothing to fear from the destruction of the cage. Our body is like the cage, and the spirit is like the bird. We see that without the cage this bird flies in the world of sleep; therefore if the cage becomes broken, the bird will continue and exist. Its feelings will be even more powerful, its perceptions greater, and its happiness increased. In truth, from hell it reaches a paradise of delights because for the thankful birds there is no paradise greater than freedom from the cage...

9.22   Can a departed soul converse with someone still on earth?'

'Abdu'l-Bahá.—'A conversation can be held, but not as our conversation. There is no doubt that the forces of the higher worlds interplay with the forces of this plane. The heart of man is open to inspiration; this is spiritual communication. As in a dream one talks with a friend while the mouth is silent, so is it in the conversation of the spirit. A man may converse with the ego within him saying: "May I do this? Would it be advisable for me to do this work?" Such as this is conversation with the higher self.'

9.23 There is no appointed length of life for man. Lengthen your life by living according to God's spiritual laws. Then you will live forever. This is true longevity, the real life. The real life is eternal happiness and existence in the Knowledge of God.

FROM THE WRITINGS AND LETTERS WRITTEN BY, OR ON BEHALF OF, SHOGHI EFFENDI

9.24 Bahá'u'lláh says that were we to have the proper vision to see the blessings of the other world we would not bear to endure one more hour of existence upon the earth. The reason why we are deprived of that vision is because otherwise no one would care to remain and the whole fabric of society will be destroyed.

Shoghi Effendi wishes you therefore to think of her blessings and rejoice in her happiness. Should we have true faith in the words of the prophets we would not fear death nor feel despondent over the passing of our loved ones.

9.25 Regarding the questions which you ask, concerning Bahá'í burials... etc. At the present time the Guardian is not stressing these matters, as their establishment might divert attention to the supreme tasks we have before us. However, the answers are as follows: under the Bahá'í teachings it seems clear that the body is not to be embalmed. The burial should take place within an hour's travel time from the place of death. The preparation for the burial is a careful washing, and placing in a shroud of white clothes, silk preferably. There is nothing in the teachings with regard to turning the body over to scientific institutions for scientific research, and therefore the individuals may do as he wishes, until such a time as the Universal House of Justice may legislate on this matter, if they ever do; sometimes even sooner; although there is no provision in the teaching as to the time limit.

9.26 The dead should be buried with their face turned toward the Qiblih. There is also a congregational to be recited. Beside this there is no other ceremony to be performed.

9.27 To 'get to heaven' as you say is dependent on two things—faith in the Manifestation of God in His Day, in other words in this Age in Bahá'u'lláh; and good deeds, in other words living to the best of our ability a noble life and doing unto others as we would be done by. But we must always remember that our existence and everything we have or ever will have is dependent upon the Mercy of God and His Bounty, and therefore He can accept into His heaven, which is really nearness to Him, even the lowliest if He pleases. We always have the hope of receiving His Mercy if we reach out for it.

9.28 The Báb has told us to bury the dead in silk (if possible) in coffins of crystal. Why? Because the body, though now dust, was once exalted by the immortal soul of man!

9.29 ... He was very sad to hear of your sadness and difficulties. Should that be only due to the passing of your son, it is not full justified, at least in the light of the teachings of Bahá'u'lláh. He explicitly states that, had we the vision to see the other world, and the mind to conceive its glory, we would not desire to remain here even for a moment. Man is destined by God to undergo a spiritual development that extends throughout eternity. His life upon this earth is only the first stage of that development. When we outgrow our physical form, and are considered by God ready to reap the fruit of our spiritual development, we proceed to the other world. We term it death only because of our short sightedness. A more proper term would be 'a more abundant life.' it is a forward step we have taken. In the light of the teachings, therefore, the proper attitude for you is to pray that God may encompass your son with His infinite blessings, that he may enhance his development and give him that felicity which awaits...every soul. "...the world is full of suffering. Bahá'u'lláh tells us that the deeper are the furrows it digs into our very being, the greater will be the fruit of our life and the more enhanced our spiritual development. All the Saints that shine in the history of society had to pass through tribulations. Their form was various but their effect has always been the same, namely, the purification of our heart and soul for receiving the light of God.

9.30 The Master has told us that gifts and good deeds done in memory of those who have passed on, are most helpful to the development of their souls in the realms beyond...

9.31 With regard to the soul of man. According to the Bahá'í Teachings the human soul starts with the formation of the embryo, and continues to develop and pass through stages of existence after its separation from the body. Its progress is thus infinite.

9.32 Concerning your question whether a soul can receive knowledge of the Truth in the world beyond. Such a knowledge is surely possible, and is but a sign of the loving Mercy of the Almighty. We can, through our prayers, help every soul to gradually attain this high station, even if it has failed to reach it in this world. The progress of the soul does not come to an end with death. It rather starts along a new line. Bahá'u'lláh teaches that great far- reaching possibilities await the soul in the other world. Spiritual progress in that realm is infinite, and no man, while on this earth, can visualize its full power and extent.

9.33 In His Tablets Bahá'u'lláh says that were we able to comprehend the facilities that await us in the world to come, death would lose its sting; nay rather we would welcome it as a gateway to a realm immeasurably higher and nobler than this home of suffering we call our earth. You should therefore think of their blessings and comfort yourself for your momentary separation. In time all of us will join our departed ones and share their joys.

9.34 ... Such earnest souls, when they pass out of this life, enter a state of being far nobler and more beautiful than this one. We fear it only because it is unknown to us and we have little faith in the words of the Prophets who bring a true message of certainty from that realm of the spirit. We should face death with joy especially if our life upon this plane of existence has been full of good deeds.

FROM THE WRITINGS AND LETTERS WRITTEN BY, OR ON BEHALF OF, THE UNIVERSAL HOUSE OF JUSTICE

9.35 Briefly the law for the burial of the dead states that it is forbidden to carry the body for more than one hour's journey from the place of death; that the body should be wrapped in a shroud of silk or cotton, and on it's finger should be placed a ring bearing inscription 'I came forth from God, and return unto Him, detached from all save Him, holding fast to His Name, the Merciful, the Compassionate'; and that the coffin should be of crystal, stone or hard fine wood. A specific 'prayer for the dead' is ordained, to be said before interment. It has been explained by 'Abdu'l-Bahá and the guardian that this law prohibits cremation of the dead. The formal prayer and the ring are meant to be for those who have attained the age of maturity.

9.36 As the law of burial, the Universal House of Justice suggests that you confine your statement to the following parts of this law which are now binding on the believers in the West:
(1) That one must be buried, not cremated.
(2) That the prayer for the dead is to be recited for a believer of the age of 15 years or over. This, as you know, is the prayers which appears as number CLXVII in *Prayers and Meditations by Bahá'u'lláh*.
(3) That the body not be transported more than one hour's journey from the place of death. The method of transport is not specified, but the journey must not take longer than one hour.

9.37 The friends should certainly be informed of the Bahá'í laws relating to burial and encouraged to do all they can to ensure after their passing they are buried according to Bahá'í law. It is not always possible to ensure this by stating it in a will and assemblies should consult upon the matter, taking legal advice if necessary, and make the best arrangements possible."

9.38 In reply to your letter of 1 May 1979, the Universal House Of Justice has instructed us to share with you the following excerpt from a letter written on behalf of Shoghi Effendi by his secretary to a believer who asked about suicide. "'suicide is forbidden in the Cause. God Who is the Author of all life can alone take it away, and dispose of it the way he deems best. Whoever commits suicide endangers his soul, and will suffer spiritually as a result in the other worlds beyond.' "the House of Justice admonishes you to put all thought of suicide and death out of your mind and concentrate on prayer and effort to serve the Cause of Bahá'u'lláh.

CHAPTER 10:

OFFERING A FULFILLING PATH TO EVERY SOUL

FROM THE WRITINGS OF BAHÁ'U'LLÁH

10.1   The whole duty of man in this Day is to attain that share of the flood of grace which God poureth forth for him.

10.2   The purpose underlying the revelation of every heavenly Book, nay, of every divinely-revealed verse, is to endue all men with righteousness and understanding, so that peace and tranquillity may be firmly established amongst them. Whatsoever instilleth assurance into the hearts of men, whatsoever exalteth their station or promoteth their contentment, is acceptable in the sight of God. How lofty is the station which man, if he but choose to fulfill his high destiny, can attain! To what depths of degradation he can sink, depths which the meanest of creatures have never reached! Seize, O friends, the chance which this Day offereth you, and deprive not yourselves of the liberal effusions of His grace. I beseech God that He may graciously enable every one of you to adorn himself, in this blessed Day, with the ornament of pure and holy deeds. He, verily, doeth whatsoever He willeth.

10.3   O COMPANION OF MY THRONE! Hear no evil, and see no evil, abase not thyself, neither sigh and weep. Speak no evil, that thou mayest not hear it spoken unto thee, and magnify not the faults of others that thine own faults may not appear great; and wish not the abasement of anyone, that thine own abasement be not exposed. Live then the days of thy life, that are less than a fleeting moment, with thy mind stainless, thy heart unsullied, thy thoughts pure, and thy nature sanctified, so that, free and content, thou mayest put away this mortal frame, and repair unto the mystic paradise and abide in the eternal kingdom for evermore.

10.4   The essence of faith is fewness of words and abundance of deeds; he whose words exceed his deeds, know verily his death is better than his life.

10.5   Let deeds, not words, be your adorning.

10.6   O SON OF MAN! Ponder and reflect. Is it thy wish to die upon thy bed, or to shed thy life-blood on the dust, a martyr in My path, and so become the manifestation of My command and the revealer of My light in the highest paradise? Judge thou aright, O servant!

10.7   Take heed lest anything deter thee from extolling the greatness of this Day—the Day whereon the Finger of majesty and power hath opened the seal of the Wine of Reunion, and called all who are in the heavens and all who are on the earth.

10.8   God willing, thou mayest accomplish a deed whose fragrance shall endure as long as the Names of God—exalted be His glory—will endure.

10.9   O CHILDREN OF NEGLIGENCE! Set not your affections on mortal sovereignty and rejoice not therein. Ye are even as the unwary bird that with full confidence warbleth upon the bough; till of a sudden the fowler Death throws it upon the dust, and the melody, the form and the color are gone, leaving not a trace. Wherefore take heed, O bondslaves of desire!

FROM THE WRITINGS AND UTTERANCES OF 'ABDU'L-BAHÁ

10.10   Unless these divine bestowals be revealed from the inner self of humankind, the bounty of the Manifestation will prove barren, and the dazzling rays of the Sun of Truth will have no effect whatever.

10.11   The most vital duty, in this day, is to purify your characters, to correct your manners, and improve your conduct. The beloved of the Merciful must show forth such character and conduct among His creatures, that the fragrance of their holiness may be shed upon the whole world, and may quicken the dead, inasmuch as the purpose of the Manifestation of God and the dawning of the limitless lights of the Invisible is to educate the souls of men, and refine the character of every living man—so that blessed individuals, who have freed themselves from the murk of the animal world, shall rise up with those qualities which are the adornings of the reality of man.

10.12 Mortal charm shall fade away, roses shall give way to thorns, and beauty and youth shall live their day and be no more. But that which eternally endureth is the Beauty of the True One, for its splendour perisheth not and its glory lasteth for ever; its charm is all-powerful and its attraction infinite.

10.13 O thou who art attracted to the Kingdom of God! Every soul seeketh an object and cherisheth a desire, and day and night striveth to attain his aim. One craveth riches, another thirsteth for glory and still another yearneth for fame, for art, for prosperity and the like. Yet finally all are doomed to loss and disappointment. One and all they leave behind them all that is theirs and empty-handed hasten to the realm beyond, and all their labours shall be in vain. To dust they shall all return, denuded, depressed, disheartened and in utter despair.

But, praised be the Lord, thou art engaged in that which secureth for thee a gain that shall eternally endure; and that is naught but thine attraction to the Kingdom of God, thy faith, and thy knowledge, the enlightenment of thine heart, and thine earnest endeavour to promote the Divine Teachings.

Verily this gift is imperishable and this wealth is a treasure from on high!

10.14 The fleeting hours of man's life on earth pass swiftly by and the little that still remaineth shall come to an end, but that which endureth and lasteth for evermore is the fruit that man reapeth from his servitude at the Divine Threshold. Behold the truth of this saying, how abundant and glorious are the proofs thereof in the world of being!

10.15 O ye friends of God! True friends are even as skilled physicians, and the Teachings of God are as healing balm, a medicine for the conscience of man. They clear the head, so that a man can breathe them in and delight in their sweet fragrance. They waken those who sleep. They bring awareness to the unheeding, and a portion to the outcast, and to the hopeless, hope.

10.16   Wherefore, look not on the degree of your capacity, ask not if you are worthy of the task: rest ye your hopes on the help and loving-kindness, the favours and bestowals of Bahá'u'lláh—may my soul be offered up for His friends! Urge on the steed of high endeavour over the field of sacrifice, and carry away from this wide arena the prize of divine grace.

10.17   O ye loved ones of God! Know ye that the world is even as a mirage rising over the sands, that the thirsty mistaketh for water. The wine of this world is but a vapour in the desert, its pity and compassion but toil and trouble, the repose it proffereth only weariness and sorrow. Abandon it to those who belong to it, and turn your faces unto the Kingdom of your Lord the All-Merciful, that His grace and bounty may cast their dawning splendours over you, and a heavenly table may be sent down for you, and your Lord may bless you, and shower His riches upon you to gladden your bosoms and fill your hearts with bliss, to attract your minds, and cleanse your souls, and console your eyes.

    O ye loved ones of God! Is there any giver save God? He singleth out for His mercy whomsoever He willeth. Erelong will He open before you the gates of His knowledge and fill up your hearts with His love. He will cheer your souls with the gentle winds of His holiness and make bright your faces with the splendours of His lights, and exalt the memory of you amongst all peoples. Your Lord is verily the Compassionate, the Merciful.

    He will come to your aid with invisible hosts, and support you with armies of inspiration from the Concourse above; He will send unto you sweet perfumes from the highest Paradise, and waft over you the pure breathings that blow from the rose gardens of the Company on high. He will breathe into your hearts the spirit of life, cause you to enter the Ark of salvation, and reveal unto you His clear tokens and signs. Verily is this abounding grace. Verily is this the victory that none can deny.

10.18   He is a true Bahá'í who strives by day and by night to progress and advance along the path of human endeavour, whose most cherished desire is so to live and act as to enrich and illuminate the world, whose source of inspiration is the essence of divine virtue, whose aim in life is so to conduct himself as to be the cause of infinite progress. Only when he attains unto such perfect gifts can it be said of him that he is a true Bahá'í.

10.19 Therefore, we learn that nearness to God is possible through devotion to Him, through entrance into the Kingdom and service to humanity; it is attained by unity with mankind and through loving-kindness to all; it is dependent upon investigation of truth, acquisition of praiseworthy virtues, service in the cause of universal peace and personal sanctification. In a word, nearness to God necessitates sacrifice of self, severance and the giving up of all to Him. Nearness is likeness.

10.20 The world for the most part is sunk in materialism, and the blessings of the Holy Spirit are ignored. There is so little real spiritual feeling, and the progress of the world is for the most part merely material. Men are becoming like unto beasts that perish, for we know that they have no spiritual feeling—they do not turn to God, they have no religion! These things belong to man alone, and if he is without them he is a prisoner of nature, and no whit better than an animal.

10.21 If you attain to such a capacity of love and unity, the Blessed Perfection will shower infinite graces of the spiritual Kingdom upon you, guide, protect and preserve you under the shadow of His Word, increase your happiness in this world and uphold you through all difficulties.

FROM THE WRITINGS AND LETTERS WRITTEN BY, OR ON BEHALF OF, SHOGHI EFFENDI

10.22 An angry Providence, the cynic might well observe, has abandoned a hapless planet to its fate, and fixed irrevocably its doom. Sore-tried and disillusioned, humanity has no doubt lost its orientation, and would seem to have lost as well its faith and hope. It is hovering, unshepherded and visionless, on the brink of disaster. A sense of fatality seems to pervade it. An ever-deepening gloom is settling on its fortunes as she recedes further and further from the outer fringes of the darkest zone of its agitated life and penetrates its very heart

10.23 Dearly beloved friends! A rectitude of conduct which, in all its manifestations, offers a striking contrast to the deceitfulness and corruption that characterize the political life of the nation and of the parties and factions that compose it; a holiness and chastity that are diametrically opposed to the moral laxity and licentiousness which defile the character of a not inconsiderable proportion of its citizens; an interracial fellowship completely purged from the curse of racial prejudice which stigmatizes the vast majority of its people—these are the weapons which the American believers can and must wield in their double crusade, first to regenerate the inward life of their own community, and next to assail the long-standing evils that have entrenched themselves in the life of their nation. The perfection of such weapons, the wise and effective utilization of every one of them, more than the furtherance of any particular plan, or the devising of any special scheme, or the accumulation of any amount of material resources, can prepare them for the time when the Hand of Destiny will have directed them to assist in creating and in bringing into operation that World Order which is now incubating within the worldwide administrative institutions of their Faith.

FROM THE WRITINGS AND LETTERS WRITTEN BY, OR ON BEHALF OF, THE UNIVERSAL HOUSE OF JUSTICE

10.24 For if we look back at one hundred years of an unexampled history of unremitting progress, we also look forward to many centuries of unfolding fulfillment of divine purpose fulfillment, which as experience has shown, is incrementally realized through the systematic advances of Plans and the wondrous leaps and thrusts of epochs.

PART II:
PRACTICES

CHAPTER 11:

PRACTICING MODERATION IN ALL THINGS

FROM THE WRITINGS OF BAHÁ'U'LLÁH

11.1 It is incumbent upon them who are in authority to exercise moderation in all things. Whatsoever passeth beyond the limits of moderation will cease to exert a beneficial influence. Consider for instance such things as liberty, civilization and the like. However much men of understanding may favorably regard them, they will, if carried to excess, exercise a pernicious influence upon men...

11.2 Fear ye God, and take heed not to outstrip the bounds of moderation, and be numbered among the extravagant.

11.3 Whoso cleaveth to justice, can, under no circumstances, transgress the limits of moderation. He discerneth the truth in all things, through the guidance of Him Who is the All-Seeing. The civilization, so often vaunted by the learned exponents of arts and sciences, will, if allowed to overleap the bounds of moderation, bring great evil upon men. Thus warneth you He Who is the All-Knowing. If carried to excess, civilization will prove as prolific a source of evil as it had been of goodness when kept within the restraints of moderation. Meditate on this, O people, and be not of them that wander distraught in the wilderness of error. The day is approaching when its flame will devour the cities, when the Tongue of Grandeur will proclaim: "The Kingdom is God's, the Almighty, the All-Praised!"

11.4 The Great Being saith: Human utterance is an essence which aspireth to exert its influence and needeth moderation. As to its influence, this is conditional upon refinement which in turn is dependent upon hearts which are detached and pure. As to its moderation, this hath to be combined with tact and wisdom as prescribed in the Holy Scriptures and Tablets.

11.5 Place not thy reliance on thy treasures. Put thy whole confidence in the grace of God, thy Lord. Let Him be thy trust in whatever thou doest, and be of them that have submitted themselves to His Will. Let Him be thy helper and enrich thyself with His treasures, for with Him are the treasuries of the heavens and of the earth. He bestoweth them upon whom He will, and from whom He will He withholdeth them. There is none other God but Him, the All-Possessing, the All-Praised. All are but paupers at the door of His mercy; all are helpless before the revelation of His sovereignty, and beseech His favors.

Overstep not the bounds of moderation, and deal justly with them that serve thee. Bestow upon them according to their needs, and not to the extent that will enable them to lay up riches for themselves, to deck their persons, to embellish their homes, to acquire the things that are of no benefit unto them, and to be numbered with the extravagant. Deal with them with undeviating justice, so that none among them may either suffer want, or be pampered with luxuries. This is but manifest justice.

11.6 Liberty must, in the end, lead to sedition, whose flames none can quench. Thus warneth you He Who is the Reckoner, the All-Knowing. Know ye that the embodiment of liberty and its symbol is the animal. That which beseemeth man is submission unto such restraints as will protect him from his own ignorance, and guard him against the harm of the mischief-maker. Liberty causeth man to overstep the bounds of propriety, and to infringe on the dignity of his station. It debaseth him to the level of extreme depravity and wickedness.

11.7 O YE THAT PRIDE YOURSELVES ON MORTAL RICHES! Know ye in truth that wealth is a mighty barrier between the seeker and his desire, the lover and his beloved. The rich, but for a few, shall in no wise attain the court of His presence nor enter the city of content and resignation. Well is it then with him, who, being rich, is not hindered by his riches from the eternal kingdom, nor deprived by them of imperishable dominion. By the Most Great Name! The splendor of such a wealthy man shall illuminate the dwellers of heaven even as the sun enlightens the people of the earth!

11.8 Say: Rejoice not in the things ye possess; tonight they are yours, tomorrow others will possess them. Thus warneth you He Who is the All-Knowing, the All-Informed. Say: Can ye claim that what ye own is lasting or secure? Nay! By Myself, the All-Merciful. The days of your life flee away as a breath of wind, and all your pomp and glory shall be folded up as were the pomp and glory of those gone before you. Reflect, O people! What hath become of your bygone days, your lost centuries? Happy the days that have been consecrated to the remembrance of God, and blessed the hours which have been spent in praise of Him Who is the All-Wise. By My life! Neither the pomp of the mighty, nor the wealth of the rich, nor even the ascendancy of the ungodly will endure. All will perish, at a word from Him. He, verily, is the All-Powerful, the All-Compelling, the Almighty. What advantage is there in the earthly things which men possess? That which shall profit them, they have utterly neglected. Erelong, they will awake from their slumber, and find themselves unable to obtain that which hath escaped them in the days of their Lord, the Almighty, the All-Praised. Did they but know it, they would renounce their all, that their names may be mentioned before His throne. They, verily, are accounted among the dead.

11.9   O peoples of the world! Forsake all evil, hold fast that which is good. Strive to be shining examples unto all mankind, and true reminders of the virtues of God amidst men. He that riseth to serve My Cause should manifest My wisdom, and bend every effort to banish ignorance from the earth. Be united in counsel, be one in thought. Let each morn be better than its eve and each morrow richer than its yesterday. Man's merit lieth in service and virtue and not in the pageantry of wealth and riches. Take heed that your words be purged from idle fancies and worldly desires and your deeds be cleansed from craftiness and suspicion. Dissipate not the wealth of your precious lives in the pursuit of evil and corrupt affection, nor let your endeavours be spent in promoting your personal interest. Be generous in your days of plenty, and be patient in the hour of loss. Adversity is followed by success and rejoicings follow woe. Guard against idleness and sloth, and cling unto that which profiteth mankind, whether young or old, whether high or low. Beware lest ye sow tares of dissension among men or plant thorns of doubt in pure and radiant hearts.

11.10   O ye beloved of the Lord! Commit not that which defileth the limpid stream of love or destroyeth the sweet fragrance of friendship. By the righteousness of the Lord! Ye were created to show love one to another and not perversity and rancour. Take pride not in love for yourselves but in love for your fellow-creatures. Glory not in love for your country, but in love for all mankind. Let your eye be chaste, your hand faithful, your tongue truthful and your heart enlightened. Abase not the station of the learned in Baha and belittle not the rank of such rulers as administer justice amidst you. Set your reliance on the army of justice, put on the armour of wisdom, let your adorning be forgiveness and mercy and that which cheereth the hearts of the well-favoured of God.

11.11   We see you rejoicing in that which ye have amassed for others and shutting out yourselves from the worlds which naught except My guarded Tablet can reckon. The treasures ye have laid up have drawn you far away from your ultimate objective. This ill beseemeth you, could ye but understand it. Wash your hearts from all earthly defilements, and hasten to enter the Kingdom of your Lord, the Creator of earth and heaven, Who caused the world to tremble and all its peoples to wail, except them that have renounced all things and clung to that which the Hidden Tablet hath ordained.

11.12   The Almighty beareth Me witness: To act like the beasts of the field is unworthy of man.

11.13   Gird up the loins of your endeavor, O people of Baha, that haply the tumult of religious dissension and strife that agitateth the peoples of the earth may be stilled, that every trace of it may be completely obliterated. For the love of God, and them that serve Him, arise to aid this most sublime and momentous Revelation. Religious fanaticism and hatred are a world-devouring fire, whose violence none can quench. The Hand of Divine power can, alone, deliver mankind from this desolating affliction....

11.14   Say: Barter not away this Youth, O people, for the vanities of this world or the delights of heaven.

11.15   In all circumstances they should conduct themselves with moderation; if the meal be only one course this is more pleasing in the sight of God; however, according to their means, they should seek to have this single dish be of good quality.

FROM THE WRITINGS AND UTTERANCES OF 'ABDU'L-BAHÁ

11.16   For desire is a flame that has reduced to ashes uncounted lifetime harvests of the learned, a devouring fire that even the vast sea of their accumulated knowledge could never quench. How often has it happened that an individual who was graced with every attribute of humanity and wore the jewel of true understanding, nevertheless followed after his passions until his excellent qualities passed beyond moderation and he was forced into excess. His pure intentions changed to evil ones, his attributes were no longer put to uses worthy of them, and the power of his desires turned him aside from righteousness and its rewards into ways that were dangerous and dark. A good character is in the sight of God and His chosen ones and the possessors of insight, the most excellent and praiseworthy of all things, but always on condition that its center of emanation should be reason and knowledge and its base should be true moderation. Were the implications of this subject to be developed as they deserve the work would grow too long and our main theme would be lost to view.

11.17   O ye the sincere loved ones of the Abhá Beauty! In these days the Cause of God, the world over, is fast growing in power and, day by day, is spreading further and further to the utmost bounds of the earth. Its enemies, therefore, from all the kindreds and peoples of the world, are growing aggressive, malevolent, envious and bitterly hostile. It is incumbent upon the loved ones of God to exercise the greatest care and prudence in all things, whether great or small, to take counsel together and unitedly resist the onslaught of the stirrers up of strife and the movers of mischief. They must endeavour to consort in a friendly spirit with everyone, must follow moderation in their conduct, must have respect and consideration one for another and show loving-kindness and tender regard to all the peoples of the world. They must be patient and long-suffering, that they may grow to become the divine magnets of the Abha Kingdom and acquire the dynamic power of the hosts of the realm on high.

The fleeting hours of man's life on earth pass swiftly by and the little that still remaineth shall come to an end, but that which endureth and lasteth for evermore is the fruit that man reapeth from his servitude at the Divine Threshold. Behold the truth of this saying, how abundant and glorious are the proofs thereof in the world of being! The glory of glories rest upon the people of Baha!

11.18   The denizens of the world are confined in the prison of nature—a prison that is continuous and eternal. If thou art at present restrained within the limits of a temporary prison, be not grieved at this; my hope is that thou mayest be emancipated from the prison of nature and may attain unto the court of everlasting life. Pray to God day and night and beg forgiveness and pardon. The omnipotence of God shall solve every difficulty.

11.19   Make ye then a mighty effort, that the purity and sanctity which, above all else, are cherished by 'Abdu'l-Bahá, shall distinguish the people of Baha; that in every kind of excellence the people of God shall surpass all other human beings; that both outwardly and inwardly they shall prove superior to the rest; that for purity, immaculacy, refinement, and the preservation of health, they shall be leaders in the vanguard of those who know. And that by their freedom from enslavement, their knowledge, their self-control, they shall be first among the pure, the free and the wise.

11.20   But man hath perversely continued to serve his lustful appetites, and he would not content himself with simple foods. Rather, he prepared for himself food that was compounded of many ingredients, of substances differing one from another. With this, and with perpetrating of vile and ignoble acts, his attention was engrossed, and he abandoned the temperance and moderation of a natural way of life. The result was the engendering of diseases both violent and diverse.

11.21   What a difference between the human world and the world of the animal, between the elevation of man and the abasement of the animal, between the perfections of man and the ignorance of the animal, between the light of man and the darkness of the animal, between the glory of man and the degradation of the animal! An Arab child of ten years can manage two or three hundred camels in the desert, and with his voice can lead them forward or turn them back. A weak Hindu can so control a huge elephant that the elephant becomes the most obedient of servants. All things are subdued by the hand of man; he can resist nature while all other creatures are captives of nature: none can depart from her requirements. Man alone can resist nature. Nature attracts bodies to the center of the earth; man through mechanical means goes far from it and soars in the air. Nature prevents man from crossing the seas; man builds a ship, and he travels and voyages across the great ocean, and so on; the subject is endless. For example, man drives engines over the mountains and through the wildernesses, and gathers in one spot the news of the events of the East and West. All this is contrary to nature. The sea with its grandeur cannot deviate by an atom from the laws of nature; the sun in all its magnificence cannot deviate as much as a needle's point from the laws of nature, and can never comprehend the conditions, the state, the qualities, the movements and the nature of man.

FROM THE WRITINGS AND LETTERS WRITTEN BY, OR ON BEHALF OF, SHOGHI EFFENDI

11.22   Such a chaste and holy life, with its implications of modesty, purity, temperance, decency, and clean-mindedness, involves no less than the exercise of moderation in all that pertains to dress, language, amusements, and all artistic and literary avocations. It demands daily vigilance in the control of one's carnal desires and corrupt inclinations. It calls for the abandonment of a frivolous conduct, with its excessive attachment to trivial and often misdirected pleasures. It requires total abstinence from all alcoholic drinks, from opium, and from similar habit-forming drugs. It condemns the prostitution of art and of literature, the practices of nudism and of companionate marriage, infidelity in marital relationships, and all manner of promiscuity, of easy familiarity, and of sexual vices. It can tolerate no compromise with the theories, the standards, the habits, and the excesses of a decadent age. Nay rather it seeks to demonstrate, through the dynamic force of its example, the pernicious character of such theories, the falsity of such standards, the hollowness of such claims, the perversity of such habits, and the sacrilegious character of such excesses.

11.23 Bahá'u'lláh urges us to always act wisely and moderately. Bahá'ís do not believe that the spread of the Cause and its principles and teachings can be effected by means of radical and violent methods. While they are loyal to all these Teachings yet they believe in the necessity of restoring to peaceful and friendly means for the realization of their aims.

11.24 We believe in balance in all things; we believe in moderation in all things—we must not be too emotional, nor cut and dried and lacking in feeling, we must not be so liberal as to cease to preserve the character and unity of our Bahá'í system, nor fanatical and dogmatic. Very few people, as you as a psychologist know, have attained perfect equilibrium in their minds or their lives—their acts—the same is certainly true of the Bahá'ís, for anyone who believes in our teachings can become a Bahá'í and they represent all elements of the population.

FROM THE WRITINGS AND LETTERS WRITTEN BY, OR ON BEHALF OF, THE UNIVERSAL HOUSE OF JUSTICE

11.25 Yet another sacred duty is that of clinging to the cord of moderation in all things, lest they who are to be the essence of detachment and moderation be deluded by the trappings of this nether world or set their hearts on its adornments and waste their lives. If they are wealthy, they should make these bestowals a means of drawing nigh unto God's Threshold, rather than being so attached to them that they forget the admonitions of the Pen of the Most High. The Voice of Truth has said, "Having attained the stage of fulfilment and reached his maturity, man standeth in need of wealth, and such wealth as he acquireth through crafts or professions is commendable and praiseworthy in the estimation of men of wisdom." If wealth and prosperity become the means of service at God's Threshold, it is highly meritorious; otherwise it would be better to avoid them. Turn to the Book of the Covenant, the Hidden Words, and other Tablets, lest the cord of your salvation become a rope of woe which will lead to your own destruction. How numerous are those negligent souls, particularly from among your own compatriots, who have been deprived of the blessings of faith and true understanding. Witness how, no sooner had they attained their newly amassed wealth and status, than they became so bewitched by them as to forget the virtues and true perfections of man's station. They clung to their empty and fruitless lifestyle. They had naught else but their homes, their commercial success, and their ornamental trappings of which to be proud. Behold their ultimate fate. Many a triumphal arch was reduced to a ruin, many an imperial palace was converted into a barn. Many a day of deceit turned into a night of despair. Vast treasures changed hands and, at the end of their lives, they were left only with tears of loss and regret. "... all that perisheth and changeth is not, and hath never been, worthy of attention, except to a recognized measure." Therefore the people of Baha must not fall prey to the corruption of the ruthless, but rather cling to contentment and moderation. They must make their homes havens for the believers, folds for their gatherings and centres for the promulgation of His Cause and the diffusion of His love, so that people of all strata, whether high or low, may feel at home and be able to consort in an atmosphere of love and fellowship.

11.26   Individuals not only have the right to express their views, but they are expected to express them fully and with the utmost devotion, courtesy, dignity, care, and moderation.

11.27   You, who live in a land where freedom is so highly prized, have not, then, to dispense with its fruits, but you are challenged and do have the obligation to uphold and vindicate the distinction between the license that limits your possibilities for genuine progress and the moderation that ensures the enjoyment of true liberty.

CHAPTER 12:

STRIVING TO FOLLOW THE BAHÁ'Í LAWS

FROM THE WRITINGS OF BAHÁ'U'LLÁH

12.1　They whom God hath endued with insight will readily recognize that the precepts laid down by God constitute the highest means for the maintenance of order in the world and the security of its peoples.

12.2　In all these journeys the traveler must stray not the breadth of a hair from the "Law," for this is indeed the secret of the "Path" and the fruit of the Tree of "Truth"; and in all these stages he must cling to the robe of obedience to the commandments, and hold fast to the cord of shunning all forbidden things, that he may be nourished from the cup of the Law and informed of the mysteries of Truth.

12.3　Think not that We have revealed unto you a mere code of laws. Nay, rather, We have unsealed the choice Wine with the fingers of might and power.

12.4　Be not grieved if thou performest it thyself alone. Let God be all-sufficient for thee.

12.5　The purpose of the one true God in manifesting Himself is to summon all mankind to truthfulness and sincerity, to piety and trustworthiness, to resignation and submissiveness to the Will of God, to forbearance and kindliness, to uprightness and wisdom. His object is to array every man with the mantle of a saintly character, and to adorn him with the ornament of holy and goodly deeds.

12.6　The All-Knowing Physician hath His finger on the pulse of mankind. He perceiveth the disease, and prescribeth, in His unerring wisdom, the remedy. Every age hath its own problem, and every soul its particular aspiration.

12.7　All men have been created to carry forward an ever-advancing civilization.

12.8   If ye believe, to your own behoof will ye believe; and if ye believe not, ye yourselves will suffer.

12.9   Were any man to taste the sweetness of the words which the lips of the All-Merciful have willed to utter, he would, though the treasures of the earth be in his possession, renounce them one and all, that he might vindicate the truth of even one of His commandments, shining above the day spring of His bountiful care and loving-kindness.

12.10   O SON OF MAN! Breathe not the sins of others so long as thou art thyself a sinner. Shouldst thou transgress this command, accursed wouldst thou be, and to this I bear witness.

12.11   He should be content with little, and be freed from all inordinate desire. He should treasure the companionship of them that have renounced the world, and regard avoidance of boastful and worldly people a precious benefit. At the dawn of every day he should commune with God, and, with all his soul, persevere in the quest of his Beloved. He should consume every wayward thought with the flame of His loving mention, and, with the swiftness of lightning, pass by all else save Him. He should succor the dispossessed, and never withhold his favor from the destitute. He should show kindness to animals, how much more unto his fellow-man, to him who is endowed with the power of utterance. He should not hesitate to offer up his life for his Beloved, nor allow the censure of the people to turn him away from the Truth. He should not wish for others that which he doth not wish for himself, nor promise that which he doth not fulfil. With all his heart he should avoid fellowship with evil-doers, and pray for the remission of their sins. He should forgive the sinful, and never despise his low estate, for none knoweth what his own end shall be. How often hath a sinner attained, at the hour of death, to the essence of faith, and, quaffing the immortal draught, hath taken his flight unto the Concourse on high! And how often hath a devout believer, at the hour of his soul's ascension, been so changed as to fall into the nethermost fire!

12.12   That seeker should, also, regard backbiting as grievous error, and keep himself aloof from its dominion, inasmuch as backbiting quencheth the light of the heart, and extinguisheth the life of the soul.

FROM THE WRITINGS AND UTTERANCES OF 'ABDU'L-BAHÁ

12.13   As to the difference between that material civilization now prevailing, and the divine civilization which will be one of the benefits to derive from the House of Justice, it is this: material civilization, through the power of punitive and retaliatory laws, restraineth the people from criminal acts; and notwithstanding this, while laws to retaliate against and punish a man are continually proliferating, as ye can see, no laws exist to reward him. In all the cities of Europe and America, vast buildings have been erected to serve as jails for the criminals.

Divine civilization, however, so traineth every member of society that no one, with the exception of a negligible few, will undertake to commit a crime. There is thus a great difference between the prevention of crime through measures that are violent and retaliatory, and so training the people, and enlightening them, and spiritualizing them, that without any fear of punishment or vengeance to come, they will shun all criminal acts. They will, indeed, look upon the very commission of a crime as a great disgrace and in itself the harshest of punishments. They will become enamoured of human perfections, and will consecrate their lives to whatever will bring light to the world and will further those qualities which are acceptable at the Holy Threshold of God.

12.14   All religious laws conform to reason, and are suited to the people for whom they are framed, and for the age in which they are to be obeyed.

Religion has two main parts:
(1) The Spiritual.
(2) The Practical.

The spiritual part never changes. All the Manifestations of God and His Prophets have taught the same truths and given the same spiritual law. They all teach the one code of morality. There is no division in the truth. The Sun has sent forth many rays to illumine human intelligence, the light is always the same.

The practical part of religion deals with exterior forms and ceremonies, and with modes of punishment for certain offences. This is the material side of the law, and guides the customs and manners of the people.

12.15   You are the reality and expression of your deeds and actions. If you abide by the precepts and teachings of the Blessed Perfection, the heavenly world and ancient Kingdom will be yours—eternal happiness, love and everlasting life. The divine bounties are flowing. Each one of you has been given the opportunity of becoming a tree yielding abundant fruits.

12.16   The phenomenal world is entirely subject to the rule and control of natural law. These myriad suns, satellites and heavenly bodies throughout endless space are all captives of nature. They cannot transgress in a single point or particular the fixed laws which govern the physical universe. The sun in its immensity, the ocean in its vastness are incapable of violating these universal laws. All phenomenal beings—the plants in their kingdom, even the animals with their intelligence—are nature's subjects and captives. All live within the bounds of natural law, and nature is the ruler of all except man. Man is not the captive of nature, for although according to natural law he is a being of the earth, yet he guides ships over the ocean, flies through the air in airplanes, descends in submarines; therefore, he has overcome natural law and made it subservient to his wishes. For instance, he imprisons in an incandescent lamp the illimitable natural energy called electricity—a material force which can cleave mountains—and bids it give him light. He takes the human voice and confines it in the phonograph for his benefit and amusement. According to his natural power man should be able to communicate a limited distance, but by overcoming the restrictions of nature he can annihilate space and send telephone messages thousands of miles. All the sciences, arts and discoveries were mysteries of nature, and according to natural law these mysteries should remain latent, hidden; but man has proceeded to break this law, free himself from this rule and bring them forth into the realm of the visible. Therefore, he is the ruler and commander of nature. Man has intelligence; nature has not. Man has volition; nature has none. Man has memory; nature is without it. Man has the reasoning faculty; nature is deprived. Man has the perceptive faculty; nature cannot perceive. It is therefore proved and evident that man is nobler than nature.

12.17   ... Thou hast written regarding aims. How blessed are these aims, especially the prevention of backbiting! I hope that you may become confirmed therein, because the worst human quality and the most great sin is backbiting; more especially when it emanates from the tongues of the believers of God. If some means were devised so that the doors of backbiting could be shut eternally and each one of the believers of God unsealed his tongue in the praise of the other, then the teachings of His Holiness Bahá'u'lláh (Bahá'u'lláh) would be spread, the hearts illuminated, the spirits glorified and the human world would attain to everlasting felicity.

I hope that the believers of God will shun completely backbiting, each one praising the other cordially and believe that backbiting is the cause of Divine Wrath, to such an extent that if a person backbites to the extent of one word, he may become dishonored among all the people, because the most hateful characteristic of man is fault-finding. One must expose the praiseworthy qualities of the souls and not their evil attributes. The friends must overlook their shortcomings and faults and speak only of their virtues and not their defects."

It is related that His Holiness Christ—May my life be a sacrifice to Him!—one day, accompanied by His apostles, passed by the corpse of a dead animal. One of them said: 'How putrid has this animal become!' The other exclaimed: 'How it is deformed!' A third cried out: 'What a stench! How cadaverous looking!' but His Holiness Christ said: "Look at its teeth! how white they are!' Consider, that He did not look at all at the defects of that animal; nay, rather, He searched well until He found the beautiful white teeth. He observed only the whiteness of the teeth and overlooked entirely the deformity of the body, the dissolution of its organs and the bad odour.

This is the attribute of the children of the Kingdom. This is the conduct and the manner of the real Bahá'ís. I hope that all the believers will attain to this lofty station."

12.18   Regarding the use of liquor: According to the text of the Book of Aqdas, both light and strong drinks are prohibited. The reason for this prohibition is that alcohol leadeth the mind astray and causeth the weakening of the body. If alcohol were beneficial, it would have been brought into the world by the Divine creation and not by the effort of man. Whatever is beneficial for man existeth in creation. Now it hath been proved and is established medically and scientifically that liquor is harmful.

12.19   I hope that the believers of God will shun completely back-biting, each one praising the other cordially and believe that backbiting is the cause of Divine Wrath, to such an extent that if a person backbites to the extent of one word, he may become dishonored among all the people, because the most hateful characteristic of man is fault-finding. One must expose the praiseworthy qualities of the souls and not their evil attributes. The friends must overlook their shortcomings and faults and speak only of their virtues and not their defects.

12.20   On the source of bad thoughts...

They come from other minds: they are reflected. One should not become a mirror for them-to reflect them, neither should one try to control them for this is impossible: it only aggravates the difficulty, causing more to appear.

One should constantly turn the mirror of his heart Squarely toward God so that the Light of the Sun of Truth may be reflected there.

This is the only cure for attacks of evil thoughts. The Face of the mirror should be turned toward God and the back of the mirror toward the evil thoughts.

FROM THE WRITINGS AND LETTERS WRITTEN BY, OR ON BEHALF OF, SHOGHI EFFENDI

12.21   As to a chaste and holy life, it should be regarded as no less essential a factor that must contribute its proper share to the strengthening and vitalization of the Bahá'í community, upon which must in turn depend the success of any Bahá'í plan or enterprise. In these days when the forces of irreligion are weakening the moral fiber, and undermining the foundations of individual morality, the obligation of chastity and holiness must claim an increasing share of the attention of the American believers, both in their individual capacities and as the responsible custodians of the interests of the Faith of Bahá'u'lláh. In the discharge of such an obligation, to which the special circumstances resulting from an excessive and enervating materialism now prevailing in their country lend particular significance, they must play a conspicuous and predominant role. All of them, be they men or women, must, at this threatening hour when the lights of religion are fading out, and its restraints are one by one being abolished, pause to examine themselves, scrutinize their conduct, and with characteristic resolution arise to purge the life of their community of every trace of moral laxity that might stain the name, or impair the integrity, of so holy and precious a Faith.

A chaste and holy life must be made the controlling principle in the behavior and conduct of all Bahá'ís, both in their social relations with the members of their own community, and in their contact with the world at large. It must adorn and reinforce the ceaseless labors and meritorious exertions of those whose enviable position is to propagate the Message, and to administer the affairs, of the Faith of Bahá'u'lláh. It must be upheld, in all its integrity and implications, in every phase of the life of those who fill the ranks of that Faith, whether in their homes, their travels, their clubs, their societies, their entertainments, their schools, and their universities. It must be accorded special consideration in the conduct of the social activities of every Bahá'í summer school and any other occasions on which Bahá'í community life is organized and fostered. It must be closely and continually identified with the mission of the Bahá'í youth, both as an element in the life of the Bahá'í community, and as a factor in the future progress and orientation of the youth of their own country.

12.22   Indeed the chief reason for the evils now rampant in society is the lack of spirituality. The materialistic civilization of our age has so much absorbed the energy and interest of mankind that people in general do no longer feel the necessity of raising themselves above the forces and conditions of their daily material existence. There is not sufficient demand for things that we call spiritual to differentiate them from the needs and requirements of our physical existence.

The universal crisis affecting mankind is, therefore, essentially spiritual in its causes. The spirit of the age, taken on the whole, is irreligious. Man's outlook on life is too crude and materialistic to enable him to elevate himself into the higher realms of the spirit.

It is this condition, so sadly morbid, into which society has fallen, that religion seeks to improve and transform. For the core of religious faith is that mystic feeling which unites Man with God. This state of spiritual communion can be brought about and maintained by means of meditation and prayer. And this is the reason why Bahá'u'lláh has so much stressed the importance of worship. It is not sufficient for a believer merely to accept and observe the teachings. He should, in addition, cultivate the sense of spirituality which he can acquire chiefly by means of prayer. The Bahá'í Faith, like all other Divine Religions, is thus fundamentally mystic in character. Its chief goal is the development of the individual and society, through the acquisition of spiritual virtues and powers. It is the soul of man which has first to be fed. And this spiritual nourishment prayer can best provide.

Laws and institutions, as viewed by Bahá'u'lláh, can become really effective only when our inner spiritual life has been perfected and transformed. Otherwise religion will degenerate into a mere organization, and becomes a dead thing. The believers, particularly the young ones, should therefore fully realize the necessity of praying. For prayer is absolutely indispensable to their inner spiritual development, and this, as already stated, is the very foundation and purpose of the religion of God."

12.23 Regarding your questions: Concerning smoking; it is not forbidden in the Bahá'í teachings and no one can enforce its prohibition. It is strongly discouraged as a habit which is not very clean or very healthy. But it is a matter left entirely to the conscience of the individual and not of major importance, whereas the use of alcohol is definitely forbidden and thus not left optional to the conscience of the believer.

12.24 The Bahá'í Faith recognizes the value of the sex impulse, but condemns its illegitimate and improper expressions such as free love, companionate marriage and others, all of which it considers positively harmful to man and to the society in which he lives. The proper use of the sex instinct is the natural right of every individual, and it is precisely for this purpose that the institution of marriage has been established. The Bahá'ís do not believe in the suppression of the sex impulse but in its regulation and control.

12.25 Amongst the many other evils afflicting society in this spiritual low water mark in history, is the question of immorality, and over- emphasis of sex. Homosexuality, according to the Writings of Bahá'u'lláh, is spiritually condemned. This does not mean that people so afflicted must not be helped and advised and sympathized with. It does mean that we do not believe that it is a permissible way of life; which, also, is all too often the accepted attitude nowadays.

We must struggle against the evils in society by spiritual means, and medical and social ones as well. We must be tolerant but uncompromising, understanding but immovable in our point of view.

The thing people need to meet this type of trouble, as well as every other type, is greater spiritual understanding and stability; and of course we Bahá'ís believe that ultimately this can only be given to mankind through the Teachings of the Manifestation of God for this Day."

12.26 No matter how devoted and fine the love may be between people of the same sex to let it find expression in sexual acts is wrong. To say that it is ideal is no excuse. Immorality of every sort is really forbidden by Bahá'u'lláh, and homosexual relationships he looks upon as such, besides being against nature.

To be afflicted this way is a great burden to an conscientious soul. But through the advice and help of doctors, through a strong and determined effort, and through prayer, a soul can overcome this handicap.

God judges each soul on its own merits. The Guardian cannot tell you what the attitude of God would be towards a person who lives a good life in most ways, but not in this way. All he can tell you is that it is forbidden by Bahá'u'lláh, and that one so afflicted should struggle and struggle again to overcome it. We must be hopeful of God's Mercy but not impose upon it.

12.27 With regard to your first question on alcohol and drinking, Bahá'u'lláh, fully aware of the great misery that it bring about, prohibits it as He expressly states that everything that takes away the mind, or in other words makes one drunk, is forbidden.

12.28 There is no need to fear opposition from without if the life within be sound and vigorous. Our Heavenly Father will always give us the strength to meet and overcome tests if we turn with all our hearts to Him, and difficulties if they are met in the right spirit only make us rely on God more firmly and completely.

12.29 As regards backbiting, i.e. discussing the faults of others in their absence, the teachings are very emphatic. In a Tablet to an American friend the Master wrote: 'The worst human quality and the most great sin is backbiting, more especially when it emanates from the tongues of the believers of God. If some means were devised so that the doors of backbiting were shut eternally and each one of the believers unsealed his lips in praise of others, then the Teachings of His Holiness Bahá'u'lláh would spread, the hearts be illumined, the spirits glorified, and the human world would attain to everlasting felicity.' (Quoted in Star of West, Vol. IV. p. 192) Bahá'u'lláh says in Hidden Words; 'Breathe not the sins of others so long as thou art a sinner. Shouldst thou transgress this command

ACCURSED ARE THOU.' The condemnation of backbiting could hardly be couched in stronger language than in these passages, and it is obviously one of the foremost obligations for Bahá'ís to set their faces against this practice. Even if what is said against another person be true, the mentioning of his faults to others still comes under the category of backbiting, and is forbidden.

12.30 There is a tremendous darkness in the world today, the darkness caused by mankind's going against the Laws of God and giving way to the animal side of human nature. People must recognize this fact, and consciously struggle against pessimism and depression.

12.31 ... he feels it his duty to explain that the Laws revealed by Bahá'u'lláh in the Aqdas are, whenever practicable and not in direct conflict with the Civil Law of the land, absolutely binding on every believer or Bahá'í institution whether in the East or in the West. Certain laws, such as fasting, obligatory prayers, the consent of the parents before marriage, avoidance of alcoholic drinks, monogamy, should be regarded by all believers as universally and vitally applicable at the present time. Others have been formulated in anticipation of a state of society destined to emerge from the chaotic conditions that prevail to-day. When the Aqdas is published this matter will be further explained and elucidated. What has not been formulated in the Aqdas, in addition to matters of detail and of secondary importance arising out of the applications of the Laws already formulated by Bahá'u'lláh, will have to be enacted by the Universal House of Justice. This body can supplement but never invalidate or modify in the least degree what has already been formulated by Bahá'u'lláh. Nor has the Guardian any right whatsoever to lessen the binding effect much less to abrogate the provisions of so fundamental and sacred a Book.

12.32 We must never dwell too much on the attitudes and feelings of our fellow believers towards us. What is most important is to foster love and harmony and ignore any rebuffs we may receive; in this way the weakness of human nature and the peculiarity or attitude of any particular person is not magnified, but pales into insignificance in comparison with our joint service to the Faith we all love.

12.33   On no subject are the Bahá'í teachings more emphatic than on the necessity to abstain from fault-finding and backbiting while being ever eager to discover and root out our own faults and overcome our own failings.

If we profess loyalty to Bahá'u'lláh, to our Beloved Master and our dear Guardian, then we must show our love by obedience to these explicit teachings. Deeds not words are what they demand, and no amount of fervour in the use of expressions of loyalty and adulation will compensate for failure to live in the spirit of the teachings.

FROM THE WRITINGS AND LETTERS WRITTEN BY, OR ON BEHALF OF, THE UNIVERSAL HOUSE OF JUSTICE

12.34   At some time or other, every Law of Bahá'u'lláh may impose a test upon the faith of a believer and the question is whether the believer will meet the test or not. As you are aware, withdrawal from the Faith in order to evade a Law of Bahá'u'lláh is not possible to a true believer.

12.35   A number of sexual problems, such as homosexuality and trans-sexuality can well have medical aspects, and in such cases recourse should certainly be had to the best medical assistance. But it is clear from the teaching of Bahá'u'lláh that homosexuality is not a condition to which a person should be reconciled, but is a distortion of his or her nature which should be controlled and overcome. This may require a hard struggle, but so also can be the struggle of a heterosexual person to control his or her desires. The exercise of self-control in this, as in so very many other aspects of life, has a beneficial effect on the progress of the soul. It should, moreover, be borne in mind that although to be, married is highly desirable, and Bahá'u'lláh has strongly recommended it, it is not the central purpose of life. If a person has to wait a considerable period before finding a spouse, or if ultimately, he or she must remain single, it does not mean that he or she is thereby unable to fulfil his or her life's purpose.

12.36   ...Any act or activity by a believer which is contrary to our teachings will surely be harmful to the spiritual future of the individual
concerned, and may give non-Bahá'ís a wrong impression of the
principles of our Faith. Whereas consider how important it is for
a believer to reflect in his actions the redeeming features of the
Cause he has embrace. Shoghi Effendi has pointed out:

'Not by the force of numbers, not by the mere exposition of
a set of new and noble principles, not by an organized campaign of
teaching—no matter how worldwide and elaborate in its character—not even by the staunchness of our faith or the exaltation of
our enthusiasm, can we ultimately hope to vindicate in the eyes of a
critical and skeptical age the supreme claim of the Abha Revelation.
One thing and only one thing will unfailingly and alone secure the
undoubted triumph of this sacred Cause, namely, the extent to which
our own inner life and private character mirror forth in their manifold aspects the splendour of those eternal principles proclaimed by
Bahá'u'lláh.'

While recognizing the Divine origin and force of the sex
impulse in man, religion teaches that it must be controlled, and
Bahá'u'lláh's Law confines its expression to the marriage relationship. The unmarried homosexual is therefore in the same position as
anyone else who does not marry. The Law of God requires them to
practise chastity.

Even though you feel that the conflict between sensuality and
spirituality is more than you can bear, your affirmation—'I do know
I am a Bahá'í' is a positive factor in the battle you must wage. Every
believer needs to remember that an essential characteristic of this
physical world is that we are constantly faced with trials, tribulations,
hardships and sufferings and that by overcoming them we achieve
our moral and spiritual development; that we must seek to accomplish in the future what we may have failed to do in the past; that
this is the way God tests His servants and we should look upon every
failure or shortcoming as an opportunity to try again and to acquire a
fuller consciousness of the Divine Will and purpose.

12.37   Of course many wayward thoughts come involuntarily to the
mind and these are merely a result of weakness and are not
blameworthy unless they become fixed or even worse, are
expressed in improper acts.

12.38   As to backbiting, the House of Justice points out that learning not to concern oneself with the faults of others seems to be one of the most difficult lessons for people to master, and that failing in this is a fertile cause of disputes among Bahá'ís as it is among men and women in general. In 'Star of the West', Volume 8, No. 10, on page 138, there is a record of a reply given by 'Abdu'l-Bahá in a private interview in Paris in 1913. He was asked 'How shall I overcome seeing the faults of others—recognizing the wrong in others?', and He replied: 'I will tell you. Whenever you recognize the fault of another, think of yourself! What are my imperfections?—and try to remove them. Do this whenever you are tried through the words or deeds of others. Thus you will grow, become more perfect. You will overcome self, you will not even have time to think of the faults of others... '

You are quite correct in your understanding of the importance of avoiding backbiting; such conduct strikes at the very unity of the Bahá'í community. In a letter written to an individual believer on behalf of the Guardian it is stated: "If we are better, if we show love, patience, and understanding of the weakness of others, if we seek to never criticize but rather encourage, others will do likewise, and we can really help the Cause through our example and spiritual strength.

12.39   Abortion merely to prevent the birth of an unwanted child is strictly forbidden in the Cause. There may, however, be instances in which an abortion would be justified by medical reasons, and legislation on this matter has been left to the Universal House of Justice. At the present time, however, the House of Justice does not intend to legislate on this very delicate issue, and therefore it is left to the consciences of those concerned who must carefully weigh the medical advice in the light of the general guidance given in the teachings.

12.40   Abortion and surgical operations for the purpose of preventing the birth of unwanted children are forbidden in the Cause unless there are circumstances which justify such actions on medical grounds, in which case the decision, at present, is left to the consciences of those concerned who must carefully weigh the medical advice in the light of the general guidance given in the Teachings. Beyond this nothing has been found in the Writings concerning specific methods or procedures to be used in family planning. It should be pointed out, however, that the Teachings state that the soul appears at conception, and that therefore it would be improper to use such a method, the effect of which would be to produce an abortion after conception has taken place.

12.41 Just as there are laws governing our physical lives, requiring that we must supply our bodies with certain foods, maintain them within a certain range of temperatures, and so forth, if we wish to avoid physical disabilities, so also there are laws governing our spiritual lives. These laws are revealed to mankind in each age by Manifestation of God, and obedience to them is of vital importance if each human being, and mankind in general, is to develop properly and harmoniously. Moreover, these various aspects are interdependent. If an individual violates the spiritual laws for his own development he will cause injury not only to himself but to the society in which he lives. Similarly, the condition of society has a direct effect on the individuals who must live within it.

12.42 As you point out, it is particularly difficult to follow the Laws of Bahá'u'lláh in present-day society whose accepted practice is so at variance with the standards of the Faith. However, there are certain laws that are so fundamental to the healthy functioning of human society that they must be upheld whatever the circumstances. Realizing the degree of human frailty, Bahá'u'lláh has provided that other laws are to be applied only gradually, but these too, once they are applied, must be followed, or else society will not be reformed but will sink into an ever worsening condition. It is the challenging task of the Bahá'ís to obey the law of God in their own lives, and gradually to win the rest of mankind to its acceptance.

CHAPTER 13:

HARNESSING THE POWER OF PRAYER IN OUR LIVES

FROM THE WRITINGS OF BAHÁ'U'LLÁH

13.1   I render Thee thanks, O Thou Who hast lighted Thy fire within my soul, and cast the beams of Thy light into my heart, that Thou hast taught Thy servants how to make mention of Thee, and revealed unto them the ways whereby they can supplicate Thee, through Thy most holy and exalted tongue, and Thy most august and precious speech. But for Thy leave, who is there that could venture to express Thy might and Thy grandeur; and were it not for Thine instruction, who is the man that could discover the ways of Thy pleasure in the kingdom of Thy creation?

13.2   This is that which hath descended from the realm of glory, uttered by the tongue of power and might, and revealed unto the Prophets of old. We have taken the inner essence thereof and clothed it in the garment of brevity, as a token of grace unto the righteous, that they may stand faithful unto the Covenant of God, may fulfill in their lives His trust, and in the realm of spirit obtain the gem of Divine virtue.

13.3   Thy name is my healing, O my God, and remembrance of Thee is my remedy. Nearness to Thee is my hope, and love for Thee is my companion. Thy mercy to me is my healing and my succor in both this world and the world to come. Thou, verily, art the All-Bountiful, the All-Knowing, the All-Wise.

13.4   O Thou Whose nearness is my wish, Whose presence is my hope, Whose remembrance is my desire, Whose court of glory is my goal, Whose abode is my aim, Whose name is my healing, Whose love is the radiance of my heart, Whose service is my highest aspiration! I beseech Thee by Thy Name, through which Thou hast enabled them that have recognized Thee to soar to the sublimest heights of the knowledge of Thee and empowered such as devoutly worship Thee to ascend into the precincts of the court of Thy holy favors, to aid me to turn my face towards Thy face, to fix mine eyes upon Thee, and to speak of Thy glory.

     I am the one, O my Lord, who hath forgotten all else but Thee, and turned towards the Day-Spring of Thy grace, who hath forsaken all save Thyself in the hope of drawing nigh unto Thy court. Behold me, then, with mine eyes lifted up towards the Seat that shineth with the splendors of the light of Thy Face. Send down, then, upon me, O my Beloved, that which will enable me to be steadfast in Thy Cause, so that the doubts of the infidels may not hinder me from turning towards Thee.

Thou art, verily, the God of Power, the Help in Peril, the All-Glorious, the Almighty.

13.5   Thou beholdest, O my Lord, the things which have befallen me in Thy days. I entreat Thee, by Him Who is the Day-Spring of Thy names and the Dawning-Place of Thine attributes, to ordain for me what will enable me to arise to serve Thee and to extol Thy virtues. Thou art, verily, the Almighty, the Most Powerful, Who art wont to answer the prayers of all men!

13.6   Recite ye the verses of God every morn and eventide. Whoso faileth to recite them hath not been faithful to the Covenant of God and His Testament, and whoso turneth away from these holy verses in this Day is of those who throughout eternity have turned away from God. Fear ye God, O My servants, one and all. Pride not yourselves on much reading of the verses or on a multitude of pious acts by night and day; for were a man to read a single verse with joy and radiance it would be better for him than to read with lassitude all the Holy Books of God, the Help in Peril, the Self-Subsisting. Read ye the sacred verses in such measure that ye be not overcome by languor and despondency. Lay not upon your souls that which will weary them and weigh them down, but rather what will lighten and uplift them, so that they may soar on the wings of the Divine verses towards the Dawning-place of His manifest signs; this will draw you nearer to God, did ye but comprehend.

13.7   O SON OF BEING! Love Me, that I may love thee. If thou lovest Me not, My love can in no wise reach thee. Know this, O servant.

FROM THE WRITINGS AND UTTERANCES OF 'ABDU'L-BAHÁ

13.8 O thou who art turning thy face towards God! Close thine eyes to all things else, and open them to the realm of the All-Glorious. Ask whatsoever thou wishest of Him alone; seek whatsoever thou seekest from Him alone. With a look He granteth a hundred thousand hopes, with a glance He healeth a hundred thousand incurable ills, with a nod He layeth balm on every wound, with a glimpse He freeth the hearts from the shackles of grief. He doeth as He doeth, and what recourse have we? He carrieth out His Will, He ordaineth what He pleaseth. Then better for thee to bow down thy head in submission, and put thy trust in the All-Merciful Lord.

13.9 Ours should be the prayer that His blessings may be vouchsafed in still greater abundance, and ours to hold fast to such means as shall ensure a fuller outpouring of His grace and a greater measure of His divine assistance.

13.10 Pray ye for all; ask ye that all be blessed, all be forgiven.

13.11 O thou who hast bowed thyself down in prayer before the Kingdom of God! Blessed art thou, for the beauty of the divine Countenance hath enraptured thy heart, and the light of inner wisdom hath filled it full, and within it shineth the brightness of the Kingdom. Know thou that God is with thee under all conditions, and that He guardeth thee from the changes and chances of this world and hath made thee a handmaid in His mighty vineyard.

13.12 O handmaid of God! Prayers are granted through the universal Manifestations of God. Nevertheless, where the wish is to obtain material things, even where the heedless are concerned, if they supplicate, humbly imploring God's help—even their prayer hath an effect.
       O handmaid of God! Although the reality of Divinity is sanctified and boundless, the aims and needs of the creatures are restricted. God's grace is like the rain that cometh down from

heaven: the water is not bounded by the limitations of form, yet on whatever place it poureth down, it taketh on limitations—dimensions, appearance, shape—according to the characteristics of that place. In a square pool, the water, previously unconfined, becometh a square; in a six-sided pool it becometh a hexagon, in an eight-sided pool an octagon, and so forth. The rain itself hath no geometry, no limits, no form, but it taketh on one form or another, according to the restrictions of its vessel. In the same way, the Holy Essence of the Lord God is boundless, immeasurable, but His graces and splendours become finite in the creatures, because of their limitations, wherefore the prayers of given persons will receive favourable answers in certain cases.

13.13   The blessings of Bahá'u'lláh are a shoreless sea, and even life everlasting is only a dewdrop therefrom. The waves of that sea are continually lapping against the hearts of the friends, and from those waves there come intimations of the spirit and ardent pulsings of the soul, until the heart giveth way, and willing or not, turneth humbly in prayer unto the Kingdom of the Lord. Wherefore do all ye can to disengage your inner selves, that ye may at every moment reflect new splendours from the Sun of Truth.

Ye live, all of you, within the heart of 'Abdu'l-Bahá, and with every breath do I turn my face toward the Threshold of Oneness and call down blessings upon you, each and all.

13.14   Praise be to God, thy heart is engaged in the commemoration of God, thy soul is gladdened by the glad tidings of God and thou art absorbed in prayer. The state of prayer is the best of conditions, for man is then associating with God. Prayer verily bestoweth life, particularly when offered in private and at times, such as midnight, when freed from daily cares.

13.15   Thou hast asked about places of worship and the underlying reason therefor. The wisdom in raising up such buildings is that at a given hour, the people should know it is time to meet, and all should gather together, and, harmoniously attuned one to another, engage in prayer; with the result that out of this coming together, unity and affection shall grow and flourish in the human heart.

13.16   The prayers which were revealed to ask for healing apply both to physical and spiritual healing. Recite them, then, to heal both the soul and the body. If healing is right for the patient, it will certainly be granted; but for some ailing persons, healing would only be the cause of other ills, and therefore wisdom doth not permit an affirmative answer to the prayer.

13.17   ... Does it matter who prays? God will answer the prayer of every servant if that prayer is urgent. His mercy is vast, illimitable. He answers the prayers of all His servants. He answers the prayer of this plant. The plant prays potentially, "O God! Send me rain!" God answers the prayer, and the plant grows. God will answer anyone. He answers prayers potentially. Before we were born into this world did we not pray, "O God! Give me a mother; give me two fountains of bright milk; purify the air for my breathing; grant me rest and comfort; prepare food for my sustenance and living"? Did we not pray potentially for these needed blessings before we were created? When we came into this world, did we not find our prayers answered? Did we not find mother, father, food, light, home and every other necessity and blessing, although we did not actually ask for them? Therefore, it is natural that God will give to us when we ask Him. His mercy is all-encircling.

But we ask for things which the divine wisdom does not desire for us, and there is no answer to our prayer. His wisdom does not sanction what we wish. We pray, "O God! Make me wealthy!" If this prayer were universally answered, human affairs would be at a standstill. There would be none left to work in the streets, none to till the soil, none to build, none to run the trains. Therefore, it is evident that it would not be well for us if all prayers were answered. The affairs of the world would be interfered with, energies crippled and progress hindered. But whatever we ask for which is in accord with divine wisdom, God will answer. Assuredly!

For instance, a very feeble patient may ask the doctor to give him food which would be positively dangerous to his life and condition. He may beg for roast meat. The doctor is kind and wise. He knows it would be dangerous to his patient so he refuses to allow it. The doctor is merciful; the patient, ignorant. Through the doctor's kindness the patient recovers; his life is saved. Yet the patient may cry out that the doctor is unkind, not good, because he refuses to answer his pleading.

God is merciful. In His mercy He answers the prayers of all His servants when according to His supreme wisdom it is necessary.

13.18   O thou spiritual friend! Thou hast asked about the wisdom of obligatory prayer. Know thou that such prayer is mandatory and binding. Man under no pretext whatsoever is excused from observing the prayer unless he is incapable of performing it or some great obstacle interveneth. The wisdom of obligatory prayer is this: That it causeth a connection between the servant and the True One, because at that time man with all his heart and soul turneth his face towards the Almighty, seeking His association and desiring His love and companionship. For a lover, there is no greater pleasure than to converse with his beloved, and for a seeker, there is no greater bounty than intimacy with the object of his desire. It is the greatest longing of every soul who is attracted to the Kingdom of God to find time to turn with entire devotion to his Beloved, so as to seek His bounty and blessing and immerse himself in the ocean of communion, entreaty and supplication. Moreover, obligatory prayer and fasting produce awareness and awakening in man, and are conducive to his protection and preservation from tests.

13.19   Remembrance of God is like the rain and dew which bestow freshness and grace on flowers and hyacinths, revive them and cause them to acquire fragrance, redolence and renewed charm.

FROM THE WRITINGS AND LETTERS WRITTEN BY, OR ON BEHALF OF, SHOGHI EFFENDI

13.20   For the core of religious faith is that mystical feeling which unites man with God. This state of spiritual communion can be brought about and maintained by means of meditation and prayer. And this is the reason why Bahá'u'lláh has so much stressed the importance of worship. It is not sufficient for a believer merely to accept and observe the teachings. He should, in addition, cultivate the sense of spirituality which he can acquire chiefly be means of prayer.

13.21 The believers, as we all know, should endeavour to set such an example in their personal lives and conduct that others will feel impelled to embrace a Faith which reforms human character. However, unfortunately, not everyone achieves easily and rapidly the victory over self. What every believer, new or old, should realize is that the Cause has the spiritual power to re-create us if we make the effort to let that power influence us, and the greatest help in this respect is prayer. We must supplicate Bahá'u'lláh to assist us to overcome the failings in our own characters, and also exert our own will power in mastering ourselves.

13.22 ...We must not be rigid about praying; there is not a set of rules governing it; the main thing is we must start out with the right concept of God, the Manifestation, the Master, the Guardian—we can turn, in thought, to any one of them when we pray. For instance you can ask Bahá'u'lláh for some thing, or, thinking of Him, ask God for it. The same is true of the Master or the Guardian. You can turn in thought to either of them and then ask their intercession, or pray direct to God. As long as you don't confuse their stations, and make them all equal, it does not matter much how you orient your thoughts.

13.23 While praying it would be better to turn one's thoughts to the Manifestation as He continues, in the other world, to be our means of contact with the Almighty. We can, however, pray directly to God Himself.

13.24 You have asked whether our prayers go beyond Bahá'u'lláh: It all depends whether we pray to Him directly and through Him to God. We may do both and also can pray directly to God, but our prayers would certainly be more effective and illuminating if they are addressed to Him through His Manifestation, Bahá'u'lláh.

   Under no circumstances, however, we can, while repeating the prayers, insert the name Bahá'u'lláh where the word 'God' is used. This would be tantamount to a blasphemy.

13.25 In connection with the question you asked about the prayer for the dead: any of the prayers which were originally revealed for a man or woman can be said for opposite sex, but the text must not be changed.

13.26 ... How to attain spirituality is indeed a question to which every young man and woman must sooner or later try to find a satisfactory answer. It is precisely because no such satisfactory answer has been given or found, that the modern youth finds itself bewildered, and is being consequently, carried away by the materialistic forces that are so powerfully undermining the foundations of man's moral and spiritual life ... It is this condition so sadly morbid, into which society has fallen, that religion seeks to improve and transform. "For the core of religious faith is that mystic feeling which unites man with God. This state of spiritual communion can be brought about and maintained by means of meditation and prayer. And this is the reason why Bahá'u'lláh has so much stressed the importance of worship.

    It is not sufficient for a believer merely to accept and observe the teachings. He should, in addition, cultivate the sense of spirituality which he can acquire chiefly by means of prayer...

    The believers, particularly the young ones, should therefore fully realize the necessity of praying. For prayer is absolutely indispensable to their inner spiritual development, and this, as already stated, is the very foundation and purpose of the religion of God.

FROM THE WRITINGS AND LETTERS WRITTEN BY, OR ON BEHALF OF, THE UNIVERSAL HOUSE OF JUSTICE

13.27 It is not easy to be burdened with long years of mental illness such as you describe. And plainly you have sought aid from many persons of scientific and non-scientific training backgrounds, apparently to little avail over the years of your prolonged illness. Possibly you should consider, if it is feasible, consulting the best specialists in a medical centre in one of the major cities, where the most advanced diagnosis and treatment can be obtained. The science of the mind, of normality and of the disabilities from which it may suffer, is in its relative infancy, but much may be possible to aid you to minimize your suffering and made possible an active life. The last ten years in the therapy of mental disorders has seen important advances from which you may well benefit.

Your discovery of the Faith, of its healing Writings and its great purposes for the individual and for all mankind, have indeed brought to you a powerful force toward a healthy life which will sustain you on a higher level, whatever your ailment may be. The best results for the healing process are to combine the spiritual with the physical, for it should be possible for you to overcome your illness through the combined and sustained power of prayer and of determined effort.

13.28 You mention that the answers to your prayers never seem to have come through clearly. Mrs Ruth Moffett has published her recollection of five steps of prayer for guidance that she was told by the beloved Guardian. When asked about these notes, Shoghi Effendi replied, in letters written by his secretary on his behalf, that the notes should be regarded as "Personal suggestions," that he considered them to be "quite sound," but that the friends need not adopt them 'strictly and universally." The House of Justice feels that they may be helpful to you and, indeed, you may already be familiar with them. They are as follows: ... use these five steps if we have a problem of any kind for which we desire a solution, or wish help. Pray and meditate about it. Use the prayers of the Manifestations, as they have the greatest power. Learn to remain in the silence of contemplation for a few moments. During this deepest communion take the next step. Arrive at a decision and hold to this. This decision is usually born in a flash at the close or during the contemplation. It may seem almost impossible of accomplishment, but if it seems to be an answer to prayer or a way of solving the problem, then immediately take the next step. Have determination to carry the decision through. Many fail here. The decision, budding into determination, is blighted and instead becomes a wish or a vague longing. When determination is born, immediately take the next step. Have faith and confidence, that the Power of the Holy Spirit will flow through you, the right way will appear, the door will open, the right message, the right principle or the right book will be given to you. Have confidence, and the right thing will come to meet your need. Then as you rise from prayer take immediately the fifth step. Act as though it had all been answered. Then act with tireless, ceaseless energy. And, as you act, you yourself will become a magnet which will attract more power to your being, until you become an unobstructed channel for the Divine Power to flow through you.

CHAPTER 14:

ALIGNING OUR LIVES WITH MEDITATION

FROM THE WRITINGS OF BAHÁ'U'LLÁH

14.1   Meditate upon that which hath streamed forth from the heaven of the Will of thy Lord, He Who is the Source of all grace, that thou mayest grasp the intended meaning which is enshrined in the sacred depths of the Holy Writings.

14.2   Meditate on that which We have, through the power of truth, revealed unto thee, and be thou of them that comprehend its meaning.

14.3   Meditate on what the poet hath written: "Wonder not, if my Best-Beloved be closer to me than mine own self; wonder at this, that I, despite such nearness, should still be so far from Him."... Considering what God hath revealed, that "We are closer to man than his life-vein," the poet hath, in allusion to this verse, stated that, though the revelation of my Best-Beloved hath so permeated my being that He is closer to me than my life-vein, yet, notwithstanding my certitude of its reality and my recognition of my station, I am still so far removed from Him. By this he meaneth that his heart, which is the seat of the All-Merciful and the throne wherein abideth the splendor of His revelation, is forgetful of its Creator, hath strayed from His path, hath shut out itself from His glory, and is stained with the defilement of earthly desires.

14.4   Our hope is that the world's religious leaders and the rulers thereof will unitedly arise for the reformation of this age and the rehabilitation of its fortunes. Let them, after meditating on its needs, take counsel together and, through anxious and full deliberation, administer to a diseased and sorely-afflicted world the remedy it requireth....

14.5   Meditate on the world and the state of its people.

14.6   If any man were to meditate on that which the Scriptures, sent down from the heaven of God's holy Will, have revealed, he would readily recognize that their purpose is that all men shall be regarded as one soul, so that the seal bearing the words 'The Kingdom shall be God's' may be stamped on every heart, and the light of Divine bounty, of grace, and mercy may envelop all mankind.

14.7   O people of Baha! The source of crafts, sciences and arts is the power of reflection. Make ye every effort that out of this ideal mine there may gleam forth such pearls of wisdom and utterance as will promote the well-being and harmony of all the kindreds of the earth.

14.8   ... The wine of renunciation must needs be quaffed, the lofty heights of detachment must needs be attained, and the meditation referred to in the words "One hour's reflection is preferable to seventy years of pious worship" must needs be observed, so that the secret of the wretched behaviour of the people might be discovered, those people who, despite the love and yearning for truth which they profess, curse the followers of Truth when once He hath been made manifest.

14.9   Meditate profoundly, that the secret of things unseen may be revealed unto you, that you may inhale the sweetness of a spiritual and imperishable fragrance, and that you may acknowledge the truth that from time immemorial even unto eternity the Almighty hath tried, and will continue to try, His servants, so that light may be distinguished from darkness, truth from falsehood, right from wrong, guidance from error, happiness from misery, and roses from thorns. Even as He hath revealed: 'Do men think when they say 'We believe' they shall be let alone and not be put to proof?' [1 Qur'án 29:2.]

14.10   O brother, we should open our eyes, meditate upon His Word, and seek the sheltering shadow of the Manifestations of God, that perchance we may be warned by the unmistakable counsels of the Book, and give heed to the admonitions recorded in the holy Tablets; that we may not cavil at the Revealer of the verses, that we may resign ourselves wholly to His Cause, and embrace wholeheartedly His law, that haply we may enter the court of His mercy, and dwell upon the shore of His grace. He, verily, is merciful, and forgiving towards His servants.

14.11   Meditate upon this, O ye beloved of God, and let your ears be attentive unto His Word, so that ye may, by His grace and mercy, drink your fill from the crystal waters of constancy, and become as steadfast and immovable as the mountain in His Cause.

14.12   Meditate upon that which hath streamed forth from the heaven of the Will of thy Lord, He Who is the Source of all grace, that thou mayest grasp the intended meaning which is enshrined in the sacred depths of the Holy Writings.

14.13   The sanctified souls should ponder and meditate in their hearts regarding the methods of teaching. From the texts of the wondrous, heavenly Scriptures they should memorize phrases and passages bearing on various instances, so that in the course of their speech they may recite divine verses whenever the occasion demands it, inasmuch as these holy verses are the most potent elixir, the greatest and mightiest talisman. So potent is their influence that the hearer will have no cause for vacillation ...

14.14   Every act ye meditate is as clear to Him as is that act when already accomplished.

14.15   Purify, O my God, the hearts of Thy creatures with the power of Thy sovereignty and might, that Thy words may sink deep into them. I know not what is in their hearts, O my God, nor can tell the thoughts they think of Thee. Methinks that they imagine that Thy purpose in calling them to Thine all-highest horizon is to heighten the glory of Thy majesty and power. For had they been satisfied that Thou summonest them to that which will recreate their hearts and immortalize their souls, they would never have fled from Thy governance, nor deserted the shadow of the tree of Thy oneness. Clear away, then, the sight of Thy creatures, O my God, that they may recognize Him Who showeth forth the Godhead as One Who is sanctified from all that pertaineth unto them, and Who, wholly for Thy sake, is summoning them to the horizon of Thy unity, at a time when every moment of His life is beset with peril. Had His aim been the preservation of His own Self, He would never have left it at the mercy of Thy foes.

FROM THE WRITINGS AND UTTERANCES OF 'ABDU'L-BAHÁ

14.16   It is incumbent upon you to ponder in your hearts and meditate upon His words, and humbly to call upon Him, and to put away self in His heavenly Cause. These are the things that will make of you signs of guidance unto all mankind, and brilliant stars shining down from the all-highest horizon, and towering trees in the Abha Paradise.

14.17   It is an axiomatic fact that while you meditate you are speaking with your own spirit. In that state of mind you put certain questions to your spirit and the spirit answers: the light breaks forth and the reality is revealed.

You cannot apply the name 'man' to any being void of this faculty of meditation; without it he would be a mere animal, lower than the beasts.

Through the faculty of meditation man attains to eternal life; through it he receives the breath of the Holy Spirit—the bestowal of the Spirit is given in reflection and meditation.

The spirit of man is itself informed and strengthened during meditation; through it affairs of which man knew nothing are unfolded before his view. Through it he receives Divine inspiration, through it he receives heavenly food.

Meditation is the key for opening the doors of mysteries. In that state man abstracts himself: in that state man withdraws himself from all outside objects; in that subjective mood he is immersed in the ocean of spiritual life and can unfold the secrets of things-in-themselves. To illustrate this, think of man as endowed with two kinds of sight; when the power of insight is being used the outward power of vision does not see.

This faculty of meditation frees man from the animal nature, discerns the reality of things, puts man in touch with God.

This faculty brings forth from the invisible plane the sciences and arts. Through the meditative faculty inventions are made possible, colossal undertakings are carried out; through it governments can run smoothly. Through this faculty man enters into the very Kingdom of God.

Nevertheless some thoughts are useless to man; they are like waves moving in the sea without result. But if the faculty of meditation is bathed in the inner light and characterized with divine attributes, the results will be confirmed.

The meditative faculty is akin to the mirror; if you put it before earthly objects it will reflect them. Therefore if the spirit of man is contemplating earthly subjects he will be informed of these.

FROM THE WRITINGS AND LETTERS WRITTEN BY, OR ON BEHALF OF, SHOGHI EFFENDI

14.18 Through meditation the doors of deeper knowledge and inspiration may be opened. Naturally, if one meditates as a Bahá'í he is connected with the Source; if a man believing in God meditates he is tuning in to the power and mercy of God; but we cannot say that any inspiration which a person, not knowing Bahá'u'lláh or not believing in God, receives is merely from his own ego. Meditation is very important, and the Guardian sees no reason why the friends should not be taught to meditate, but they should guard against superstitious or foolish ideas creeping into it.

14.19 ...There are no set forms of meditation prescribed in the teachings, no plan, as such, for inner development. The friends are urged—nay enjoined—to pray, and they also should meditate, but the manner of doing the latter is left entirely to the individual...

The inspiration received through meditation is of a nature that one cannot measure or determine. God can inspire into our minds things that we had no previous knowledge of, if He desires to do so.

14.20 Regarding your question concerning a deep and profound study of the teachings: of course the Bahá'ís can and should meditate upon the significances of the Writings, and endeavour to grasp their meaning to the uttermost. There can be no possible objection to this. However certain things are, by their very nature, a mystery to us, at least in our present stage of development. One of these is what the next world, the purely spiritual world, is like.

14.21 Prayer and meditation are very important factors in deepening the spiritual life of the individual, but with them must go also action and example, as these are the tangible result of the former. Both are essential."

FROM THE WRITINGS AND LETTERS WRITTEN BY, OR ON BEHALF OF, THE UNIVERSAL HOUSE OF JUSTICE

14.22 These points, expressed in other words, have already been conveyed to the friends... by the counsellors, but the House of Justice wishes to stress them, because they represent the path towards the attainment of true spirituality that has been laid down by the Manifestation of God for this age.

It is striking how private and personal the most fundamental spiritual exercises of prayer and meditation are in the Faith. Bahá'ís do, of course, have meetings for devotions, as in the Mashriqu'l-Adhkar or at Nineteen Day Feasts, but the daily obligatory prayers are ordained to be said in the privacy of one's chamber, and meditation on the Teachings is, likewise, a private individual activity, not a form of group therapy. In His talks 'Abdu'l-Bahá describes prayer as 'Conversation with God', and concerning meditation He says that 'while you meditate you are speaking with your own spirit. In that state of mind you put certain questions to your spirit and the spirit answers: the light breaks forth and the reality is revealed."

14.23 As to your question about prayer and whether it is necessary to recite the prayers of only the Central Figures of our Faith, we have been asked to quote here the following two excerpts on this subject, from letters written by Shoghi Effendi's secretary on his behalf:

"... as the Cause embraces members of all races and religions we should be careful not to introduce into it the customs of our previous beliefs. Bahá'u'lláh has given us the obligatory prayers, also prayers before sleeping, for travellers, etc. We should not introduce a new set of prayers He has not specified, when He has given us already so many, for so many occasions.'

'He thinks it would be wiser for the Bahá'ís to use the meditations given by Bahá'u'lláh, and not any set form of meditation recommended by someone else; but the believers must be left free in these details and allowed to have personal latitude in finding their own level of communion with God.'

As to the reading of prayers or selections from the Sacred Writings of other religions such readings are permissible, and indeed from time to time are included in the devotional programmes of Bahá'í Houses of Worship, demonstrating thereby the universality of our Faith."

CHAPTER 15:

ENJOYING THE LASTING REWARDS OF FASTING

FROM THE WRITINGS OF BAHÁ'U'LLÁH

15.1 The days of fasting have arrived wherein those servants who circle round Thy throne and have attained Thy presence have fasted. Say: O God of names and creator of heaven and earth! I beg of Thee by Thy Name, the All-Glorious, to accept the fast of those who have fasted for love of Thee and for the sake of Thy good-pleasure and have carried out what Thou hast bidden them in Thy Books and Tablets.

15.2 There are various stages and stations for the Fast and innumerable effects and benefits are concealed therein. Well is it with those who have attained unto them.

15.3 Even though outwardly the Fast is difficult and toilsome, yet inwardly it is bounty and tranquillity. Purification and training are conditioned and dependent only on such rigorous exercises as are in accord with the Book of God and sanctioned by Divine law, not those which the deluded have inflicted upon the people. Whatsoever God hath revealed is beloved of the soul. We beseech Him that He may graciously assist us to do that which is pleasing and acceptable unto Him.

15.4 Cling firmly to obligatory prayer and fasting. Verily, the religion of God is like unto heaven; fasting is its sun, and obligatory prayer is its moon. In truth, they are the pillars of religion whereby the righteous are distinguished from those who transgress His commandments. We entreat God, exalted and glorified be He, that he may graciously enable all to observe that which He hath revealed in His Ancient Book.

15.5 All praise be unto God, Who hath revealed the law of obligatory prayer as a reminder to His servants, and enjoined on them the Fast that those possessed of means may become apprised of the woes and sufferings of the destitute.

15.6 Verily, I say, fasting is the supreme remedy and the most great healing for the disease of self and passion.

15.7   Be not neglectful of obligatory prayer and fasting. He who faileth to observe them hath not been nor will ever be acceptable in the sight of God. Follow ye wisdom under all conditions. He, verily, hath bidden all to observe that which hath been and will be of profit to them. He, in truth, is the All-Sufficing, the Most High.

15.8   Praise be unto Him Who hath revealed laws in accordance with His good-pleasure. Verily, He is sovereign over whatsoever He wisheth. O My friends! Act ye in accordance with what ye have been commanded in the Book. Fasting hath been decreed for you in the month of 'Ala. Fast ye for the sake of your Lord, the Mighty, the Most High. Restrain yourselves from sunrise to sunset. Thus doth the Beloved of mankind instruct you as bidden by God, the All-Powerful, the Unconstrained. It is not for anyone to exceed the limits laid down by God and His law, nor should anyone follow his own idle imaginings. Well is it with the one who fulfilleth My decrees for the love of My Beauty, and woe to the one who neglecteth the Dayspring of Command in the days of his Lord, the Almighty, the Omnipotent.

15.9   This is one of the nights of the Fast, and during it the Tongue of Grandeur and Glory proclaimed: There is no God beside Me, the Omnipotent Protector, the Self-Subsisting. We, verily, have commanded all to observe the Fast in these days as a bounty on Our part, but the people remain unaware, except for those who have attained unto the purpose of God as revealed in His laws and have comprehended His wisdom that pervadeth all things visible and invisible. Say: By God! His Law is a fortress unto you, could ye but understand. Verily, He hath no purpose therein save to benefit the souls of His servants, but, alas, the generality of mankind remain heedless thereof. Cling ye to the cord of God's laws, and follow not those who have turned away from the Book, for verily they have opposed God, the Mighty, the Beloved.

15.10 We beseech God to assist His people that they may observe the most great and exalted Fast, which is to protect one's eye from beholding whatever is forbidden and to withhold one's self from food, drink and whatever is not of Him. We pray God to confirm His loved ones that they may succeed in accomplishing that which they have been commanded in this Day.

15.11 In clear cases of weakness, illness, or injury the law of the Fast is not binding. This injunction is in conformity with the precepts of God, eternal in the past, eternal in the future. Well is it with them who act accordingly.

15.12 Praise be unto Thee, O Lord my God! We have observed the Fast in conformity with Thy bidding and break it now through Thy love and Thy good-pleasure. Deign to accept, O my God, the deeds that we have performed in Thy path wholly for the sake of Thy beauty with our faces set towards Thy Cause, free from aught else but Thee. Bestow, then, Thy forgiveness upon us, upon our forefathers, and upon all such as have believed in Thee and in Thy mighty signs in this most great, this most glorious Revelation. Potent art Thou to do what Thou choosest. Thou art, verily, the Most Exalted, the Almighty, the Unconstrained.

15.13 All praise be to the one true God Who hath assisted His loved ones to observe the Fast and hath aided them to fulfill that which hath been decreed in the Book. In truth, ceaseless praise and gratitude are due unto Him for having graciously confirmed His loved ones to perform that which is the cause of the exaltation of His Word. If a man possessed ten thousand lives and offered them all to establish the truth of God's laws and commandments, he would still be beholden unto Him, since whatsoever proceedeth from His irresistible decree serveth solely to benefit His friends and loved ones.

15.14 We have fasted this day, O my Lord, by Thy command and Thy bidding in accordance with what Thou hast revealed in Thy perspicuous Book. We have withheld our souls from passion and from whatsoever Thou abhorest until the day drew to an end and the time arrived to break the Fast. Wherefore, I implore Thee, O Desire of the hearts of ardent lovers and Beloved of the souls of them who are endued with understanding, O Rapture of the breasts of them that yearn after Thee and Object of the desire of them that seek Thee, to cause us to soar in the atmosphere of Thy nearness and the heaven of Thy presence, and to accept from us what we have performed in the pathway of Thy love and good-pleasure. Write down our names, then, among those who have acknowledged Thy oneness and confessed to Thy singleness and who have humbled themselves before the evidences of Thy majesty and the tokens of Thy grandeur, those who have taken refuge in Thy nearness and sought shelter in Thee, who have expended their lives in their eagerness to meet Thee and attain the court of Thy presence, and who have cast the world behind their backs for love of Thee and severed every tie with aught save Thee in their eagerness to draw nigh unto Thee. These are servants whose hearts melt in ardent desire for Thy beauty at the mention of Thy Name, and whose eyes overflow with tears in their longing to find Thee and enter the precincts of Thy court.

15.15 All glory be to Thee, O my God, for Thou hast graciously enabled me to fast during this month which Thou hast related to Thy Name, the Most Exalted, and called 'Ala (Loftiness). Thou hast commanded that Thy servants and Thy people should fast therein and seek thereby to draw nearer unto Thee. The days and months of the year have culminated with the Fast, even as the first month began with Thy Name, Baha, that all might testify that Thou art the First and the Last, the Manifest and the Hidden, and be well assured that the glory of all names is conferred only through the glory of Thy Cause and the word expounded by Thy will and revealed through Thy purpose. Thou hast ordained that this month be a remembrance and honor from Thee, and a sign of Thy presence amongst them, that they may not forget Thy grandeur and Thy majesty, Thy sovereignty and Thy glory, and may be well assured that from time immemorial Thou hast ever been and wilt ever be Ruler over the entire creation. Nothing created in the heavens or on the earth can hinder Thee in Thy governance, nor can anyone in the realms of Revelation and creation prevent Thee from fulfilling Thy purpose.

FROM THE WRITINGS AND UTTERANCES OF 'ABDU'L-BAHÁ

15.16   Obligatory prayer and fasting are among the most great ordinances of this holy Dispensation.

15.17   In the realm of worship, fasting and obligatory prayer constitute the two mightiest pillars of God's holy Law. Neglecting them is in no wise permitted, and falling short in their performance is of a certainty not acceptable.

15.18   Fasting is the cause of the elevation of one's spiritual station.

15.19   Moreover, obligatory prayer and fasting produce awareness and awakening in man, and are conducive to his protection and preservation from tests.

15.20   Thou hast written about the Fast. This is a most weighty matter and thou shouldst exert thine utmost in its observance. It is a fundamental of the Divine law, and one of the pillars of the religion of God.

15.21   Well is it with you, as you have followed the Law of God and arisen to observe the Fast during these blessed days, for this physical fast is a symbol of the spiritual fast. This Fast leadeth to the cleansing of the soul from all selfish desires, the acquisition of spiritual attributes, attraction to the breezes of the All-Merciful, and enkindlement with the fire of divine love.

15.22   Ye had written of the fasting month. Fortunate are ye to have obeyed the commandment of God, and kept this fast during the holy season. For this material fast is an outer token of the spiritual fast; it is a symbol of self-restraint, the withholding of oneself from all appetites of the self, taking on the characteristics of the spirit, being carried away by the breathings of heaven and catching fire from the love of God.

FROM THE WRITINGS AND LETTERS WRITTEN BY, OR ON BEHALF OF, SHOGHI EFFENDI

15.23 Regarding your question concerning the Fast: travellers are exempt from fasting, but if they want to fast while they are travelling, they are free to do so. You are exempt the whole period of your travel, not just the hours you are in a train or car, etc. If one eats unconsciously during the fasting hours, this is not breaking the Fast as it is an accident. The age limit is seventy years, but if one desires to fast after the age limit is passed, and is strong enough to, one is free to do so. If during the Fast period a person falls ill and is unable to fast, but recovers before the Fast period is over, he can start to Fast again and continue until the end. Of course the Fast, as you know, can only be kept during the month set aside for that purpose.

15.24 The fasting period, which lasts nineteen days starting as a rule from the second of March every year and ending on the twentieth of the same month, involves complete abstention from food and drink from sunrise till sunset. It essentially a period of meditation and prayer, of spiritual recuperation, during which the believer must strive to make the necessary readjustments in his inner life, and to refresh and reinvigorate the spiritual forces latent in his soul. Its significance and purpose are, fundamentally spiritual in character. Fasting is symbolic, and a reminder of abstinence from selfish and carnal desired.

15.25 Regarding the nineteen-day fast; its observance has been enjoined by Bahá'u'lláh upon all believers, once they attain the age of fifteen and until they reach seventy. Children of all countries, nationalities and classes, who are fifteen years old are under this obligation. It matters not whether they mature later in one country than in another. The command of Bahá'u'lláh is universal, irrespective of any variance in the age of maturity in different countries and among different peoples. "In the 'Aqdas' Bahá'u'lláh permits certain exceptions to this general obligation of fasting, among them are included those who do hard work, such as workers in heavy industries. "But while a universal obligation, the observance of the nineteen day fast has been made by Bahá'u'lláh the sole responsibility of the individual believer. No Assembly has the right to enforce it on the friends, or to hold anybody responsible for not observing it. The believer is free, however, to ask the advice of his Assembly as to the circumstances that would justify him to conscientiously break such a fast. But he is by no means required to do so.

15.26 Keeping the Fast is enjoined upon all Bahá'ís, regardless of nationality; it has a very salutary effect both physically and spiritually, and the friends should realize Bahá'u'lláh never would have instituted it if it were detrimental to the health.

15.27 As to your question regarding the Fast: if there is any doubt in the mind of a person as to whether it will really be bad for that person's health to keep it, the best doctor's advice should be obtained. But generally speaking most people can keep it, anywhere in the world, with no detriment to their health. It is very good for the health and, once one forms the habit, each year it becomes easier to keep, unless one is rundown. No one is obliged to keep it if it really harms them.

FROM THE WRITINGS AND LETTERS WRITTEN BY, OR ON BEHALF OF, THE UNIVERSAL HOUSE OF JUSTICE

15.28 In one of His Tablets 'Abdu'l-Bahá, after stating that fasting consists of abstinence from food and drink, categorically says that smoking is a form of 'drink'. (In Arabic the verb 'drink' applies equally to smoking.) "In the East, therefore, the friends abstain from smoking during the hours of fasting, and friends from the East living in the West do likewise. But, as stated in our letter to the National Spiritual Assembly of New Zealand, this application of the Divine Law has not been extended to the friends in the West for the present, and therefore it should not be made an issue.

CHAPTER 16:

CHERISHING THE DAILY BENEFITS OF OBLIGATORY PRAYER

FROM THE WRITINGS OF BAHÁ'U'LLÁH

16.1 O My brother! How great, how very great, can the law of obligatory prayer be, when, through His mercy and loving kindness, one is enabled to observe it. When a man commenceth the recitation of the Obligatory Prayer, he should see himself severed from all created things and regard himself as utter nothingness before the will and purpose of God, in such wise that he seeth naught but Him in the world of being. This is the station of God's well-favored ones and those who are wholly devoted to Him. Should one perform the Obligatory Prayer in this manner, he will be accounted by God and the Concourse on high among those who have truly offered the prayer.

16.2 As for obligatory prayer, it hath been sent down by the Pen of the Most High in such wise that it setteth ablaze the hearts and captivateth the souls and minds of men.

16.3 Concerning obligatory prayer, it hath been revealed in such wise that whosoever reciteth it, even one time, with a detached heart, will find himself wholly severed from the world.

16.4 One of the deeds in obedience to the law is obligatory prayer. He Who is the Bearer of divine mysteries hath called it the ladder of ascent. He saith: "Obligatory prayer is a ladder of ascent for the believer." Within it are hidden and concealed a myriad effects and benefits. Indeed, they are beyond computation. How great would be a man's indolence and his injustice to himself if he were to abandon this ladder of ascent and attach himself to earthly treasures. It is our hope that we may be assisted to perform pure and acceptable deeds. We beseech God, exalted and glorified be He, to confirm us in that which He desireth and pleaseth and in that which will draw us nigh unto Him. Verily, He is the Almighty, the All-Powerful, He Who is wont to answer the prayers of all men.

16.5 Of the new Obligatory Prayers that were later revealed, the long Obligatory Prayer should be said at those times when one feeleth himself in a prayerful mood. In truth, it hath been revealed in such wise that if it be recited to a rock, that rock would stir and speak forth; and if it be recited to a mountain, that mountain would move and flow. Well is it with the one who reciteth it and fulfilleth God's precepts. Whichever prayer is read will suffice.

FROM THE WRITINGS AND UTTERANCES OF ʻABDUʼL-BAHÁ

16.6   Obligatory prayer is the very foundation of the Cause of God. Through it joy and vitality infuse the heart. Even if every grief should surround Me, as soon as I engage in conversing with God in obligatory prayer, all My sorrows disappear and I attain joy and gladness. A condition descendeth upon Me which I am unable to describe or express. Whenever, with full awareness and humility, we undertake to perform the Obligatory Prayer before God, and recite it with heartfelt tenderness, we shall taste such sweetness as to endow all existence with eternal life.

16.7   O thou spiritual friend! Thou hast asked about the wisdom of obligatory prayer. Know thou that such prayer is mandatory and binding. Man under no pretext whatsoever is excused from observing the prayer unless he is incapable of performing it or some great obstacle interveneth. The wisdom of obligatory prayer is this: That it causeth a connection between the servant and the True One, because at that time man with all his heart and soul turneth his face towards the Almighty, seeking His association and desiring His love and companionship. For a lover, there is no greater pleasure than to converse with his beloved, and for a seeker, there is no greater bounty than intimacy with the object of his desire. It is the greatest longing of every soul who is attracted to the Kingdom of God to find time to turn with entire devotion to his Beloved, so as to seek His bounty and blessing and immerse himself in the ocean of communion, entreaty and supplication. Moreover, obligatory prayer and fasting produce awareness and awakening in man, and are conducive to his protection and preservation from tests.

16.8   The Obligatory Prayers are binding inasmuch as they are conducive to humility and submissiveness, to setting one's face
towards God and expressing devotion to Him. Through such
prayer man holdeth communion with God, seeketh to draw
near unto Him, converseth with the true Beloved of his heart,
and attaineth spiritual stations.

16.9   Obligatory prayer causeth the heart to become attentive to
the Divine kingdom. One is alone with God, converseth with
Him, and acquireth bounties. Likewise, if one performeth the
Obligatory Prayer with his heart in a state of utmost purity, he
will obtain the confirmations of the Holy Spirit, and this will
entirely obliterate love of self. I hope that thou wilt persevere
in the recitation of the Obligatory Prayer, and thus will come to
witness the power of entreaty and supplication.

16.10   Persevere in the use of the Obligatory Prayer and early
morning supplications, so that day by day thine awareness
may increase, and, through the power of the knowledge of
God, thou mayest rend asunder the veil of error of the people
of doubt and lead them to His unfailing guidance. In every
assembly, like unto a candle, thou shouldst give forth the light
of Divine knowledge.

16.11   Strengthen thou the foundation of the Faith of God, and worship the Almighty. Be constant in offering obligatory prayer,
and be mindful of fasting. Day and night devote thyself to
prayer, supplication and entreaty, especially at the prescribed
times.

16.12   O thou servant of God! Each morn God's infinite grace con-
firmeth the ardent and tearful invocations of 'Abdu'l-Bahá.
Accordingly, let every awakened soul obtain, to the extent
of its capacity, a portion of this spiritual grace. This can be
achieved by fervently offering unto God prayers and supplications at every dawn and observing the law of obligatory prayer.
Thus may his nostrils delight in the sweet savors wafting from
the garden of the bounty of God, his soul attain new life, and
his reality mirror forth the effulgences of the All- Merciful.

16.13   Thou hast written concerning obligatory prayer. Such prayer is binding and mandatory for everyone. Most certainly guide all to its observance, because it is like unto a ladder for the souls, a lamp unto the hearts of the righteous, and the water of life from the garden of paradise. It is a clear duty prescribed by the All-Merciful, in the observance of which it is in no wise permissible to be dilatory or neglectful

16.14   Obligatory prayer and supplication cause man to reach the kingdom of mystery, and the worship of the Supreme One. They bestow nearness unto His threshold. There is a pleasure in offering prayers that transcendeth all other pleasures, and there is a sweetness in chanting and singing the verses of God which is the greatest desire of all the believers, men and women alike. While reciting the Obligatory Prayer, one converseth intimately and shareth secrets with the true Beloved. No pleasure is greater than this, if one proceedeth with a detached soul, with tears overflowing, with a trusting heart and an eager spirit. Every joy is earthly save this one, the sweetness of which is divine.

16.15   Obligatory prayer is the very foundation of the Cause of God. Through it joy and vitality infuse the heart. Even if every grief should surround Me, as soon as I engage in conversing with God in obligatory prayer, all My sorrows disappear and I attain joy and gladness. A condition descendeth upon Me which I am unable to describe or express. Whenever, with full awareness and humility, we undertake to perform the Obligatory Prayer before God, and recite it with heartfelt tenderness, we shall taste such sweetness as to endow all existence with eternal life.

16.16   Obligatory prayers and supplications are the very water of life. They are the cause of existence, of the refinement of souls, and of their attainment to the utmost joy. Exercise the greatest care in this regard, and encourage others to recite the Obligatory Prayers and supplications.

FROM THE WRITINGS AND LETTERS WRITTEN BY, OR ON BEHALF OF, SHOGHI EFFENDI

16.17 He would advise you to only use the short mid-day Obligatory Prayer. This has no genuflections and only requires that when saying in the believer turn his face towards 'Akká where Bahá'u'lláh is buried. This is a physical symbol of an inner reality, just as the plant stretches out to the sunlight—from which it receives life and growth—so we turn our hearts to the Manifestation if God, Bahá'u'lláh, when we pray; and we turn our faces, during this short prayer, to where His dust lies on this earth as a symbol of the inner act.

Bahá'u'lláh has reduced all ritual and form to an absolute minimum in His Faith. The few forms that there are—like those associated with the two longer obligatory daily prayers, are only symbols of the inner attitude. There is a wisdom in them, and a great blessing but we cannot force ourselves to understand or feel these things, that is why He gave us also the very short and simple prayer, for those who did not feel the desire to perform the acts associated with the other two."

16.18 Concerning the times for prayer and fasting, it is correct that, in the high latitudes, where the lengths of day and night vary considerably from season to season of the year, it is permissible to observe the laws of prayer and fasting in accordance with the lock rather than with the rising and setting of the sun. As Iceland lies in such latitudes, it is for your Assembly to decide this matter for the believers in your country. All should then abide by whatever your Assembly lays down.

16.19 As regards the questions about the proper use of the long Obligatory Prayer: All the writing of the Faith may be read and should be read for the instruction and inspiration of the friends. This includes the specific prayers. If a believer is physical incapable of performing the genuflections accompanying one of the prayers, and yet he longs to say it as an obligatory prayer, then he may do so. By physically incapable is meant a real physical incapacity which a physician would attest as genuine.

FROM THE WRITINGS AND LETTERS WRITTEN BY, OR ON BEHALF OF, THE UNIVERSAL HOUSE OF JUSTICE

16.20 The Universal House of Justice received your letter of 7 January 1975, enquiring about the correct way of following certain instructions in the Long Obligatory Prayer, and has asked us to give you this reply.

In following the direction stating: 'Let him then stand and raise his hands twice in supplication, and say': ... the believer does not have to read twice the paragraph which follows. Whether the believer raises his hands twice before the reciting of the paragraph, or commences the reciting after having raised his hands once, and raises them a second time soon thereafter, is left to his choice.

As to the direction which states: 'Let him then raise his hands thrice, and say: ... ', and individual believer asked the beloved Guardian the following question: "... the direction to raise the hands thrice and say 'greater is God than every great one.' Does this mean after every raising of the hands, or only to be said once, after the three raisings?'

Shoghi Effendi's secretary answered on his behalf as follows:

The hands should be raised three times and each time the sentence be repeated in conjunction with the act.

CHAPTER 17:

EXPERIENCING PILGRIMAGE AND DIVINE CONNECTIONS

FROM THE WRITINGS OF BAHÁ'U'LLÁH

17.1 The Lord hath ordained that those of you who are able shall make pilgrimage to the sacred House, and from this He hath exempted women as a mercy on His part. He, of a truth, is the All-Bountiful, the Most Generous.

17.2 Hear Me, ye mortal birds! In the Rose Garden of changeless splendor a Flower hath begun to bloom, compared to which every other flower is but a thorn, and before the brightness of Whose glory the very essence of beauty must pale and wither. Arise, therefore, and, with the whole enthusiasm of your hearts, with all the eagerness of your souls, the full fervor of your will, and the concentrated efforts of your entire being, strive to attain the paradise of His presence, and endeavor to inhale the fragrance of the incorruptible Flower, to breathe the sweet savors of holiness, and to obtain a portion of this perfume of celestial glory. Whoso followeth this counsel will break his chains asunder, will taste the abandonment of enraptured love, will attain unto his heart's desire, and will surrender his soul into the hands of his Beloved. Bursting through his cage, he will, even as the bird of the spirit, wing his flight to his holy and everlasting nest.

17.3 The purpose of God in creating man hath been, and will ever be, to enable him to know his Creator and to attain His Presence. To this most excellent aim, this supreme objective, all the heavenly Books and the divinely-revealed and weighty Scriptures unequivocally bear witness. Whoso hath recognized the Day Spring of Divine guidance and entered His holy court hath drawn nigh unto God and attained His Presence, a Presence which is the real Paradise, and of which the loftiest mansions of heaven are but a symbol.

17.4 'Call out to Zion, O Carmel, and announce the joyful tidings: He that was hidden from mortal eyes is come! His all-conquering sovereignty is manifest; His all-encompassing splendour is revealed. Beware lest thou hesitate or halt. Hasten forth and circumambulate the City of God that hath descended from heaven, the celestial

Kaaba round which have circled in adoration the favoured of God, the pure in heart, and the company of the most exalted angels. Oh, how I long to announce unto every spot on the surface of the earth, and to carry to each one of its cities, the glad-tidings of this Revelation—a Revelation to which the heart of Sinai hath been attracted, and in whose name the Burning Bush is calling: "Unto God, the Lord of Lords, belong the kingdoms of earth and heaven." Verily this is the Day in which both land and sea rejoice at this announcement, the Day for which have been laid up those things which God, through a bounty beyond the ken of mortal mind or heart, hath destined for revelation. Ere long will God sail His Ark upon thee, and will manifest the people of Baha who have been mentioned in the Book of Names.

17.5 By pilgrimage to the sacred House, which is enjoined upon men, is intended both the Most Great House in Baghdad and the House of the Primal Point in Shiraz; pilgrimage to either of these Houses sufficeth. They may thus make pilgrimage to whichever lieth nearer to the place where they reside.

FROM THE WRITINGS AND UTTERANCES OF 'ABDU'L-BAHÁ

17.6 At every instant, I beg for you assistance, bounty, and a fresh favour and blessing, so that the confirmations of Bahá'u'lláh may, like unto the sea, be constantly surging, the lights of the Sun of Truth may shine upon you all and that ye may be confirmed in service, may become the manifestations of bounty and that each one of you may, at dawn, turn unto the Holy Land and may experience spiritual emotions with all intensity.

17.7 Remember the saying: 'Of all pilgrimages the greatest is to relieve the sorrow-laden heart.'

17.8 O ye loved ones of God! Be ye firm of foot, and fixed of heart, and through the power of the Blessed Beauty's help, stand ye committed to your purpose. Serve ye the Cause of God. Face ye all nations of the world with the constancy and the endurance of the people of Baha, that all men may be astounded and ask how this could be, that your hearts are as well-springs of confidence and faith, and as mines so rich in the love of God. Be ye so, that ye shall neither fail nor falter on account of these tragedies in the Holy Land; let not these dread events make you despondent. And if all the believers be put to the sword, and only one be left, let that one cry out in the name of the Lord and tell the joyous tidings; let that one rise up and confront all the peoples of the earth.

Gaze ye not upon the dire happenings at this Illumined Spot. The Holy Land is in danger at all times, and here, the tide of calamities is ever at the flood; for this upraised call hath now been heard around the world, and the fame of it hath gone forth to the ends of the earth. It is because of this that foes, both from within and from without, have turned themselves with subtlety and craft to spreading slander. It is clear that such a place as this would be exposed to danger, for there is no defender here, none to arise and take our side in the face of calumny: here are only a few souls that are homeless, hapless, held captive in this stronghold. No champion have they; there is none to succour them, none to ward off the arrows of lies, the darts of defamation that are hurled against them: none except God.

17.9 One of the great events which is to occur in the Day of the manifestation of that Incomparable Branch (Bahá'u'lláh) is the hoisting of the Standard of God among all nations. By this is meant that all nations and kindreds will be gathered together under the shadow of this Divine Banner, which is no other than the Lordly Branch itself, and will become a single nation. Religious and sectarian antagonism, the hostility of races and peoples, and differences among nations, will be eliminated. All men will adhere to one religion, will have one common faith, will be blended into one race, and become a single people. All will dwell in one common fatherland, which is the planet itself. Universal peace and concord will be realized between all the nations, and that Incomparable Branch will gather together all Israel, signifying that in this cycle Israel will be gathered in the Holy Land, and that the Jewish people who are scattered to the East and West, South and North, will be assembled together.

17.10 Finally, they consulted together and said, "We have banished Bahá'u'lláh from place to place, but each time he is exiled his cause is more widely extended, his proclamation increases in power, and day by day his lamp is becoming brighter. This is due to the fact that we have exiled him to large cities and populous centers. Therefore, we will send him to a penal colony as a prisoner so that all may know he is the associate of murderers, robbers and criminals; in a short time he and his followers will perish." The Sultan of Turkey then banished Him to the prison of Akká in Syria.

　　When Bahá'u'lláh arrived at Akká, through the power of God He was able to hoist His banner. His light at first had been a star; now it became a mighty sun, and the illumination of His Cause expanded from the East to the West. Inside prison walls He wrote Epistles to all the kings and rulers of nations, summoning them to arbitration and universal peace. Some of the kings received His words with disdain and contempt. One of these was the Sultan of the Ottoman kingdom. Napoleon III of France did not reply. A second Epistle was addressed to him. It stated, "I have written you an Epistle before this, summoning you to the Cause of God, but you are of the heedless. You have proclaimed that you were the defender of the oppressed; now it hath become evident that you are not. Nor are you kind to your own suffering and oppressed people. Your actions are contrary to your own interests, and your kingly pride must fall. Because of your arrogance God shortly will destroy your sovereignty. France will flee away from you, and you will be overwhelmed by a great conquest. There will be lamentation and mourning, women bemoaning the loss of their sons." This arraignment of Napoleon III was published and spread.

　　Read it and consider: one prisoner, single and solitary, without assistant or defender, a foreigner and stranger imprisoned in the fortress of Akká, writing such letters to the Emperor of France and Sultan of Turkey. Reflect upon this: how Bahá'u'lláh upraised the standard of His Cause in prison. Refer to history. It is without parallel. No such thing has happened before that time nor since—a prisoner and an exile advancing His Cause and spreading His teachings broadcast so that eventually He became powerful enough to conquer the very king who banished Him.

His Cause spread more and more. The Blessed Perfection was a prisoner twenty-five years. During all this time He was subjected to the indignities and revilement of the people. He was persecuted, mocked and put in chains. In Persia His properties were pillaged and His possessions confiscated. First, there was banishment from Persia to Baghdad, then to Constantinople, then to Adrianople, finally from Rumelia to the prison fortress of Akká.

During His lifetime He was intensely active. His energy was unlimited. Scarcely one night was passed in restful sleep. He bore these ordeals, suffered these calamities and difficulties in order that a manifestation of selflessness and service might become apparent in the world of humanity; that the Most Great Peace should become a reality; that human souls might appear as the angels of heaven; that heavenly miracles would be wrought among men; that human faith should be strengthened and perfected; that the precious, priceless bestowal of God—the human mind—might be developed to its fullest capacity in the temple of the body; and that man might become the reflection and likeness of God, even as it hath been revealed in the Bible, "Let us make man in our image."

Briefly, the Blessed Perfection bore all these ordeals and calamities in order that our hearts might become enkindled and radiant, our spirits be glorified, our faults become virtues, our ignorance be transformed into knowledge; in order that we might attain the real fruits of humanity and acquire heavenly graces; in order that, although pilgrims upon earth, we should travel the road of the heavenly Kingdom, and, although needy and poor, we might receive the treasures of eternal life. For this has He borne these difficulties and sorrows.

Trust all to God. The lights of God are resplendent. The blessed Epistles are spreading. The blessed teachings are promulgated throughout the East and West. Soon you will see that the heavenly Words have established the oneness of the world of humanity. The banner of the Most Great Peace has been unfurled, and the great community is appearing.

FROM THE WRITINGS AND LETTERS WRITTEN BY, OR ON BEHALF OF, SHOGHI EFFENDI

17.11 ... the Holy Land—the Land promised by God to Abraham, sanctified by the Revelation of Moses, honored by the lives and labors of the Hebrew patriarchs, judges, kings and prophets, revered as the cradle of Christianity, and as the place where Zoroaster, according to 'Abdu'l-Bahá's testimony, had 'held converse with some of the Prophets of Israel,' and associated by Islam with the Apostle's night-journey, through the seven heavens, to the throne of the Almighty. Within the confines of this holy and enviable country, 'the nest of all the Prophets of God,' 'the Vale of God's unsearchable Decree, the snow-white Spot, the Land of unfading splendor' was the Exile of Baghdad, of Constantinople and Adrianople condemned to spend no less than a third of the allotted span of His life, and over half of the total period of His Mission. 'It is difficult,' declares 'Abdu'l-Bahá, 'to understand how Bahá'u'lláh could have been obliged to leave Persia, and to pitch His tent in this Holy Land, but for the persecution of His enemies, His banishment and exile.'

17.12 For, just as in the realm of the spirit, the reality of the Báb has been hailed by the Author of the Bahá'í Revelation as "The Point round Whom the realities of the Prophets and Messengers revolve," so, on this visible plane, His sacred remains constitute the heart and center of what may be regarded as nine concentric circles, paralleling thereby, and adding further emphasis to the central position accorded by the Founder of our Faith to One "from Whom God hath caused to proceed the knowledge of all that was and shall be," "the Primal Point from which have been generated all created things."

The outermost circle in this vast system, the visible counterpart of the pivotal position conferred on the Herald of our Faith, is none other than the entire planet. Within the heart of this planet lies the "Most Holy Land," acclaimed by 'Abdu'l-Bahá as "the Nest of the Prophets" and which must be regarded as the center of the world and the Qiblih of the nations. Within this Most Holy Land rises the Mountain of God of immemorial sanctity, the Vineyard of the Lord, the Retreat of Elijah, Whose return the Báb Himself symbolizes. Reposing on the breast of this holy mountain are the extensive properties permanently dedicated to, and constituting the sacred precincts of, the Báb's holy Sepulcher. In the midst of these properties, recognized as the international endowment-sof the Faith, is situated the most holy court, an enclosure comprising gardens and terraces which at once embellish, and lend a peculiar charm to, these sacred precincts. Embosomed in these lovely and verdant surroundings stands in all its exquisite beauty the mausoleum of the Báb, the shell designed to preserve and adorn the original structure raised by 'Abdu'l-Bahá as the tomb of the Martyr-Herald of our Faith. Within this shell is enshrined that Pearl of Great Price, the holy of holies, those chambers which constitute the tomb itself, and which were constructed by 'Abdu'l-Bahá. Within the heart of this holy of holies is the tabernacle, the vault wherein reposes the most holy casket. Within this vault rests the alabaster sarcophagus in which is deposited that inestimable jewel, the Báb's holy dust. So precious is this dust that the very earth surrounding the edifice enshrining this dust has been extolled by the Center of Bahá'u'lláh's Covenant, in one of His Tablets in which He named the five doors belonging to the six chambers which He originally erected after five of the believers associated with the construction of the Shrine, as being endowed with such potency as to have inspired Him in bestowing these names, whilst the tomb itself housing this dust He acclaimed as the spot round which the Concourse on high circle in adoration.

17.13 The arrival of fifteen pilgrims, in three successive parties, the first of which, including Dr. and Mrs. Getsinger, reached the prison-city of 'Akká on December 10, 1898; the intimate personal contact established between the Center of Bahá'u'lláh's Covenant and the newly arisen heralds of His Revelation in the West; the moving circumstances attending their visit to His Tomb and the great honor bestowed upon them of being conducted by Abdu'l-Bahá Himself into its innermost chamber; the spirit which, through precept and example, despite the briefness of their stay, a loving and bountiful Host so powerfully infused into them; and the passionate zeal and unyielding resolve which His inspiring exhortations, His illuminating instructions and the multiple evidences of His divine love kindled in their hearts—all these marked the opening of a new epoch in the development of the Faith in the West, an epoch whose significance the acts subsequently performed by some of these same pilgrims and their fellow-disciples have amply demonstrated.

"Of that first meeting," one of these pilgrims, recording her impressions, has written, "I can remember neither joy nor pain, nor anything that I can name. I had been carried suddenly to too great a height, my soul had come in contact with the Divine Spirit, and this force, so pure, so holy, so mighty, had overwhelmed me... We could not remove our eyes from His glorious face; we heard all that He said; we drank tea with Him at His bidding; but existence seemed suspended; and when He arose and suddenly left us, we came back with a start to life; but never again, oh! never again, thank God, the same life on this earth." "In the might and majesty of His presence," that same pilgrim, recalling the last interview accorded the party of which she was a member, has testified, "our fear was turned to perfect faith, our weakness into strength, our sorrow into hope, and ourselves forgotten in our love for Him. As we all sat before Him, waiting to hear His words, some of the believers wept bitterly. He bade them dry their tears, but they could not for a moment. So again He asked them for His sake not to weep, nor would He talk to us and teach us until all tears were banished..."

..."Those three days," Mrs. Hearst herself has, in one of her letters, testified, "were the most memorable days of my life... The Master I will not attempt to describe: I will only state that I believe with all my heart that He is the Master, and my greatest blessing in this world is that I have been privileged to be in His presence, and look upon His sanctified face... Without a doubt Abbas Effendi is the Messiah of this day and generation, and we need not look for another." "I must say," she, moreover, has in another letter written, "He is the most wonderful Being I have ever met or ever expect to meet in this world... The spiritual atmosphere which surrounds Him and most powerfully affects all those who are blest by being near Him, is indescribable... I believe in Him with all my heart and soul, and I hope all who call themselves believers will concede to Him all the greatness, all the glory, and all the praise, for surely He is the Son of God—and 'the spirit of the Father abideth in Him.'"

Even Mrs. Hearst's butler, a negro named Robert Turner, the first member of his race to embrace the Cause of Bahá'u'lláh in the West, had been transported by the influence exerted by Abdu'l-Bahá in the course of that epoch-making pilgrimage. Such was the tenacity of his faith that even the subsequent estrangement of his beloved mistress from the Cause she had spontaneously embraced failed to becloud its radiance, or to lessen the intensity of the emotions which the loving-kindness showered by Abdu'l-Bahá upon him had excited in his breast.

FROM THE WRITINGS AND LETTERS WRITTEN BY, OR ON BEHALF OF, THE UNIVERSAL HOUSE OF JUSTICE

17.14　In harmony with the worldwide growth of the Cause the World Center of the Faith is also developing rapidly. The pilgrims, the beloved Guardian has said, are the lifeblood of this World Center and it has long been our cherished hope and desire to be able to grant the bounty of pilgrimage to the Holy Land to all who can avail themselves of it. It is therefore with great joy that we now find it possible to open the door of pilgrimage to a much greater number of believers. Beginning in October of this year the size of each group of friends to be invited will be quadrupled and the number of groups each year will be increased so that nearly six times the present number of pilgrims will have the opportunity each year to pray in the Shrines of the Central Figures of their Faith, to visit the places hallowed by the footsteps, sufferings and triumphs of Bahá'u'lláh and 'Abdu'l-Bahá, and to meditate in the tranquillity of these sacred precincts, beautified with so much loving care by our beloved Guardian.

This increased flow of pilgrims will greatly augment the spiritual development of the Bahá'í World Community which now, after five years of strenuous labor and bearing the laurels of outstanding victories, is entering the fourth phase of the Nine Year Plan.

17.15   The majestic buildings that now stand along the Arc traced for them by Shoghi Effendi on the slope of the Mountain of God, together with the magnificent flight of garden terraces that embrace the Shrine of the Báb, are an outward expression of the immense power animating the Cause we serve. They offer timeless witness to the fact that the followers of Bahá'u'lláh have successfully laid the foundations of a worldwide community transcending all differences that divide the human race, and have brought into existence the principal institutions of a unique and unassailable Administrative Order that shapes this community's life. In the transformation that has taken place on Mount Carmel, the Bahá'í Cause emerges as a visible and compelling reality on the global stage, as the focal center of forces that will, in God's good time, bring about the reconstruction of society, and as a mystic source of spiritual renewal for all who turn to it.

OTHER SOURCES

17.16   Two sacred Houses are covered by this ordinance, the House of the Báb in Shiraz and the House of Bahá'u'lláh in Baghdad... In this sense, the performance of a pilgrimage is more than simply visiting these two Houses. After the passing of Bahá'u'lláh, 'Abdu'l-Bahá designated the Shrine of Bahá'u'lláh at Bahji as a place of pilgrimage. In a Tablet, He indicates that the "Most Holy Shrine, the Blessed House in Baghdad and the venerated House of the Báb in Shiraz" are "consecrated to pilgrimage", and that it is "obligatory" to visit these places "if one can afford it and is able to do so, and if no obstacle stands in one's way". No rites have been prescribed for pilgrimage to the Most Holy Shrine. (Bahá'í World Center, Notes on The Kitáb-i-Aqdas, p. 191)

17.17 In the Bayan, the Báb enjoined the ordinance of pilgrimage once in a lifetime upon those of His followers who were financially able to undertake the journey. He stated that the obligation was not binding on women in order to spare them the rigours of travel.

Bahá'u'lláh likewise exempts women from His pilgrimage requirements. The Universal House of Justice has clarified that this exemption is not a prohibition, and that women are free to perform the pilgrimage. (Bahá'í World Center, Notes on The *Kitáb-i-Aqdas*, p. 191)

17.18 It shall blossom abundantly, and rejoice even with joy and singing: the glory of Lebanon shall be given unto it, the excellency of Carmel and Sharon, they shall see the glory of the Lord, and the excellency of our God. (Isaiah 35:2, KJV)

CHAPTER 18:

CULTIVATING A NEW MODEL FOR MARRIAGE AND FAMILY LIFE

FROM THE WRITINGS OF BAHÁ'U'LLÁH

18.1   Enter into wedlock, O people, that ye may bring forth one who will make mention of Me amid My servants. This is My bidding unto you; hold fast to it as an assistance to yourselves.

18.2   Teach your children the verses revealed from the heaven of majesty and power, so that, in most melodious tones, they may recite the Tablets of the All-Merciful in the alcoves within the Mashriqu'l-Adhkárs.

18.3   Should resentment or antipathy arise between husband and wife, he is not to divorce her but to bide in patience through-out the course of one whole year, that perchance the fragrance of affection may be renewed between them. If, upon the completion of this period, their love hath not returned, it is permissible for divorce to take place.

18.4   The parents must exert every effort to rear their offspring to be religious, for should the children not attain this greatest of adornments, they will not obey their parents, which in a certain sense means that they will not obey God. Indeed, such children will show no consideration to anyone, and will do exactly as they please.

18.5   He that bringeth up his son or the son of another, it is as though he hath brought up a son of Mine; upon him rest My glory, My loving-kindness, My mercy, that have compassed the world.

FROM THE WRITINGS AND UTTERANCES OF 'ABDU'L-BAHÁ

18.6   O ye my two beloved children! The news of your union, as soon as it reached me, imparted infinite joy and gratitude. Praise be to God, those two faithful birds have sought shelter in one nest. I beseech God that He may enable them to raise an honoured family, for the importance of marriage lieth in the bringing up of a richly blessed family, so that with entire gladness they may, even as candles, illuminate the world. For the enlightenment of the world dependeth upon the existence of man. If man did not exist in this world, it would have been like a tree without fruit. My hope is that you both may become even as one tree, and may, through the outpourings of the cloud of loving-kindness, acquire freshness and charm, and may blossom and yield fruit, so that your line may eternally endure.

Upon ye be the Glory of the Most Glorious.

18.7 The true marriage of Bahá'ís is this, that husband and wife should be united both physically and spiritually, that they may ever improve the spiritual life of each other, and may enjoy everlasting unity throughout all the worlds of God. This is Bahá'í marriage.

18.8 Note ye how easily, where unity existeth in a given family, the affairs of that family are conducted; what progress the members of that family make, how they prosper in the world. Their concerns are in order, they enjoy comfort and tranquillity, they are secure, their position is assured, they come to be envied by all. Such a family but addeth to its stature and its lasting honour, as day succeedeth day.

18.9 Bahá'í marriage is the commitment of the two parties one to the other, and their mutual attachment of mind and heart. Each must, however, exercise the utmost care to become thoroughly acquainted with the character of the other, that the binding covenant between them may be a tie that will endure forever. Their purpose must be this: to become loving companions and comrades and at one with each other for time and eternity....

18.10 Happy the soul that shall forget his own good, and like the chosen ones of God, vie with his fellows in service to the good of all...

18.11   As to thy question regarding the education of children: it
behoveth thee to nurture them at the breast of the love of God,
and urge them onward to the things of the spirit, that they may
turn their faces unto God; that their ways may conform to the
rules of good conduct and their character be second to none; that
they make their own all the graces and praiseworthy qualities of
humankind; acquire a sound knowledge of the various branches
of learning, so that from the very beginning of life they may
become spiritual beings, dwellers in the Kingdom, enamoured
of the sweet breaths of holiness, and may receive an education
religious, spiritual, and of the Heavenly Realm. Verily will I call
upon God to grant them a happy outcome in this.

18.12   In a time to come, morals will degenerate to an extreme
degree. It is essential that children be reared in the Bahá'í way,
that they may find happiness both in this world and the next.
If not, they shall be beset by sorrows and troubles, for human
happiness is founded upon spiritual behaviour.

18.13   O ye two believers in God! The Lord, peerless is He, hath
made woman and man to abide with each other in the closest
companionship, and to be even as a single soul. They are two
helpmates, two intimate friends, who should be concerned
about the welfare of each other.
      If they live thus, they will pass through this world with
perfect contentment, bliss, and peace of heart, and become the
object of divine grace and favour in the Kingdom of heaven.
But if they do other than this, they will live out their lives in
great bitterness, longing at every moment for death, and will
be shamefaced in the heavenly realm.
      Strive, then, to abide, heart and soul, with each other as
two doves in the nest, for this is to be blessed in both worlds.

18.14   Ye should consider the question of goodly character as of
the first importance. It is incumbent upon every father and
mother to counsel their children over a long period, and guide
them unto those things which lead to everlasting honour.
      Encourage ye the school children, from their earliest
years, to deliver speeches of high quality, so that in their leisure

time they will engage in giving cogent and effective talks, expressing themselves with clarity and eloquence.

18.15   Train your children from their earliest days to be infinitely tender and loving to animals. If an animal be sick, let the children try to heal it, if it be hungry, let them feed it, if thirsty, let them quench its thirst, if weary, let them see that it rests.

18.16   Children are even as a branch that is fresh and green; they will grow up in whatever way ye train them. Take the utmost care to give them high ideals and goals, so that once they come of age, they will cast their beams like brilliant candles on the world, and will not be defiled by lusts and passions in the way of animals, heedless and unaware, but instead will set their hearts on achieving everlasting honour and acquiring all the excellences of humankind.

18.17   Praised be God, ye two have demonstrated the truth of your words by your deeds, and have won the confirmations of the Lord God. Every day at first light, ye gather the Bahá'í children together and teach them the communes and prayers. This is a most praiseworthy act, and bringeth joy to the children's hearts: that they should, at every morn, turn their faces toward the Kingdom and make mention of the Lord and praise His Name, and in the sweetest of voices, chant and recite.

These children are even as young plants, and teaching them the prayers is as letting the rain pour down upon them, that they may wax tender and fresh, and the soft breezes of the love of God may blow over them, making them to tremble with joy.

18.18   Thou didst write as to the children: from the very beginning, the children must receive divine education and must continually be reminded to remember their God. Let the love of God pervade their inmost being, commingled with their mother's milk.

18.19   ...Work ye for the guidance of the women in that land, teach the young girls and the children, so that the mothers may educate their little ones from their earliest days, thoroughly train them, rear them to have a goodly character and good morals, guide them to all the virtues of humankind, prevent the development of any behaviour that would be worthy of blame, and foster them in the embrace of Bahá'í education. Thus shall these tender infants be nurtured at the breast of the knowledge of God and His love. Thus shall they grow and flourish, and be taught righteousness and the dignity of humankind, resolution and the will to strive and to endure. Thus shall they learn perseverance in all things, the will to advance, high mindedness and high resolve, chastity and purity of life. Thus shall they be enabled to carry to a successful conclusion whatsoever they undertake.

18.20 This gathering must be completely spiritual. That is, the discussions must be confined to marshalling clear and conclusive proofs that the Sun of Truth hath indeed arisen. And further, those present should concern themselves with every means of training the girl children; with teaching the various branches of knowledge, good behaviour, a proper way of life, the cultivation of a good character, chastity and constancy, perseverance, strength, determination, firmness of purpose; with household management, the education of children, and whatever especially applieth to the needs of girls—to the end that these girls, reared in the stronghold of all perfections, and with the protection of a goodly character, will, when they themselves become mothers, bring up their children from earliest infancy to have a good character and conduct themselves well.

Let them also study whatever will nurture the health of the body and its physical soundness, and how to guard their children from disease.

18.21 In short, the foundation of the Kingdom of God is based upon harmony and love, oneness, relationship and union, not upon differences, especially between husband and wife. If one of these two become the cause of divorce, that one will unquestionably fall into great difficulties, will become the victim of formidable calamities and experience deep remorse.

18.22 It is highly important for man to raise a family. So long as he is young, because of youthful self-complacency, he does not realize its significance, but this will be a source of regret when he grows old ...

In this glorious Cause the life of a married couple should resemble the life of the angels in heaven—a life full of joy and spiritual delight, a life of unity and concord, a friendship both mental and physical. The home should be orderly and well- organized. Their ideas and thoughts should be like the rays of the sun of truth and the radiance of the brilliant stars in the heavens. Even as two birds they should warble melodies upon the branches of the tree of fellowship and harmony. They should always be elated with joy and gladness and be a source of happiness to the hearts of others. They should set an example to their fellow-men, manifest true and sincere love towards each other and educate their children in such a manner as to blazon the fame and glory of their family.

18.23 O Thou kind Lord! These lovely children are the handiwork of the fingers of Thy might and the wondrous signs of Thy greatness. O God! Protect these children, graciously assist them to be educated and enable them to render service to the world of humanity. O God! These children are pearls, cause them to be nurtured within the shell of Thy loving-kindness. Thou art the Bountiful, the All-Loving.

18.24 Hold thou fast to this kind of teaching, for the fruits of it will be very great. The children must, from their infancy, be raised to be spiritual and godly Bahá'ís. If such be their training, they will remain safe from every test.

18.25 Among these children many blessed souls will arise, if they be trained according to the Bahá'í Teachings. If a plant is carefully nurtured by a gardener, it will become good, and produce better fruit. These children must be given a good training from their earliest childhood. They must be given a systematic training which will further their development from day to day, in order that they may receive greater insight, so that their spiritual receptivity be broadened. Beginning in childhood they must receive instruction. They cannot be taught through books. Many elementary sciences must be made clear to them in the nursery; they must learn in play, in amusement. Most ideas must be taught them through speech, not by book learning. One child must question the other concerning these things, and the other child must give the answer. In this way, they will make great progress. For example, mathematical problems must also be taught in the form of questions and answers. One of the children asks a question and the other must give the answer. Later on, the children will of their own accord speak with each other concerning these same subjects. The children who are at the head of the class must receive premiums. They must be encouraged and when any one of them shows good advancement, for the further development they must be praised and encouraged therein. Even so in God-like affairs. Oral questions must be asked and the answers must be given orally. They must discuss with each other in this manner.

18.26 Let the mothers consider that whatever concerneth the education of children is of the first importance. Let them put forth every effort in this regard, for when the bough is green and tender it will grow in whatever way ye train it. Therefore is it incumbent upon the mothers to rear their little ones even as a gardener tendeth his young plants. Let them strive by day and by night to establish within their children faith and certitude, the fear of God, the love of the Beloved of the worlds, and all good qualities and traits. Whensoever a mother seeth that her child hath done well, let her praise and applaud him and cheer his heart; and if the slightest undesirable trait should manifest itself, let her counsel the child and punish him, and use means based on reason, even a slight verbal chastisement should this be necessary. It is not, however, permissible to strike a child, or vilify him, for the child's character will be totally perverted if he be subjected to blows or verbal abuse.

FROM THE WRITINGS AND LETTERS WRITTEN BY, OR ON BEHALF OF, SHOGHI EFFENDI

18.27 Regarding your questions: by holiness in our Bahá'í teachings is meant attachment to God, His Precepts and His Will. We are not ascetics in any sense of the word. On the contrary, Bahá'u'lláh says God has created all the good things in the world for us to enjoy and partake. But we must not become attached to them and put them before the spiritual things. Chastity in the strict sense means not to have sexual intercourse, or sexual intimacies, before marriage. In the general sense it means not to be licentious. This does not mean we Bahá'ís believe sexual relations to be impure or wrong. On the contrary they are natural and should be considered one of God's many blessings. He does not know anything about whether albumen and delicious food affect sex; this is a medical question. Sex is a very individual matter, some people are more passionate by nature than others, and might consequently suffer more if forced to be continent. But when the world becomes more spiritual there will not be such an exaggerated emphasis on sex, as there is today, and consequently it will be easier for young people to be chaste and control their passions. A man of noble character and strong willpower, could certainly remain faithful to his wife during a long absence!

18.28 There is no doubt about it that the believers in America, probably unconsciously influenced by the extremely lax morals prevalent and the flippant attitude towards divorce which seems to be increasingly prevailing, do not take divorce seriously enough and do not seem to grasp the fact that although Bahá'u'lláh has permitted it, He has only permitted it as a last resort and strongly condemns it.

The presence of children, as a factor in divorce, cannot be ignored, for surely it places an even greater weight of moral responsibility on the man and wife in considering such a step. Divorce under such circumstances no longer just concerns them and their desires and feelings but also concerns the children's entire future and their own attitude towards marriage."

18.29 He was very sorry to hear that you are contemplating separation from your husband. As you no doubt know, Bahá'u'lláh considers the marriage bond very sacred; and only under very exceptional and unbearable circumstances is divorce advisable for Bahá'ís.

The Guardian does not tell you that you must not divorce your husband; but he does urge you to consider prayerfully, not only because you are a believer and anxious to obey the Laws of God, but also for the sake of the happiness of your children, whether it is not possible for you to rise above the limitations you have felt in your marriage hitherto, and make a go of it together.

We often feel that our happiness lies in a certain direction; and yet, if we have to pay too heavy a price for it in the end we may discover that we have not really purchased either freedom or happiness, but must some new situation of frustration and disillusion.

18.30 Shoghi Effendi wishes me to add this note in connection with your marriage; he does not feel that any believer, under any circumstances whatsoever, can ever use the Cause or service to it as a reason for abandoning their marriage; divorce, as we know, is very strongly condemned by Bahá'u'lláh, and only grounds of extreme gravity justify it.

18.31 The task of bringing up a Bahá'í child, as emphasized time and again in Bahá'í writings, is the chief responsibility of the mother, whose unique privilege is indeed to create in her home such conditions as would be most conducive to both his material and spiritual welfare and advancement. The training which the child first receives through his mother constitutes the strongest foundation for his future development...

18.32 It was a pleasure to Shoghi Effendi to receive your letter of May 26th and to hear about your adopted children. This is a truly Bahá'í act especially as it was often lauded both by Bahá'u'lláh and 'Abdu'l-Bahá, and the Guardian trusts that they will grow to become Bahá'í workers, and thus repay your kind generosity.

18.33 The Guardian will pray that each of you may become a brilliant light in this dark world, and in due time, lead many seeking souls to the Splendor of the Cause of God. This is the real object of life, and he hopes all your training, will be a means of training your characters, and enriching your spirits, so you may teach the Faith, and become strong supporters of its institutions.

FROM THE WRITINGS AND LETTERS WRITTEN BY, OR ON BEHALF OF, THE UNIVERSAL HOUSE OF JUSTICE

18.34 Unlike the children of some other religions, Bahá'í children do not automatically inherit the Faith of their parents. However, the parents are responsible for the upbringing and spiritual welfare of their children, and Spiritual Assemblies have the duty to assist parents, if necessary, in fulfilling these obligations, so that the children will be reared in the light of the Revelation of Bahá'u'lláh and from their earliest years will learn to love God and His Manifestations and to walk in the way of God's Law. It is natural, therefore, to regard the children of Bahá'ís as Bahá'ís unless there is a reason to conclude the contrary. It is quite wrong to think of Bahá'í children as existing in some sort of spiritual limbo until the age of fifteen at which point they can "become" Bahá'ís. In the light of this one can conclude the following:

Children born to a Bahá'í couple are regarded as Bahá'ís from the beginning of their lives, and their births should be registered by the Spiritual Assembly.

The birth of a child to a couple, one of whom is a Bahá'í, should also be registered unless the non-Bahá'í parent objects.

A Spiritual Assembly may accept the declaration of faith of a child of non-Bahá'í parents, and register him as a Bahá'í child, provided the parents give their consent.

In the cases of children whose parents become Bahá'ís, much depends upon the ages and reactions of the children concerned. They will require great love and understanding, and each case must be judged on its own merits. This applies to an added degree, of course, if only one of the parents has accepted the Faith, in which case the attitude of the other parent is an important factor; the aim of the Bahá'ís should be to foster family unity. The important thing is that the children, whether registered as Bahá'ís or not, should be made to feel welcome at Bahá'í children's classes and other community gatherings.

It is within a Spiritual Assembly's discretion to request Bahá'í children to undertake work of which they are capable in service to the Faith, such as service on suitable committees.

18.35 The relationship between husband and wife must be viewed in the context of the Bahá'í ideal of family life. Bahá'u'lláh came to bring unity to the world, and a fundamental unity is that of the family. Therefore, one must believe that the Faith is intended to strengthen the family, not weaken it, and one of the keys to the strengthening of unity is loving consultation. The atmosphere within a Bahá'í family as within the community as a whole should express 'the keynote of the Cause of God' which, the beloved Guardian has stated, 'is not dictatorial authority but humble fellowship, not arbitrary power, but the spirit of frank and loving consultation'.

18.36 The Tablet of 'Abdu'l-Bahá concerning the education of children refers particularly to their formal education which He says must begin at the age of five. The Master makes it clear that during the daytime children of that age and older should be looked after in a place where there are teachers. They should learn good conduct and be taught how to spell and to read and He indicates that spelling and reading can be learned by the use of simple games. Children of all ages can benefit from the guidance given to mothers by 'Abdu'l-Bahá in which He advises that when the children are ready for bed their mothers should read or sing to them verses of Bahá'u'lláh so that from their earliest years the children will be educated by these words of the Blessed Beauty. The House of Justice adds that you should feel free to hold classes for children under the age of five provided you keep in mind that their attention span is relatively short and so the duration of their class periods should be measured accordingly.

18.37 There are many texts included in A Compilation on Bahá'í Education, from the writings of Bahá'u'lláh, 'Abdu'l-Bahá and the Guardian, which indicate that 'children must, from their infancy, be raised to be spiritual and godly Bahá'ís. If such be their training, they will remain safe from every test.' (Abdu'l-Bahá, p.36). Bahá'u'lláh Himself has written: 'As to the children: We have directed that in the beginning they should be trained in the observances and laws of religion; ... and in deeds that will further the victory of God's Cause...'(p. 8). They should even be trained from an early age to make their own sacrifices for the Faith, as indicated in these words: 'Bring them up to work and strive, and accustom them to hardship. Teach them to dedicate their lives to matters of great import...' ('Abdu'l-Bahá, p. 31).

18.38   The Universal House of Justice has noted with increasing concern that the undisciplined attitude of present-day society towards divorce is reflected in some parts of the Bahá'í World Community. Our Teachings on this subject are clear and in direct contrast to the loose and casual attitude of the 'permissive society' and it is vital that the Bahá'í Community practise these Teachings.

18.39   The Spiritual Assembly should always be concerned that the believers in its community are being deepened in their understanding of the Bahá'í concept of marriage, especially the young people, so that the very thought of divorce will be abhorrent to them.

18.40   It is clear that the separation of a child from its natural parents is a tragedy that society must do its best to prevent or mitigate. It is also clear that in certain cases the actual separation may be better for the child than to continue living with a parent whose conduct and character make him unworthy of this sacred function, for the Guardian has explicitly stated that the serving of family ties and renunciation of responsibilities between parents and the children is, in certain cases, permissible under the Law of God, but that the Universal House of Justice has to make the law governing such matters.

Whenever the law of the land or the agreement of adoption prohibits future contact between an adopted child and its natural parents, the Bahá'í law does not require the child to seek the consent of those parents to its marriage.

In the situation, however, where contact with the natural parent is permitted, it should be a matter of wise discretion at what stage contact, in cases where it has been broken, should be re- established. Just as love for one person need not reduce the love one bears to another, so unity with the adoptive parents need not destroy or reduce the unity a child has with its natural parents, or vice versa. The characters and attitudes of the individuals concerned will have an effect upon this...

18.41 Concerning the definition of the term 'aversion' in relation to Bahá'í divorce law, the Universal House of Justice points out that there are no specific 'grounds' for Bahá'í divorce such as there are in some codes of civil law. Bahá'í Law permits divorce but, as both Bahá'u'lláh and 'Abdu'l-Bahá have made very clear, divorce is abhorred. Thus, from the point of view of the individual believer he should do all he can to refrain from divorce. Bahá'ís should be profoundly aware of the sanctity of marriage and should strive to make their marriages an eternal bond of unity and harmony. This requires effort and sacrifice and wisdom and self-abnegation. A Bahá'í should consider the possibility of divorce only if the situation is intolerable and he or she has a strong aversion to being married to the other partner. This is the standard help up to the individual. It is not a law, but an exhortation. It is a goal to which we should strive.

CHAPTER 19

MASTERING A SPIRITUAL PERSPECTIVE IN WORK AND CAREERS

FROM THE WRITINGS OF BAHÁ'U'LLÁH

19.1   O people of Bahá! It is incumbent upon each one of you to engage in some occupation—such as a craft, a trade or the like. We have exalted your engagement in such work to the rank of worship of the one true God. Reflect, O people, on the grace and blessings of your Lord, and yield Him thanks at eventide and dawn. Waste not your hours in idleness and sloth, but occupy yourselves with what will profit you and others.

19.2   Man's merit lieth in service and virtue and not in the pageantry of wealth and riches.

19.3   O MY SERVANTS! Ye are the trees of My garden; ye must give forth goodly and wondrous fruits, that ye yourselves and others may profit therefrom. Thus it is incumbent on every one to engage in crafts and professions, for therein lies the secret of wealth, O men of understanding! For results depend upon means, and the grace of God shall be all-sufficient unto you. Trees that yield no fruit have been and will ever be for the fire.

19.4   O MY SERVANT! The best of men are they that earn a livelihood by their calling and spend upon themselves and upon their kindred for the love of God, the Lord of all worlds.

19.5   Say: Should your conduct, O people, contradict your professions, how think ye, then, to be able to distinguish yourselves from them who, though professing their faith in the Lord their God, have, as soon as He came unto them in the cloud of holiness, refused to acknowledge Him, and repudiated His truth?

19.6   Let your acts be a guide unto all mankind, for the professions of most men, be they high or low, differ from their conduct. It is through your deeds that ye can distinguish yourselves from others. Through them the brightness of your light can be shed upon the whole earth. Happy is the man that heedeth My counsel, and keepeth the precepts prescribed by Him Who is the All-Knowing, the All-Wise.

19.7   True reliance is for the servant to pursue his profession and calling in this world, to hold fast unto the Lord, to seek naught but His grace, inasmuch as in His Hands is the destiny of all His servants.

19.8   Concerning thine own affairs, if thou wouldst content thyself with whatever might come to pass it would be praiseworthy. To engage in some profession is highly commendable, for when occupied with work one is less likely to dwell on the unpleasant aspects of life. God willing thou mayest experience joy and radiance, gladness and exultation in any city or land where thou mayest happen to sojourn. This lowly servant will never forget that distinguished and kind friend. He hath remembered and will continue to remember thee. The decree lieth with God, the Lord of all worlds. I fain would hope He may vouchsafe divine assistance and grant confirmation in that which is pleasing and acceptable unto Him.

19.9   The first Taraz and the first effulgence which hath dawned from the horizon of the Mother Book is that man should know his own self and recognize that which leadeth unto loftiness or lowliness, glory or abasement, wealth or poverty. Having attained the stage of fulfilment and reached his maturity, man standeth in need of wealth, and such wealth as he acquireth through crafts or professions is commendable and praiseworthy in the estimation of men of wisdom, and especially in the eyes of servants who dedicate themselves to the education of the world and to the edification of its peoples. They are, in truth, cup-bearers of the life-giving water of knowledge and guides unto the ideal way. They direct the peoples of the world to the straight path and acquaint them with that which is conducive to human upliftment and exaltation. The straight path is the one which guideth man to the dayspring of perception and to the dawning-place of true understanding and leadeth him to that which will redound to glory, honour and greatness.

19.10   The most despised of men in the sight of God are those who sit idly and beg. Hold ye fast unto the cord of material means, placing your whole trust in God, the Provider of all means. When anyone occupieth himself in a craft or trade, such occupation itself is regarded in the estimation of God as an act of worship; and this is naught but a token of His infinite and all-pervasive bounty.

19.11   O MY SERVANT! The basest of men are they that yield no fruit on earth. Such men are verily counted as among the dead, nay better are the dead in the sight of God than those idle and worthless souls.

19.12   Please God, the poor may exert themselves and strive to earn the means of livelihood. This is a duty which, in this most great Revelation, hath been prescribed unto every one, and is accounted in the sight of God as a goodly deed. Whoso observeth this duty, the help of the invisible One shall most certainly aid him. He can enrich, through His grace, whomsoever He pleaseth. He, verily, hath power over all things...

19.13   Knowledge is as wings to man's life, and a ladder for his ascent. Its acquisition is incumbent upon everyone. The knowledge of such sciences, however, should be acquired as can profit the peoples of the earth, and not those which begin with words and end with words. Great indeed is the claim of scientists and craftsmen on the peoples of the world.

FROM THE WRITINGS AND UTTERANCES OF 'ABDU'L-BAHÁ

19.14   It behoveth the craftsmen of the world at each moment to offer a thousand tokens of gratitude at the Sacred Threshold, and to exert their highest endeavour and diligently pursue their professions so that their efforts may produce that which will manifest the greatest beauty and perfection before the eyes of all men.

19.15   Thy letter was received. I hope that thou mayest be protected and assisted under the providence of the True One, be occupied always in mentioning the Lord and display effort to complete thy profession. Thou must endeavour greatly so that thou mayest become unique in thy profession and famous in those parts, because attaining perfection in one's profession in this merciful period is considered to be worship of God. And whilst thou art occupied with thy profession, thou canst remember the True One.

19.16 He teaches that it is incumbent upon all mankind to become fitted for some useful trade, craft or profession by which subsistence may be assured, and this efficiency is to be considered as an act of worship.

19.17 Make ye a mighty effort till you yourselves betoken this advancement and all these confirmations, and become focal centres of God's blessings, daysprings of the light of His unity, promoters of the gifts and graces of civilized life. Be ye in that land vanguards of the perfections of humankind; carry forward the various branches of knowledge, be active and progressive in the field of inventions and the arts. Endeavour to rectify the conduct of men, and seek to excel the whole world in moral character. While the children are yet in their infancy feed them from the breast of heavenly grace, foster them in the cradle of all excellence, rear them in the embrace of bounty. Give them the advantage of every useful kind of knowledge. Let them share in every new and rare and wondrous craft and art. Bring them up to work and strive, and accustom them to hardship. Teach them to dedicate their lives to matters of great import, and inspire them to undertake studies that will benefit mankind.

19.18 Wealth is most commendable, provided the entire population is wealthy. If, however, a few have inordinate riches while the rest are impoverished, and no fruit or benefit accrues from that wealth, then it is only a liability to its possessor. If, on the other hand, it is expended for the promotion of knowledge, the founding of elementary and other schools, the encouragement of art and industry, the training of orphans and the poor—in brief, if it is dedicated to the welfare of society—its possessor will stand out before God and man as the most excellent of all who live on earth and will be accounted as one of the people of paradise.

19.19 Strain every nerve to acquire both inner and outer perfections, for the fruit of the human tree hath ever been and will ever be perfections both within and without. It is not desirable that a man be left without knowledge or skills, for he is then but a barren tree. Then, so much as capacity and capability allow, ye needs must deck the tree of being with fruits such as knowledge, wisdom, spiritual perception and eloquent speech.

19.20 There are no solitaries and no hermits among the Bahá'ís. Man must work with his fellows. Everyone should have some trade, or art or profession, be he rich or poor, and with this he must serve humanity. This service is acceptable as the highest form of worship.

19.21 If we are true Bahá'ís speech is not needed. Our actions will help in the world, will spread civilization, will help the progress of science, and cause the arts to develop. Without action nothing in the material world can be accomplished, neither can words unaided advance a man in the spiritual Kingdom. It is not through lip-service only that the elect of God have attained to holiness, but by patient lives of active service they have brought light into the world.

19.22 If a man is successful in his business, art, or profession he is thereby enabled to increase his physical wellbeing and to give his body the amount of ease and comfort in which it delights. All around us today we see how man surrounds himself with every modern convenience and luxury, and denies nothing to the physical and material side of his nature. But, take heed, lest in thinking too earnestly of the things of the body you forget the things of the soul: for material advantages do not elevate the spirit of a man. Perfection in worldly things is a joy to the body of a man but in no wise does it glorify his soul.

It may be that a man who has every material benefit, and who lives surrounded by all the greatest comfort modern civilization can give him, is denied the all important gift of the Holy Spirit.

It is indeed a good and praiseworthy thing to progress materially, but in so doing, let us not neglect the more important spiritual progress, and close our eyes to the Divine light shining in our midst.

Only by improving spiritually as well as materially can we make any real progress, and become perfect beings. It was in order to bring this spiritual life and light into the world that all the great Teachers have appeared. They came so that the Sun of Truth might be manifested, and shine in the hearts of men, and that through its wondrous power men might attain unto Everlasting Light.

19.23 In like manner, the members of each profession, such as in industry, should consult, and those in commerce should similarly consult on business affairs. In short, consultation is desirable and acceptable in all things and on all issues."

FROM THE WRITINGS AND LETTERS WRITTEN BY, OR ON BEHALF OF, SHOGHI EFFENDI

19.24 With reference to Bahá'u'lláh's command concerning the engagement of the believers in some sort of profession; the Teachings are most emphatic on this matter, particularly the statement in the "Aqdas" to this effect which makes it quite clear that idle people who lack the desire to work can have no place in the new World Order. As a corollary of this principle, Bahá'u'lláh further states that mendacity should not only be discouraged but entirely wiped out from the face of society. It is the duty of those who are in charge of the organization of society to give every individual the opportunity of acquiring the necessary talent in some kind of profession, and also the means of utilizing such a talent, both for its own sake and for the sake of earning the means of his livelihood. Every individual, no matter how handicapped and limited he may be, is under the obligation of engaging in some work or profession, for work, specially when performed in the spirit of service, is according to Bahá'u'lláh a form of worship. It has not only a utilitarian purpose, but has a value in itself, because it draws us nearer to God, and enables us to better grasp His purpose for us in this world. It is obvious, therefore, that the inheritance of wealth cannot make anyone immune from daily work."

19.25   The Guardian fully realizes that from the material standpoint it would be quite easy for you to devote all your time to the service of the Cause, and he deeply appreciates the strong desire you have expressed to consecrate your full life to this noble aim, which should certainly be the chief and constant ambition of every loyal believer.

But he thinks that in view of Bahá'u'lláh's emphatic command, as recorded in His Book of Laws, that every person should be engaged in some sort of profession it would be better and more in conformity with the Teachings if you remain in your profession and teach the Cause at the same time. As you rightly suggest, the middle path, that is to say practicing one's profession and also teaching the Cause is the best way for you to follow.

19.26   In connection with your dear husband, Shoghi Effendi would consider it in full and happy accord with the expressed desire of the Master that every man should have some permanent work. Much as he desires to see you both devote your entire energies to a well-thought out, progressive and attractive presentation of the Cause—a thing he feels we lack lamentably—he would be very pleased to see your husband follow what the Master often repeated even to His own immediate family, namely the necessity of a profession. Of course you know that He always said His had been mat-making."

19.27   In the teaching there is nothing against dancing, but the friends should remember that the standard of Bahá'u'lláh is modesty and chastity. The atmosphere of modern dance halls, where so much smoking and drinking and promiscuity goes on, is very bad, but decent dances are not harmful in themselves. There is certainly no harm in classical dancing or learning dancing in school. There is also no harm in taking part in dramas. Likewise in cinema acting. The harmful thing, nowadays, is not the art itself but the unfortunate corruption which often surrounds these arts. As Bahá'ís we need to avoid none of the arts, but acts and the atmosphere that sometimes go with these professions we should avoid."

19.28   The advice that Shoghi Effendi gave you regarding the division of your time between serving the Cause and attending to your other duties was also given to many other friends both by Bahá'u'lláh and the Master. It is a compromise between the two verses of the Aqdas one making it incumbent upon every Bahá'í to serve the promotion of the Faith and the other that every soul should be occupied in some form of occupation that will benefit society. In one of His Tablets Bahá'u'lláh says that the highest form of detachment in this day is to be occupied with some profession and be self-supporting. A good Bahá'í, therefore Is the one who so arranges his life as to devote time both to his material needs and also to the service of the Cause.

FROM THE WRITINGS AND LETTERS WRITTEN BY, OR ON BEHALF OF, THE UNIVERSAL HOUSE OF JUSTICE

19.29   The delicate balance between the claims of the Cause of God and the claims of one's profession is an intensely personal matter which can only be resolved eventually in the heart and soul of each individual. Many Bahá'ís have become, and are, distinguished in their professions and at the same time have rendered and are rendering great services to the Cause and it is obviously possible to achieve distinction in one's profession and calling and to serve the Cause of God at the same time. The House of Justice realizes, however that circumstances can conspire at critical times in the fortunes of the Faith, to require individuals to make the heart- searching decision of sacrificing one's own prospect for the apparent good of the Cause. Here again, the history of the Cause provides many examples of believers who have willingly forgone promotion in, or even the continued practice of, their professions in order to meet the needs of the Faith. As in all difficult decisions facing individual officer, such as a Counsellor or Board member, or even one or two friends of his own choosing. Even then, however, the eventual decisions rests with the individual himself."

19.30   We have been asked to share with you the following extract from one of the Tablets of 'Abdu'l- Bahá on the subject of begging: "By the Sacred Verse: "Begging is forbidden, and it is also prohibited to dispense alms to a beggar' is meant that mendicancy is forbidden and that giving charity to people who take up begging as their profession is also prohibited. The object is to wipe out mendicancy altogether. However, if a person is disabled, stricken by dire poverty or becomes helpless, then it is incumbent upon the rich or the trustees to provide him with a monthly allowance for his subsistence. when the House of Justice comes into being it will set up homes for the incapacitated. Thus no one will be obliged to beg, even as the supplementary part of the Blessed Verse denotes: 'It is enjoined upon everyone to earn his livelihood'; then He says: 'As to those who are disabled, it devolveth upon the trustees and the rich to make adequate provision for them.' By 'trustees' is meant the representatives of the people, that is to say the members of the House of Justice."

The Universal House of Justice does not wish to go beyond the elucidation given by the Master in the above passage and wishes, for the time being, to leave any matter not entirely covered by this text to the conscience of individual believers.

CHAPTER 20:

EMBARKING ON A LIFETIME OF STUDY

FROM THE WRITINGS OF BAHÁ'U'LLÁH

20.1 Immerse yourselves in the ocean of My words, that ye may unravel its secrets, and discover all the pearls of wisdom that lie hid in its depths. Take heed that ye do not vacillate in your determination to embrace the truth of this Cause—a Cause through which the potentialities of the might of God have been revealed, and His sovereignty established. With faces beaming with joy, hasten ye unto Him. This is the changeless Faith of God, eternal in the past, eternal in the future. Let him that seeketh, attain it; and as to him that hath refused to seek it—verily, God is Self-Sufficient, above any need of His creatures.

20.2 Pride not yourselves on much reading of the verses or on a multitude of pious acts by night and day; for were a man to read a single verse with joy and radiance it would be better for him than to read with lassitude all the Holy Books of God, the Help in Peril, the Self-Subsisting.

20.3 Ponder a while thereon, that with both your inner and outer eye, ye may perceive the subtleties of Divine wisdom and discover the gems of heavenly knowledge which, in clear and weighty language, I have revealed in this exalted and incorruptible Tablet, and that ye may not stray far from the All-Highest Throne, from the Tree beyond which there is no passing, from the Habitation of everlasting might and glory.

20.4 Arise in the name of Him Who is the Object of all knowledge, and, with absolute detachment from the learning of men, lift up your voices and proclaim His Cause. I swear by the Day Star of Divine Revelation! The very moment ye arise, ye will witness how a flood of Divine knowledge will gush out of your hearts, and will behold the wonders of His heavenly wisdom manifested in all their glory before you. Were ye to taste of the sweetness of the sayings of the All-Merciful, ye would unhesitatingly forsake your selves, and would lay down your lives for the Well-Beloved.

20.5   The signs of God shine as manifest and resplendent as the sun amidst the works of His creatures. Whatsoever proceedeth from Him is apart, and will always remain distinguished, from the inventions of men. From the Source of His knowledge countless Luminaries of learning and wisdom have risen, and out of the Paradise of His Pen the breath of the All-Merciful hath continually been wafted to the hearts and souls of men. Happy are they that have recognized this truth.

20.6   Of these truths some can be disclosed only to the extent of the capacity of the repositories of the light of Our knowledge, and the recipients of Our hidden grace. We beseech God to strengthen thee with His power, and enable thee to recognize Him Who is the Source of all knowledge, that thou mayest detach thyself from all human learning, for, "what would it profit any man to strive after learning when he hath already found and recognized Him Who is the Object of all knowledge?" Cleave to the Root of Knowledge, and to Him Who is the Fountain thereof, that thou mayest find thyself independent of all who claim to be well versed in human learning, and whose claim no clear proof, nor the testimony of any enlightening book, can support.

20.7   Only when the lamp of search, of earnest striving, of longing desire, of passionate devotion, of fervid love, of rapture, and ecstasy, is kindled within the seeker's heart, and the breeze of His loving-kindness is wafted upon his soul, will the darkness of error be dispelled, the mists of doubts and misgivings be dissipated, and the lights of knowledge and certitude envelop his being. At that hour will the Mystic Herald, bearing the joyful tidings of the Spirit, shine forth from the City of God resplendent as the morn, and, through the trumpet-blast of knowledge, will awaken the heart, the soul, and the spirit from the slumber of heedlessness. Then will the manifold favors and outpouring grace of the holy and everlasting Spirit confer such new life upon the seeker that he will find himself endowed with a new eye, a new ear, a new heart, and a new mind. He will contemplate the manifest signs of the universe, and will penetrate the hidden mysteries of the soul. Gazing with the eye of God, he will perceive within every atom a door that leadeth him to the stations of absolute certitude. He will discover in all things the mysteries of Divine Revelation, and the evidences of an everlasting Manifestation.

20.8 Be an ornament to the countenance of truth, a crown to the brow of fidelity, a pillar of the temple of righteousness, a breath of life to the body of mankind, an ensign of the hosts of justice, a luminary above the horizon of virtue, a dew to the soil of the human heart, an ark on the ocean of knowledge, a sun in the heaven of bounty, a gem on the diadem of wisdom, a shining light in the firmament of thy generation, a fruit upon the tree of humility

20.9 The spirit that animateth the human heart is the knowledge of God, and its truest adorning is the recognition of the truth that "He doeth whatsoever He willeth, and ordaineth that which He pleaseth." Its raiment is the fear of God, and its perfection steadfastness in His Faith. Thus God instructeth whosoever seeketh Him. He, verily, loveth the one that turneth towards Him. There is none other God but Him, the Forgiving, the Most Bountiful. All praise be to God, the Lord of all worlds.

20.10 O My servants! Could ye apprehend with what wonders of My munificence and bounty I have willed to entrust your souls, ye would, of a truth, rid yourselves of attachment to all created things, and would gain a true knowledge of your own selves—a knowledge which is the same as the comprehension of Mine own Being. Ye would find yourselves independent of all else but Me, and would perceive, with your inner and outer eye, and as manifest as the revelation of My effulgent Name, the seas of My loving-kindness and bounty moving within you. Suffer not your idle fancies, your evil passions, your insincerity and blindness of heart to dim the luster, or stain the sanctity, of so lofty a station. Ye are even as the bird which soareth, with the full force of its mighty wings and with complete and joyous confidence, through the immensity of the heavens, until, impelled to satisfy its hunger, it turneth longingly to the water and clay of the earth below it, and, having been entrapped in the mesh of its desire, findeth itself impotent to resume its flight to the realms whence it came. Powerless to shake off the burden weighing on its sullied wings, that bird, hitherto an inmate of the heavens, is now forced to seek a dwelling-place upon the dust. Wherefore, O My servants, defile not your wings with the clay of waywardness and vain desires, and suffer them not to be stained with the dust of envy and hate, that ye may not be hindered from soaring in the heavens of My divine knowledge.

O My servants! Through the might of God and His power, and out of the treasury of His knowledge and wisdom, I have brought forth and revealed unto you the pearls that lay concealed in the depths of His everlasting ocean. I have summoned the Maids of Heaven to emerge from behind the veil of concealment, and have clothed them with these words of Mine—words of consummate power and wisdom. I have, moreover, with the hand of divine power, unsealed the choice wine of My Revelation, and have wafted its holy, its hidden, and musk-laden fragrance upon all created things. Who else but yourselves is to be blamed if ye choose to remain unendowed with so great an outpouring of God's transcendent and all-encompassing grace, with so bright a revelation of His resplendent mercy?

20.11 O MAN OF TWO VISIONS! Close one eye and open the other. Close one to the world and all that is therein, and open the other to the hallowed beauty of the Beloved.

20.12 O MY BROTHER! Hearken to the delightsome words of My honeyed tongue, and quaff the stream of mystic holiness from My sugar-shedding lips. Sow the seeds of My divine wisdom in the pure soil of thy heart, and water them with the water of certitude, that the hyacinths of My knowledge and wisdom may spring up fresh and green in the sacred city of thy heart.

20.13 O DWELLERS OF MY PARADISE! With the hands of loving-kindness I have planted in the holy garden of paradise the young tree of your love and friendship, and have watered it with the goodly showers of My tender grace; now that the hour of its fruiting is come, strive that it may be protected, and be not consumed with the flame of desire and passion.

20.14 The Word of God hath set the heart of the world afire; how regrettable if ye fail to be enkindled with its flame!

20.15 Incline your hearts, O people of God, unto the counsels of your true, your incomparable Friend. The Word of God may be likened unto a sapling, whose roots have been implanted in the hearts of men. It is incumbent upon you to foster its growth through the living waters of wisdom, of sanctified and holy words, so that its root may become firmly fixed and its branches may spread out as high as the heavens and beyond.

20.16 Know assuredly that just as thou firmly believest that the Word of God, exalted be His glory, endureth for ever, thou must, likewise, believe with undoubting faith that its meaning can never be exhausted.

FROM THE WRITINGS AND UTTERANCES OF 'ABDU'L-BAHÁ

20.17 O ye loved ones of God! Is there any giver save God? He singleth out for His mercy whomsoever He willeth. Erelong will He open before you the gates of His knowledge and fill up your hearts with His love. He will cheer your souls with the gentle winds of His holiness and make bright your faces with the splendours of His lights, and exalt the memory of you amongst all peoples. Your Lord is verily the Compassionate, the Merciful.

He will come to your aid with invisible hosts, and support you with armies of inspiration from the Concourse above; He will send unto you sweet perfumes from the highest Paradise, and waft over you the pure breathings that blow from the rose gardens of the Company on high. He will breathe into your hearts the spirit of life, cause you to enter the Ark of salvation, and reveal unto you His clear tokens and signs. Verily is this abounding grace. Verily is this the victory that none can deny.

20.18 It is therefore urgent that beneficial articles and books be written, clearly and definitely establishing what the present-day requirements of the people are, and what will conduce to the happiness and advancement of society. These should be published and spread throughout the nation, so that at least the leaders among the people should become, to some degree, awakened, and arise to exert themselves along those lines which will lead to their abiding honour. The publication of high thoughts is the dynamic power in the arteries of life; it is the very soul of the world. Thoughts are boundless sea, and the effects and varying conditions of existence are as the separate forms and individual limits of the waves; not until the sea boils up will the waves rise and scatter their pearls of knowledge on the shore of life....

20.19 We should continually be establishing new bases for human happiness and creating and promoting new instrumentalities toward this end.

20.20 As to those persons who, here and there, are considered leaders of the people: because this is only the beginning of the new administrative process, they are not yet sufficiently advanced in their education to have experienced the delights of dispensing justice or to have tasted the exhilaration of pro- moting righteousness or to have drunk from the springs of a clear conscience and a sincere intent. They have not properly understood that man's supreme honor and real happiness lie in self-respect, in high resolves and noble purposes, in integrity and moral quality, in immaculacy of mind. They have, rather, imagined that their greatness consists in the accumulation, by whatever means may offer, of worldly goods.

20.21 These are the counsels of 'Abdu'l-Bahá. It is my hope that out of the bestowals of the Lord of Hosts ye will become the spiritual essence and the very radiance of humankind, binding the hearts of all with bonds of love; that through the power of the Word of God ye will bring to life the dead now buried in the graves of their sensual desires; that ye will, with the rays of the Sun of Truth, restore the sight of those whose inner eye is blind; that ye will bring spiritual healing to the spiritually sick. These things do I hope for, out of the bounties and the bestowals of the Beloved.

20.22 O ye beloved of God, these are days for steadfastness, for firmness and perseverance in the Cause of God. Ye must not focus your attention upon the person of 'Abdu'l-Bahá, for erelong he will bid you farewell. Rather must ye fix your gaze upon the Word of God.

20.23 For the Word of God is collective wisdom, absolute knowledge and eternal truth

20.24 I pray that the divine blessings may descend upon you day by day, that your hearts may be opened to perceive the inner significances of the Word of God.

20.25 An humble man without learning, but filled with the Holy Spirit, is more powerful than the most nobly-born profound scholar without that inspiration. He who is educated by the Divine Spirit can, in his time, lead others to receive the same Spirit.

FROM THE WRITINGS AND LETTERS WRITTEN BY, OR ON BEHALF OF, SHOGHI EFFENDI

20.26 Another essential thing is that those who do embrace the Faith should be constantly urged to study the literature of the Cause. It is not sufficient that our numbers should increase, we want people whose faith stands on a rock and no trial can move. We want people who in turn arise and carry the message to other people and guide other souls.

20.27 The world is in great turmoil and its problems seem to become daily more acute. We should therefore not sit idle; otherwise we would be failing in carrying out our sacred duty. Bahá'u'lláh has not given us His teachings to treasure them and hide them for our personal delight and pleasure. He gave them to us so that we may pass them from mouth to mouth until all the world becomes familiar with them and enjoys their blessings and uplifting influence.

FROM THE WRITINGS AND LETTERS WRITTEN BY, OR ON BEHALF OF, THE UNIVERSAL HOUSE OF JUSTICE

20.28 The Holy Word has been extolled by the Prophets of God as the medium of celestial power and the wellspring of all spiritual, social and material progress. Access to it, constant study of it and daily use of it in our individual lives are vital to the inner personal transformation towards which we strive and whose ultimate outer manifestation will be the emergence of that divine civilization which is the promise of the World Order of Bahá'u'lláh....

20.29 It is neither possible nor desirable for the Universal House of Justice to set forth a set of rules covering every situation. Rather it is the task of the individual believer to determine, according to his own prayerful understanding of the Writings, precisely what his course of conduct should be in relation to situations which he encounters in his daily life. If he is to fulfill his true mission in life as a follower of the Blessed Perfection, he will pattern his life according to the Teachings. The believer cannot attain this objective merely by living according to a set of rigid regulations. When his life is oriented toward service to Bahá'u'lláh, and when every conscious act is performed within this frame of reference, he will not fail to achieve the true purpose of his life.

Therefore, every believer must continually study the sacred Writings and the instructions of the beloved Guardian, striving always to attain a new and better understanding of their import to him and to his society. He should pray fervently for Divine Guidance, wisdom and strength to do what is pleasing to God, and to serve Him at all times and to the best of his ability.

20.30 ... This is the theme we must pursue in our efforts to deepen in the Cause. What is Bahá'u'lláh's purpose for the human race? For what ends did He submit to the appalling cruelties and indignities heaped upon Him? What does He mean by a 'new race of men'? What are the profound changes which He will bring about? The answers are to be found in the Sacred

Writings of our Faith and in their interpretation by 'Abdu'l-Bahá and our beloved Guardian. Let the friends immerse themselves in this ocean, let them organize regular study classes for its constant consideration, and as reinforcements of daily prayers and reading of the Word of God enjoined upon all Bahá'ís by Bahá'u'lláh.

20.31 A clear distinction is made in our Faith between authoritative interpretation and the interpretation or understanding that each individual arrives at for himself from his study of its teachings. While the former is confined to the Guardian, the latter, according to the guidance given to us by the Guardian himself, should by no means be suppressed. In fact such individual interpretation is considered the fruit of man's rational power and conducive to a better understanding of the teachings, provided that no disputes or arguments arise among the friends and the individual himself understands and makes it clear that his views are merely his own. Individual interpretations continually change as one grows in comprehension of the teachings. In a letter written on behalf of Shoghi Effendi it is stated, 'To deepen in the Cause means to read the Writings of Bahá'u'lláh and the Master so thoroughly as to be able to give it to others in its pure form. They, therefore, present it together with all sorts of ideas that are their own. As the Cause is still in its early days we must be most careful lest we fall into this error and injure the Movement we so much adore. There is no limit to the study of the Cause. The more we read the Writings, the more truths we can find in Them, the more we will see that our previous notions were erroneous.' So, although individual insights can be enlightening and helpful, they can also be misleading. The friends must therefore learn to listen to the views of others without being over-awed or allowing their faith to be shaken, and to express their own views without pressing them on their fellow Bahá'ís. "The Cause of God is organic, growing and developing like a living being. Time and again it has faced crisis which have perplexed the believers, but each time the Cause, impelled by the immutable purpose of God, overcame the crisis and went on to greater heights."

CHAPTER 21

GROWING FROM TEACHING THE BAHÁ'Í FAITH

FROM THE WRITINGS OF BAHÁ'U'LLÁH

21.1   Consort with all men, O people of Baha, in a spirit of friendliness and fellowship. If ye be aware of a certain truth, if ye possess a jewel, of which others are deprived, share it with them in a language of utmost kindliness and good-will. If it be accepted, if it fulfil its purpose, your object is attained. If any one should refuse it, leave him unto himself, and beseech God to guide him. Beware lest ye deal unkindly with him. A kindly tongue is the lodestone of the hearts of men. It is the bread of the spirit, it clotheth the words with meaning, it is the fountain of the light of wisdom and understanding....

21.2   Whoso ariseth among you to teach the Cause of his Lord, let him, before all else, teach his own self, that his speech may attract the hearts of them that hear him. Unless he teacheth his own self, the words of his mouth will not influence the heart of the seeker...

21.3   O Friends! You must all be so ablaze in this day with the fire of the love of God that the heat thereof may be manifest in all your veins, your limbs and members of your body, and the peoples of the world may be ignited by this heat and turn to the horizon of the Beloved.

21.4   Say: Teach ye the Cause of God, O people of Baha, for God hath prescribed unto every one the duty of proclaiming His Message, and regardeth it as the most meritorious of all deeds. Such a deed is acceptable only when he that teacheth the Cause is already a firm believer in God, the Supreme Protector, the Gracious, the Almighty. He hath, moreover, ordained that His Cause be taught through the power of men's utterance, and not through resort to violence. Thus hath His ordinance been sent down from the Kingdom of Him Who is the Most Exalted, the All-Wise.

21.5   Beware lest ye contend with any one, nay, strive to make him aware of the truth with kindly manner and most convincing exhortation. If your hearer respond, he will have responded to his own behoof, and if not, turn ye away from him, and set your faces towards God's sacred Court, the seat of resplendent holiness.

21.6   Dispute not with any one concerning the things of this world
        and its affairs, for God hath abandoned them to such as have
        set their affection upon them. Out of the whole world He
        hath chosen for Himself the hearts of men—hearts which the
        hosts of revelation and of utterance can subdue. Thus hath
        it been ordained by the Fingers of Baha, upon the Tablet of
        God's irrevocable decree, by the behest of Him Who is the
        Supreme Ordainer, the All-Knowing.

21.7   Teach thou the Cause of God with an utterance which will cause
        the bushes to be enkindled, and the call 'Verily, there is no God but
        Me, the Almighty, the Unconstrained' to be raised therefrom. Say:
        Human utterance is an essence which aspireth to exert its influence
        and needeth moderation. As to its influence, this is conditional
        upon refinement which in turn is dependent upon hearts which are
        detached and pure. As to its moderation, this hath to be combined
        with tact and wisdom as prescribed in the Holy Scriptures and Tab-
        lets. Meditate upon that which hath streamed forth from the heaven
        of the Will of thy Lord, He Who is the Source of all grace, that thou
        mayest grasp the intended meaning which is enshrined in the sacred
        depths of the Holy Writings.

21.8   Verily, We behold you from Our realm of glory, and shall aid
        whosoever will arise for the triumph of Our Cause with the
        hosts of the Concourse on high and a company of Our favored
        angels.

21.9   O SON OF MY HANDMAID! Guidance hath ever been
        given by words, and now it is given by deeds. Every one must
        show forth deeds that are pure and holy, for words are the
        property of all alike, whereas such deeds as these belong only
        to Our loved ones. Strive then with heart and soul to distin-
        guish yourselves by your deeds. In this wise We counsel you in
        this holy and resplendent tablet.

21.10   ...Say: O people of God! That which can insure the victory of
        Him Who is the Eternal Truth, His hosts and helpers on earth,
        have been set down in the sacred Books and Scriptures, and are
        as clear and manifest as the sun. These hosts are such righteous

deeds, such conduct and character, as are acceptable in His sight. Whoso ariseth, in this Day, to aid Our Cause, and summoneth to his assistance the hosts of a praiseworthy character and upright conduct, the influence from such an action will, most certainly, be diffused throughout the whole world.

21.11　The sanctified souls should ponder and meditate in their hearts regarding the methods of teaching. From the texts of the wondrous, heavenly Scriptures they should memorize phrases and passages bearing on various instances, so that in the course of their speech they may recite divine verses whenever the occasion demandeth it, inasmuch as these holy verses are the most potent elixir, the greatest and mightiest talisman. So potent is their influence that the hearer will have no cause for vacillation. I swear by My life! This Revelation is endowed with such a power that it will act as the lodestone for all nations and kindreds of the earth. Should one pause to meditate attentively he would recognize that no place is there, nor can there be, for anyone to flee to.

21.12　Should such a man ever succeed in influencing any one, this success should be attributed not to him, but rather to the influence of the words of God, as decreed by Him Who is the Almighty, the All-Wise

FROM THE WRITINGS AND UTTERANCES OF 'ABDU'L-BAHÁ

21.13　It is essential that the deeds of the teacher should attest the truth of his words.

21.14　O ye friends of God! True friends are even as skilled physicians, and the Teachings of God are as healing balm, a medicine for the conscience of man. They clear the head, so that a man can breathe them in and delight in their sweet fragrance. They waken those who sleep. They bring awareness to the unheeding, and a portion to the outcast, and to the hopeless, hope.

21.15   O ye servants of the Blessed Beauty!... It is clear that in this day, confirmations from the unseen world are encompassing all those who deliver the divine Message. Should the work of teaching lapse, these confirmations   would be entirely cut off, since it is impossible for the loved ones of God to receive assistance unless they teach.

21.16   The teaching work should under all conditions be actively pursued by the believers because divine confirmations are dependent upon it. Should a Bahá'í refrain from being fully, vigorously and wholeheartedly involved in the teaching work he will undoubtedly be deprived of the blessings of the Abha Kingdom. Even so, this activity should be tempered with wisdom—not that wisdom which requireth one to be silent and forgetful of such an obligation, but rather that which requireth one to display divine tolerance, love, kindness, patience, a goodly character, and holy deeds. In brief, encourage the friends individually to teach the Cause of God and draw their attention to this meaning of wisdom mentioned in the Writings, which is itself the essence of teaching the Faith—but all this to be done with the greatest tolerance, so that heavenly assistance and divine confirmation may aid the friends.

21.17   As to his question about the permissibility of promulgating the divine teachings without relating them to the Most Great Name, you should answer: 'This blessed Name hath an effect on the reality of things. If these teachings are spread without identifying them with this holy Name, they will fail to exert an abiding influence in the world. The teachings are like the body, and this holy Name is like the spirit. It imparteth life to the body. It causeth the people of the world to be aroused from their slumber.'

21.18   The teacher, when teaching, must be himself fully enkindled, so that his utterance, like unto a flame of fire, may exert influence and consume the veil of self and passion. He must also be utterly humble and lowly, so that others may be edified and be totally self-effaced and evanescent so that he may teach with the melody of the Concourse of high—otherwise his teaching will have no effect.

21.19 When the friends do not endeavor to spread the message, they fail to remember God befittingly, and will not witness the tokens of assistance and confirmation from the Abha Kingdom nor comprehend the divine mysteries. However, when the tongue of the teacher is engaged in teaching, he will naturally himself be stimulated, will become a magnet attracting the divine aid and bounty of the Kingdom, and will be like unto the bird at the hour of dawn, which itself becometh exhilarated by its own singing, its warbling and its melody.

21.20 When a speaker's brow shineth with the radiance of the love of God, at the time of his exposition of a subject, and he is exhilarated with the wine of true understanding, he becometh the center of a potent force which like unto a magnet will attract the hearts. This is why the expounder must be in the utmost enkindlement.

21.21 The friends of God should weave bonds of fellowship with others and show absolute love and affection towards them. These links have a deep influence on people and they will listen. When the friends sense receptivity to the Word of God, they should deliver the Message with wisdom. They must first try and remove any apprehensions in the people they teach. In fact, every one of the believers should choose one person every year and try to establish ties of friendship with him, so that all his fear would disappear. Only then, and gradually, must he teach that person. This is the best method.

21.22 If thou wishest to guide the souls, it is incumbent on thee to be firm, to be good and to be imbued with praiseworthy attributes and divine qualities under all circumstances. Be a sign of love, a manifestation of mercy, a fountain of tenderness, kindhearted, good to all and gentle to the servants of God, and especially to those who bear relation to thee, both men and women. Bear every ordeal that befalleth thee from the people and confront them not save with kindness, with great love and good wishes.

21.23 By the Lord of the Kingdom! If one arise to promote the Word of God with a pure heart, overflowing with the love of God and severed from the world, the Lord of Hosts will assist him with such a power as will penetrate the core of the existent beings.

FROM THE WRITINGS AND LETTERS WRITTEN BY, OR ON BEHALF OF, SHOGHI EFFENDI

21.24   ... Let him remember the example set by 'Abdu'l-Bahá, and his constant admonition to shower such kindness upon the seeker, and exemplify to such a degree the spirit of the teachings he hopes to instill into him, that the recipient will be spontaneously impelled to identify himself with the Cause embodying such teachings. Let him refrain, at the outset from insisting on such laws and observances as might impose too severe a strain on the seeker's newly-awakened faith, and endeavor to nurse him, patiently, tactfully, and yet determinedly, into full maturity, and aid him to proclaim his unqualified acceptance of whatever has been ordained by Bahá'u'lláh. Let him, as soon as that stage has been attained, introduce him to the body of his fellow-believers, and seek, through constant fellowship and active participation in the local activities of his community... Let him not be content until he has infused into his spiritual child so deep a longing as to impel him to arise independently, in his turn, and devote his energies to the quickening of other souls, and the upholding of the laws and principles laid down by his newly-adopted Faith.

21.25   Whether it be by an open and bold assertion of the fundamental verities of the Cause, or the adoption of a less direct and more cautious method of teaching; whether by the dissemination of our literature or the example of our conduct, our one aim and sole object should be to help in the eventual recognition by all mankind of the indispensability, the uniqueness and the supreme station of the Bahá'í Revelation. Whatever method he adopts, and however indirect the course he chooses to pursue, every true believer should regard such a recognition as the supreme goal of his endeavor. Whilst consciously laboring towards the attainment of this end, he should, by supporting every branch of the administrative activities of his national and local assembly, seek and obtain the fullest information on the character and extent of the worldwide progress of the Cause, and strive to contribute his share towards the strengthening of the spirit of solidarity among the component parts of the Bahá'í world.

21.26 Sincerity, devotion and faith are not the sole conditions of successful teaching. Tactfulness, extreme caution and wisdom are equally important. we should not be in a hurry when we announce the message to the public and we should be careful to present the teachings in their entirety and not to alter them for the sake of others.

21.27 First and foremost one should resort to every possible means to purge one's heart and motives, otherwise it would be futile to engage in any form of enterprise. It is also essential to abstain from hypocrisy and blind imitation, inasmuch as their foul odor would soon be detected by every man of understanding and wisdom. Moreover the friends must observe the specific times for the remembrance of God, meditation, devotion and prayer, as it is highly unlikely, nay, rather impossible, that any enterprise should prosper and develop short of divine bestowals and confirmation. One can hardly imagine what a great influence genuine love, truthfulness and purity of motives exert on the souls of men. But these traits cannot be acquired unless every believer makes a daily effort to gain them....

It is primarily through the potency of noble deeds and character, then by the power of exposition and proofs that the friends of God should demonstrate to the world the fact that what has been promised by God is bound to happen, that it is already taking place and that the divine glad-tidings are clear, evident and complete.

21.28 The individual alone must assess its [the individual's duty] character, consult his conscience, prayerfully consider all its aspects, manfully struggle against the natural inertia that weighs him down in his effort to arise, shed, heroically and irrevocably, the trivial and superfluous attachments which hold him back, empty himself of every thought that may tend to obstruct his path, mix, in obedience to the counsels of the Author of His Faith, and in imitation of the One Who is its true Exemplar, with men and women, in all walks of life, seek to touch their hearts, through the distinction which characterizes his thoughts, his words and acts, and win them over tactfully, lovingly, prayerfully and persistently, to the Faith he himself has espoused.

21.29   It should not be overlooked, however, that the most powerful and effective teaching medium that has been found so far is the fireside meeting, because in the fireside meeting, intimate personal questions can be answered, and the student find the spirit of the Faith more abundant there.

21.30   Perhaps the reason why you have not accomplished so much in the field of teaching, is the extent you looked upon your own weaknesses and inabilities to spread the Message. Bahá'u'lláh and the Master have both urged us repeatedly to disregard our own handicaps and lay our whole reliance upon God. He will come to our help if we only arise and become an active channel for God's grace. Do you think it is the teachers who make converts and change human hearts? No, surely not. They are only pure souls who take the first step, and then let the spirit of Bahá'u'lláh move them and make use of them. If any one of them should even for a second consider his achievements as due to his own capacities, his work is ended and his fall starts. This is in fact the reason why so many competent souls have after wonderful services suddenly found themselves absolutely impotent and perhaps thrown aside by the Spirit of the Cause as useless souls. The criterion is the extent to which we are ready to have the will of God operate through us.

Stop to be conscious of your frailties, therefore; have a perfect reliance upon God; let your heart burn with the desire to serve His Mission and proclaim His call; and you will observe how eloquence and the power to change human hearts will come as a matter of course.

Shoghi Effendi will surely pray for your success if you should arise and start to teach. In fact the mere act of arising will win for you God's help and blessings.

21.31 ... The Bahá'í teacher must be all confidence. Therein lies his strength and the secret of his success. Though single-handed, and no matter how great the apathy of the people around you may be, you should have faith that the hosts of the Kingdom are on your side, and that through their help you are bound to overcome the forces of darkness that are facing the Cause of God. Persevere, be happy and confident, therefore.

21.32 ... refrain, under any circumstances, from involving yourselves, much less the Cause, in lengthy discussions of a controversial character, as these besides being fruitless actually cause incalculable harm to the Faith. Bahá'u'lláh has repeatedly urged us not to engage in religious controversies, as the adepts of former religions have done. The Bahá'í teacher should be concerned above all else with presenting the Message, in explaining and clarifying all its aspects rather than in attacking other religions. He should avoid all situations that, he feels, would lead to strife, to hairsplitting and interminable discussions.

21.33 The love we bear mankind, our conviction that Bahá'u'lláh's Faith contains the only and the Divine remedy for all its ills, must be demonstrated today in action by bringing the Cause before the public. No doubt the majority are not yet able to see its true significance, but they must not be deprived, through our failure in obligation, of the opportunity of hearing of it. And there are many precious souls who are seeking for it and ready to embrace it.

21.34 We should never insist on teaching those who are not really ready for the Cause. If a man is not hungry you cannot make him eat. Among the Theosophists there are, no doubt, many receptive souls, but those who are satisfied should be just associated with in a friendly way, but let alone. Once a seeker comes to accept the concept of progressive religion, and accepts Bahá'u'lláh as the Manifestation for this day, the reincarnation concept will fade away in the light of truth; we should try and avoid controversial issues in the beginning, if possible.

21.35 Just one mature soul, with spiritual understanding and a profound knowledge of the Faith, can set a whole country ablaze —so great is the power of the Cause to work through a pure and selfless channel.

21.36 ... At all times we must look at the greatness of the Cause, and remember that Bahá'u'lláh will assist all who arise in His service. When we look at ourselves, we are sure to feel discouraged by our shortcomings and insignificance!

21.37 Consecration, dedication and enthusiastic service is the Keynote to successful teaching. One must become like a reed through which the Holy Spirit descends to reach the student of the Faith. We give the Message, and explain the Teachings, but it is the Holy Spirit that quickens and confirms.

21.38 The greatest glory and honor which can come to an individual is to bring the light of guidance to some new soul. The quickening power of the Holy Spirit, which has come into the world through Bahá'u'lláh, is the source of immortal life; and those who are quickened by this spirit in this world will find themselves in great honor and glory in the next world. The most meritorious service which anyone could render is to bring the light of divine guidance and the quickening power of the spirit to an entirely new area. Humanity is crying for salvation; and it is only by the Bahá'ís going into the various areas of the world, that it can be brought to them. This is the reason the Guardian has encouraged all of the friends to disperse to new territories, for this is the hour for the quickening of the world.

21.39 The need of the Hour is Teaching on the Home Front. Its goals can only be won, by a new spirit of dedication and consecration on the part of the friends, each in his own country, in his own home.

   ... Never must they let a day pass without teaching some soul, trusting to Bahá'u'lláh that the seed will grow. The friends should seek pure souls, gain their confidence, and then teach that person carefully until he becomes a Bahá'í, and then nurture him until he becomes a firm and active supporter of the Faith.

   ... Everyone must remember that it is the 'Holy Spirit that quickens' and therefore the teacher must become like a reed through with the Holy Spirit may reach the seeking soul.

The beloved Guardian has stressed over and over again, that to effectively teach the Faith, the individual must study deeply, the Divine Word, imbibe Its life-giving waters, and feast upon Its glorious teachings. He should then /meditate/ on the import of the Word, and finding its spiritual depths, /pray/ for guidance and assistance. But most important, after prayer is /action/. After one has prayed and meditated, he must arise, relying fully on the guidance and confirmation of Bahá'u'lláh, to teach His Faith. /Perseverance/ in action is essential, just as wisdom and audacity are necessary for effective teaching. The individual must sacrifice all things to this great goal, and then the victories will be won.

21.40 The Master assured us that when we forget ourselves, and strive with all our powers to serve and teach the Faith, we receive divine assistance. It is not we who do the work, but we are the instruments used at that time for the purpose of teaching His Cause.

21.41 Divine Truth is relative and that is why we are enjoined to constantly refer the seeker to the Word itself—and why any explanations we make to ease the journey of the soul of any individual must be based on the Word—and the Word alone.

FROM THE WRITINGS AND LETTERS WRITTEN BY, OR ON BEHALF OF, THE UNIVERSAL HOUSE OF JUSTICE

21.42 Every Bahá'í, however humble or inarticulate, must become intent on fulfilling his role as bearer of the Divine Message. Indeed, how can true believer remain silent while around us men cry out in anguish for truth, love and unity to descend upon this world?

PART III: VISION

CHAPTER 22:

REALIZING THE VISION OF BAHÁ'U'LLÁH

FROM THE WRITINGS OF BAHÁ'U'LLÁH

22.1 Say: O men! This is a matchless Day. Matchless must, likewise, be the tongue that celebrateth the praise of the Desire of all nations, and matchless the deed that aspireth to be acceptable in His sight. The whole human race hath longed for this Day, that perchance it may fulfil that which well beseemeth its station, and is worthy of its destiny. Blessed is the man whom the affairs of the world have failed to deter from recognizing Him Who is the Lord of all things.

   So blind hath become the human heart that neither the disruption of the city, nor the reduction of the mountain in dust, nor even the cleaving of the earth, can shake off its torpor. The allusions made in the Scriptures have been unfolded, and the signs recorded therein have been revealed, and the prophetic cry is continually being raised. And yet all, except such as God was pleased to guide, are bewildered in the drunkenness of their heedlessness!

22.2 God willing, thou mayest accomplish a deed whose fragrance shall endure as long as the Names of God—exalted be His glory—will endure.

22.3 That which the Lord hath ordained as the sovereign remedy and mightiest instrument for the healing of all the world is the union of all its peoples in one universal Cause, one common Faith. This can in no wise be achieved except through the power of a skilled, an all-powerful and inspired Physician. This, verily, is the truth, and all else naught but error.

22.4 With the utmost friendliness and in a spirit of perfect fellowship take ye counsel together, and dedicate the precious days of your lives to the betterment of the world and the promotion of the Cause of Him Who is the Ancient and Sovereign Lord of all. He, verily, enjoineth upon all men what is right, and forbiddeth whatsoever degradeth their station.

22.5 ... they who are the people of God must, with fixed resolve and perfect confidence, keep their eyes directed towards the

Day Spring of Glory, and be busied in whatever may be conducive to the betterment of the world and the education of its peoples.

22.6　The world's equilibrium hath been upset through the vibrating influence of this most great, this new World Order. Mankind's ordered life hath been revolutionized through the agency of this unique, this wondrous System—the like of which mortal eyes have never witnessed.

22.7　God grant that, with a penetrating vision and radiant heart, thou mayest observe the things that have come to pass and are now happening, and, pondering them in thine heart, mayest recognize that which most men have, in this Day, failed to perceive.

22.8　By the righteousness of God, my Well-Beloved! I have never aspired after worldly leadership. My sole purpose hath been to hand down unto men that which I was bidden to deliver by God, the Gracious, the Incomparable, that it may detach them from all that pertaineth to this world, and cause them to attain such heights as neither the ungodly can conceive, nor the froward imagine.

22.9　By the righteousness of God! The world and its vanities, and its glory, and whatever delights it can offer, are all, in the sight of God, as worthless as, nay, even more contemptible than, dust and ashes. Would that the hearts of men could comprehend it! Cleanse yourselves thoroughly, O people of Baha, from the defilement of the world, and of all that pertaineth unto it. God Himself beareth Me witness. The things of the earth ill beseem you. Cast them away unto such as may desire them, and fasten your eyes upon this most holy and effulgent Vision

22.10　O contending peoples and kindreds of the earth! Set your faces towards unity, and let the radiance of its light shine upon you. Gather ye together, and for the sake of God resolve to root out whatever is the source of contention amongst you. Then will the effulgence of the world's great Luminary envelop the whole earth, and its inhabitants become the citizens of one city, and the occupants of one and the same throne. This wronged One hath, ever since the early days of His life, cherished none other desire but this, and will continue to entertain no wish except this wish.

FROM THE WRITINGS AND UTTERANCES OF 'ABDU'L-BAHÁ

22.11   The divine religions must be the cause of oneness among men, and the means of unity and love; they must promulgate universal peace, free man from every prejudice, bestow joy and gladness, exercise kindness to all men and do away with every difference and distinction. Just as Bahá'u'lláh addressing the world of humanity saith: 'O people! Ye are the fruits of one tree and the leaves of one branch.' At most it is this, that some souls are ignorant, they must be educated; some are sick, they must be healed; some are still of tender age, they must be helped to attain maturity, and the utmost kindness must be shown to them. This is the conduct of the people of Baha.

22.12   Every universal cause is divine and every particular one is temporal. The principles of the divine Manifestations of God were, therefore, all-universal and all-inclusive.

Every imperfect soul is self-centred and thinketh only of his own good. But as his thoughts expand a little he will begin to think of the welfare and comfort of his family. If his ideas still more widen, his concern will be the felicity of his fellow citizens; and if still they widen, he will be thinking of the glory of his land and of his race. But when ideas and views reach the utmost degree of expansion and attain the stage of perfection, then will he be interested in the exaltation of humankind. He will then be the well-wisher of all men and the seeker of the weal and prosperity of all lands. This is indicative of perfection.

Thus, the divine Manifestations of God had a universal and all-inclusive conception. They endeavoured for the sake of

everyone's life and engaged in the service of universal education. The area of their aims was not limited—nay, rather, it was
wide and all-inclusive.

Therefore, ye must also be thinking of everyone, so that
mankind may be educated, character moderated and this world
may turn into a Garden of Eden.

Love ye all religions and all races with a love that is true
and sincere and show that love through deeds and not through
the tongue; for the latter hath no importance, as the majority
of men are, in speech, well-wishers, while action is the best.

22.13 O phoenix of that immortal flame kindled in the sacred Tree!
Bahá'u'lláh—may my life, my soul, my spirit be offered up as
a sacrifice unto His lowly servants—hath, during His last days
on earth, given the most emphatic promise that, through the
outpourings of the grace of God and the aid and assistance
vouchsafed from His Kingdom on high, souls will arise and
holy beings appear who, as stars, would adorn the firmament
of divine guidance; illumine the dayspring of loving-kindness
and bounty; manifest the signs of the unity of God; shine with
the light of sanctity and purity; receive their full measure of
divine inspiration; raise high the sacred torch of faith; stand
firm as the rock and immoveable as the mountain; and grow to
become luminaries in the heavens of His Revelation, mighty
channels of His grace, means for the bestowal of God's bountiful care, heralds calling forth the name of the One true God,
and establishers of the world's supreme foundation.

These shall labour ceaselessly, by day and by night,
shall heed neither trials nor woe, shall suffer no respite in
their efforts, shall seek no repose, shall disregard all ease and
comfort, and, detached and unsullied, shall consecrate every
fleeting moment of their lives to the diffusion of the divine
fragrance and the exaltation of God's holy Word. Their faces
will radiate heavenly gladness, and their hearts be filled with
joy. Their souls will be inspired, and their foundation stand
secure. They shall scatter in the world, and travel throughout
all regions. They shall raise their voices in every assembly, and
adorn and revive every gathering. They shall speak in every
tongue, and interpret every hidden meaning. They shall reveal

the mysteries of the Kingdom, and manifest unto everyone the signs of God. They shall burn brightly even as a candle in the heart of every assembly, and beam forth as a star upon every horizon. The gentle breezes wafted from the garden of their hearts shall perfume and revive the souls of men, and the revelations of their minds, even as showers, will reinvigorate the peoples and nations of the world.

I am waiting, eagerly waiting for these holy ones to appear; and yet, how long will they delay their coming? My prayer and ardent supplication, at eventide and at dawn, is that these shining stars may soon shed their radiance upon the world, that their sacred countenances may be unveiled to mortal eyes, that the hosts of divine assistance may achieve their victory, and the billows of grace, rising from His oceans above, may flow upon all mankind. Pray ye also and supplicate unto Him that through the bountiful aid of the Ancient Beauty these souls may be unveiled to the eyes of the world.

The glory of God rest upon thee, and upon him whose face is illumined with that everlasting light that shineth from His Kingdom of Glory.

22.14　The world of humanity is in need of great improvement, for it is a material jungle wherein trees without fruit flourish and useless weeds abound. If at all there is a tree that beareth fruit it is overshadowed by the fruitless ones, and if a flower groweth in this jungle it is hidden and concealed. The world of mankind is in need of expert gardeners who may convert these forests into delectable rose gardens, may substitute for these barren trees ones that yield fruit, and may replace these useless weeds with roses and fragrant herbs. Thus active souls and vigilant people rest neither by day nor by night; they strive to be closely linked to the divine Kingdom and thereby become the manifestations of infinite bounty and ideal gardeners for these forests. Thus the world of humanity will be wholly transformed and the merciful bounties become manifest.

22.15　The second pathway is that of religion, the road of the divine Kingdom. It involves the acquisition of praiseworthy attributes, heavenly illumination and righteous actions in the world of humanity. This pathway is conducive to the progress and uplift of the world. It is the source of human enlightenment, training and ethical improvement; the magnet which attracts the love of God because of the knowledge of God it bestows. This is the road of the holy Manifestations of God for they are in reality the foundation of the divine religion of oneness. There is no change or transformation in this pathway. It is the cause of human betterment, the acquisition of heavenly virtues and the illumination of mankind.

22.16 Then wilt thou see that today these heavenly Teachings are the remedy for a sick and suffering world, and a healing balm for the sores on the body of mankind. They are the spirit of life, the ark of salvation, the magnet to draw down eternal glory, the dynamic power to motivate the inner self of man.

22.17 My hope is that through the zeal and ardour of the pure of heart, the darkness of hatred and difference will be entirely abolished, and the light of love and unity shall shine; this world shall become a new world; things material shall become the mirror of the divine; human hearts shall meet and embrace each other; the whole world become as a man's native country and the different races be counted as one race.

22.18 For man two wings are necessary. One wing is physical power and material civilization; the other is spiritual power and divine civilization. With one wing only, flight is impossible. Two wings are essential. Therefore, no matter how much material civilization advances, it cannot attain to perfection except through the uplift of spiritual civilization.

22.19 The foundations of human society are changing and strengthening. Today sciences of the past are useless. The Ptolemaic system of astronomy and numberless other systems and theories of scientific and philosophical explanation are discarded, known to be false and worthless. Ethical precedents and principles cannot be applied to the needs of the modern world. Thoughts and theories of past ages are fruitless now. Thrones and governments are crumbling and falling. All conditions and requisites of the past unfitted and inadequate for the present time are undergoing radical reform. It is evident, therefore, that counterfeit and spurious religious teaching, antiquated forms of belief and ancestral imitations which are at variance with the foundations of divine reality must also pass away and be reformed. They must be abandoned and new conditions be recognized.

FROM THE WRITINGS AND LETTERS WRITTEN BY, OR ON BEHALF OF, SHOGHI EFFENDI

22.20 We are indeed living in an age which, if we would correctly appraise it, should be regarded as one which is witnessing a dual phenomenon. The first signalizes the death pangs of an order, effete and godless, that has stubbornly refused, despite the signs and portents of a century-old Revelation, to attune its processes to the precepts and ideals which that Heaven-sent Faith proffered it. The second proclaims the birth pangs of an Order, divine and redemptive, that will inevitably supplant the former, and within Whose administrative structure an embryonic civilization, incomparable and world-embracing, is imperceptibly maturing. The one is being rolled up, and is crashing in oppression, bloodshed, and ruin. The other opens up vistas of a justice, a unity, a peace, a culture, such as no age has ever seen. The former has spent its force, demonstrated its falsity and barrenness, lost irretrievably its opportunity, and is hurrying to its doom. The latter, virile and unconquerable, is plucking asunder its chains, and is vindicating its title to be the one refuge within which a sore-tried humanity, purged from its dross, can attain its destiny.

22.21 Unification of the whole of mankind is the hall-mark of the stage which human society is now approaching. Unity of family, of tribe, of city-state, and nation have been successively attempted and fully established. World unity is the goal towards which a harassed humanity is striving. Nation-building has come to an end. The anarchy inherent in state sovereignty is moving towards a climax. A world, growing to maturity, must abandon this fetish, recognize the oneness and wholeness of human relationships, and establish once for all the machinery that can best incarnate this fundamental principle of its life.

22.22 Ours, dearly-beloved co-workers, is the paramount duty to continue, with undimmed vision and unabated zeal, to assist in the final erection of that Edifice the foundations of which Bahá'u'lláh has laid in our hearts, to derive added hope and strength from the general trend of recent events, however dark their immediate effects, and to pray with unremitting fervour that He may hasten the approach of the realization of that Wondrous Vision which constitutes the brightest emanation of His Mind and the fairest fruit of the fairest civilization the world has yet seen.

22.23 In the passage 'eschew all fellowship with the ungodly, 'Bahá'u'lláh means that we should shun the company of those who disbelieve in God and are wayward. The word 'ungodly' is a reference to such perverse people. The words 'Be thou as a flame of fire to My enemies and a river of life eternal to My loved ones', should flee from the enemies of God and instead seek the fellowship of His lovers.

22.24 People are so markedly lacking in spirituality these days that the Bahá'ís should consciously guard themselves against being caught in what one might call the undertow of materialism and atheism, sweeping the world these days. Skepticism, cynicism, disbelief, immorality and hard-heartedness are rife, and as friends are those who stand for the antithesis of all these things they should beware lest the atmosphere of the present world affects them without their being conscious of it.

22.25 There are two kinds of Bahá'ís, one might say: those whose religion is Bahá'í and those who live for the Faith. Needless to say if one can belong to the latter category, if one can be in the vanguard of heroes, martyrs and saints, it is more praiseworthy in the sight of God.

22.26 After Bahá'u'lláh many Prophets will, no doubt, appear, but they will be all under His shadow. Although they may abrogate the laws of the Dispensation, in accordance with the needs and requirements of the age in which they appear, they nevertheless draw their spiritual force from this mighty Revelation. The Faith of Bahá'u'lláh constitutes, indeed, the stage of maturity in the development of mankind. His appearance has released such spiritual forces which will continue to animate, for many long years to come, the world in its development. Whatever progress may be achieved in the later ages-after the unification of the whole human race is achieved—will be but improvements in the machinery of the world. For the machinery itself has already been created by Bahá'u'lláh. The task of continually improving and perfecting this machinery is one which later Prophets will be called upon to achieve. They will move and work within the orbit of Bahá'í cycle.

FROM THE WRITINGS AND LETTERS WRITTEN BY, OR ON BEHALF OF, THE UNIVERSAL HOUSE OF JUSTICE

22.27 The dark horizon faced by a world which has failed to recognize the Promised One, the Source of its salvation, acutely affects the outlook of the younger generations; their distressing lack of hope and their indulgence in desperate but futile and even dangerous solutions make a direct claim on the remedial attention of Bahá'í youth, who, through their knowledge of that Source and the bright vision with which they have thus been endowed, cannot hesitate to impart to their despairing fellow youth the restorative joy, the constructive hope, the radiant assurances of Bahá'u'lláh's stupendous Revelation.

The words, the deeds, the attitudes, the lack of prejudice, the nobility of character, the high sense of service to others-in a word, those qualities and actions which distinguish a Bahá'í must unfailingly characterize their inner life and outer behavior, and their interactions with friend or foe.

Rejecting the low sights of mediocrity, let them scale the ascending heights of excellence in all they aspire to do. May they resolve to elevate the very atmosphere in which they move, whether it be in the school rooms or halls of higher learning, in their work, their recreation, their Bahá'í activity or social service.

Indeed, let them welcome with confidence the challenges awaiting them. Imbued with this excellence and a corresponding humility, with tenacity and a loving servitude, today's youth must move towards the front ranks of the professions, trades, arts and crafts which are necessary to the further progress of humankind—this to ensure that the spirit of the Cause will cast its illumination on all these important areas of human endeavor. Moreover, while aiming at mastering the unifying concepts and swiftly advancing technologies of this era of communications, they can, indeed they must also guarantee the transmittal to the future of those skills which will preserve the marvelous, indispensable achievements of the past. The transformation which is to occur in the functioning of society will certainly depend to a great extent on the effectiveness of the preparations the youth make for the world they will inherit.

22.28 The experience of the Bahá'í community may be seen as an example of this enlarging unity. It is a community of some three to four million people drawn from many nations, cultures, classes and creeds, engaged in a wide range of activities serving the spiritual, social and economic needs of the peoples of many lands. It is a single social organism, representative of the diversity of the human family, conducting its affairs through a system of commonly accepted consultative principles, and cherishing equally all the great outpourings of divine guidance in human history. Its existence is yet another convincing proof of the practicality of its Founder's vision of a united world, another evidence that humanity can live as one global society, equal to whatever challenges its coming of age may entail. If the Bahá'í experience can contribute in whatever measure to reinforcing hope in the unity of the human race, we are happy to offer it as a model for study.

22.29 In the midst of a civilization torn by strifes and enfeebled by materialism, the people of Baha are building a new world. We face at this time opportunities and responsibilities of vast magnitude and great urgency. Let each believer in his inmost heart resolve not to be seduced by the ephemeral allurements of the society around him, nor to be drawn into its feuds and short-lived enthusiasms, but instead to transfer all he can from the old world to that new one which is the vision of his longing and will be the fruit of his labours.

CHAPTER 23:

HEALING YOUR HEART IN THE BAHÁ'Í COMMUNITY

FROM THE WRITINGS OF BAHÁ'U'LLÁH

23.1 It is Our wish and desire that every one of you may become a source of all goodness unto men, and an example of uprightness to mankind. Beware lest ye prefer yourselves above your neighbors. Fix your gaze upon Him Who is the Temple of God amongst men. He, in truth, hath offered up His life as a ransom for the redemption of the world. He, verily, is the All-Bountiful, the Gracious, the Most High. If any differences arise amongst you, behold Me standing before your face, and overlook the faults of one another for My name's sake and as a token of your love for My manifest and resplendent Cause. We love to see you at all times consorting in amity and concord within the paradise of My good-pleasure, and to inhale from your acts the fragrance of friendliness and unity, of loving-kindness and fellowship. Thus counselleth you the All-Knowing, the Faithful. We shall always be with you; if We inhale the perfume of your fellowship, Our heart will assuredly rejoice, for naught else can satisfy Us. To this beareth witness every man of true understanding.

23.2 They who are the people of God have no ambition except to revive the world, to ennoble its life, and regenerate its peoples. Truthfulness and good-will have, at all times, marked their relations with all men. Their outward conduct is but a reflection of their inward life, and their inward life a mirror of their outward conduct. No veil hideth or obscureth the verities on which their Faith is established. Before the eyes of all men these verities have been laid bare, and can be unmistakably recognized. Their very acts attest the truth of these words.

23.3 O MY SON! The company of the ungodly increaseth sorrow, whilst fellowship with the righteous cleanseth the rust from off the heart. He that seeketh to commune with God, let him betake himself to the companionship of His loved ones; and he that desireth to hearken unto the word of God, let him give ear to the words of His chosen ones.

23.4   That seeker should also regard backbiting as grievous error, and keep himself aloof from its dominion, inasmuch as back-biting quencheth the light of the heart, and extinguisheth the life of the soul. He should be content with little, and be freed from all inordinate desire. He should treasure the companionship of those that have renounced the world, and regard avoidance of boastful and worldly people a precious benefit.

23.5   O SON OF MAN! Breathe not the sins of others so long as thou art thyself a sinner. Shouldst thou transgress this command, accursed wouldst thou be, and to this I bear witness.

FROM THE WRITINGS AND UTTERANCES OF 'ABDU'L-BAHÁ

23.6   Look ye not upon the fewness of thy numbers, rather, seek ye out hearts that are pure. One consecrated soul is preferable to a thousand other souls. If a small number of people gather lovingly together, with absolute purity and sanctity, with their hearts free of the world, experiencing the emotions of the Kingdom and the powerful magnetic forces of the Divine, and being at one in their happy fellowship, that gathering will exert its influence over all the earth. The nature of that band of people, the words they speak, the deeds they do, will unleash the bestowals of Heaven, and provide a foretaste of eternal bliss. The hosts of the Company on high will defend them, and the angels of the Abha Paradise, in continuous succession, will come down to their aid.

23.7   In brief, O ye believers of God! The text of the divine Book is this: If two souls quarrel and contend about a question of the divine questions, differing and disputing, both are wrong. The wisdom of this incontrovertible law of God is this: That between two souls from amongst the believers of God, no contention and dispute may arise; that they may speak with each other with infinite amity and love. Should there appear the least trace of controversy, they must remain silent, and both parties must continue their discussions no longer, but ask the reality of the question from the Interpreter. This is the irrefutable command!

23.8 How unpleasing to the eye if all the flowers and plants, the leaves and blossoms, the fruits, the branches and the trees of that garden were all of the same shape and colour! Diversity of hues, form and shape, enricheth and adorneth the garden, and heighteneth the effect thereof. In like manner, when divers shades of thought, temperament and character, are brought together under the power and influence of one central agency, the beauty and glory of human perfection will be revealed and made manifest. Naught but the celestial potency of the Word of God, which ruleth and transcendeth the realities of all things, is capable of harmonizing the divergent thoughts, sentiments, ideas, and convictions of the children of men. Verily, it is the penetrating power in all things, the mover of souls and the binder and regulator in the world of humanity.

23.9 O ye lovers of God! The world is even as a human being who is diseased and impotent, whose eyes can see no longer, whose ears have gone deaf, all of whose powers are corroded and used up. Wherefore must the friends of God be competent physicians who, following the holy Teachings, will nurse this patient back to health. Perhaps, God willing, the world will mend, and become permanently whole, and its exhausted faculties will be restored, and its person will take on such vigour, freshness and verdancy that it will shine out with comeliness and grace.

The first remedy of all is to guide the people aright, so that they will turn themselves unto God, and listen to His counsellings, and go forth with hearing ears and seeing eyes. Once this speedily effective draught is given them, then, in accordance with the Teachings, they must be led to acquire the characteristics and the behaviour of the Concourse on high, and encouraged to seek out all the bounties of the Abha Realm. They must cleanse their hearts from even the slightest trace of hatred and spite, and they must set about being truthful and honest, conciliatory and loving to all humankind—so that East and West will, even as two lovers, hold each other close; that hatred and hostility will perish from the earth, and universal peace be firmly rooted in their place.

23.10 Strive with heart and soul in order to bring about union and harmony among the white and the black and prove thereby the unity of the Bahá'í world wherein distinction of colour findeth no place, but where hearts only are considered. Praise be to God, the hearts of the friends are united and linked together, whether they be from the east or the west, from north or from south, whether they be German, French, Japanese, American, and whether they pertain to the white, the black, the red, the yellow or the brown race. Variations of colour, of land and of race are of no importance in the Bahá'í Faith; on the contrary, Bahá'í unity overcometh them all and doeth away with all these fancies and imaginations.

23.11 O beloved of the Lord! If any soul speak ill of an absent one, the only result will clearly be this: he will dampen the zeal of the friends and tend to make them indifferent. For back-biting is divisive, it is the leading cause among the friends of a disposition to withdraw. If any individual should speak ill of one who is absent, it is incumbent on his hearers, in a spiritual and friendly manner, to stop him, and say in effect: would this detraction serve any useful purpose? Would it please the Blessed Beauty, contribute to the lasting honour of the friends, promote the holy Faith, support the Covenant, or be of any possible benefit to any soul? No, never! On the contrary, it would make the dust to settle so thickly on the heart that the ears would hear no more, and the eyes would no longer behold the light of truth.

　　If, however, a person setteth about speaking well of another, opening his lips to praise another, he will touch an answering chord in his hearers and they will be stirred up by the breathings of God. Their hearts and souls will rejoice to know that, God be thanked, here is a soul in the Faith who is a focus of human perfections, a very embodiment of the bounties of the Lord, one whose tongue is eloquent, and whose face shineth, in whatever gathering he may be, one who hath victory upon his brow, and who is a being sustained by the sweet savours of God.

　　Now which is the better way? I swear this by the beauty of the Lord: whensoever I hear good of the friends, my heart filleth up with joy; but whensoever I find even a hint that they are on bad terms one with another, I am overwhelmed by grief. Such is the condition of 'Abdu'l-Bahá. Then judge from this where your duty lieth.

23.12   If a man has ten good qualities and one bad one, to look at the ten and forget the one; and if a man has ten bad qualities and one good one, to look at the one and forget the ten. Never to allow ourselves to speak one unkind word about another, even though that other be our enemy.

23.13   But some souls are weak; we must endeavor to strengthen them. Some are ignorant, uninformed of the bounties of God; we must strive to make them knowing. Some are ailing; we must seek to restore them to health. Some are immature as children; they must be trained and assisted to attain maturity. We nurse the sick in tenderness and the kindly spirit of love; we do not despise them because they are ill. Therefore, we must exercise extreme patience, sympathy and love toward all mankind, considering no soul as rejected. If we look upon a soul as rejected, we have disobeyed the teachings of God. God is loving to all.

23.14   Act in such a way that your heart may be free from hatred. Let not your heart be offended with anyone. If someone commits an error and wrong toward you, you must instantly forgive him. Do not complain of others. Refrain from reprimanding them, and if you wish to give admonition or advice, let it be offered in such a way that it will not burden the bearer. Turn all your thoughts toward bringing joy to hearts. Beware! Beware! lest ye offend any heart. Assist the world of humanity as much as possible. Be the source of consolation to every sad one, assist every weak one, be helpful to every indigent one, care for every sick one, be the cause of glorification to every lowly one, and shelter those who are overshadowed by fear.

FROM THE WRITINGS AND LETTERS WRITTEN BY, OR ON BEHALF OF, SHOGHI EFFENDI

23.15   ...The generality of mankind, blind and enslaved, is wholly unaware of the healing power with which this community has been endowed, nor can it as yet suspect the role which this same community is destined to play in its redemption. Fierce and manifold will be the assaults with which governments, races, classes and religions, jealous of its rising prestige and fearful of its consolidating strength, will seek to silence its voice and sap its foundations. Unmoved by the relative obscurity that surrounds it at the present time, and undaunted by the forces that will be arrayed against it in the future, this community, I cannot but feel confident, will, no matter how afflictive the agonies of a travailing age, pursue its destiny, undeflected in its course, undimmed in its serenity, unyielding in its resolve, unshaken in its convictions.

FROM THE WRITINGS AND LETTERS WRITTEN BY, OR ON BEHALF OF, THE UNIVERSAL HOUSE OF JUSTICE

23.16   Each of us is responsible for one life only, and that is our own. Each of us is immeasurably far from being 'perfect as our Heavenly Father is perfect' and the task of perfecting our own life and character is one that requires all our attention, our will-power and energy... On no subject are the Bahá'í teachings more emphatic than on the necessity to abstain from fault- finding, while being ever eager to discover and root out our own faults and overcome our own failings.

23.17   In the human body, every cell, every organ, every nerve has its part to play. When all do so the body is healthy, vigorous, radiant, ready for very call made upon it. No cell, however humble, lives apart from the body, whether in serving it or receiving from it. This is true of the body of mankind in which God has endowed each humble being with ability and talent', and is supremely true of the body of the Bahá'í World Community, for this body is already an organism, united in its aspirations, unified in its methods, seeking assistance and confirmation from the same Source, and illumined with the conscious knowledge of its unity... The Bahá'í World community, growing like a healthy new body, develops new cells, new organs, new functions and powers as it presses on to its maturity, when every soul, living for the Cause of God, will receive from that Cause, health, assurance, and the overflowing bounties of Bahá'u'lláh which are diffused through His Divinely-ordained Order.

CHAPTER 24:

BUILDING A NEW WORLD ORDER WITH THE BAHÁ'Í ADMINISTRATION

FROM THE WRITINGS OF BAHÁ'U'LLÁH

24.1   Soon will the present-day order be rolled up, and a new one spread out in its stead.

24.2   The Lord hath ordained that in every city a House of Justice be established wherein shall gather counselors to the number of Baha, and should it exceed this number it doth not matter. They should consider themselves as entering the Court of the presence of God, the Exalted, the Most High, and as beholding Him Who is the Unseen. It behoveth them to be the trusted ones of the Merciful among men and to regard themselves as the guardians appointed of God for all that dwell on earth. It is incumbent upon them to take counsel together and to have regard for the interests of the servants of God, for His sake, even as they regard their own interests, and to choose that which is meet and seemly. Thus hath the Lord your God commanded you. Beware lest ye put away that which is clearly revealed in His Tablet...

24.3   Please God, the peoples of the world may be led, as the result of the high endeavors exerted by their rulers and the wise and learned amongst men, to recognize their best interests. How long will humanity persist in its waywardness? How long will injustice continue? How long is chaos and confusion to reign amongst men? How long will discord agitate the face of society?... The winds of despair are, alas, blowing from every direction, and the strife that divideth and afflicteth the human race is daily increasing. The signs of impending convulsions and chaos can now be discerned, inasmuch as the prevailing order appeareth to be lamentably defective. I beseech God, exalted be His glory, that He may graciously awaken the peoples of the earth, may grant that the end of their conduct may be profitable unto them, and aid them to accomplish that which beseemeth their station.

24.4   It is incumbent upon everyone to aid those daysprings of authority and sources of command who are adorned with the ornament of equity and justice. Blessed are the rulers and the learned among the people of Baha. They are My trustees

among My servants and the manifestations of My commandments amidst My people. Upon them rest My glory, My blessings and My grace which have pervaded the world of being. In
this connection the utterances revealed in the *Kitáb-i-Aqdas* are
such that from the horizon of their words the light of divine
grace shineth luminous and resplendent.

24.5 Abase not the station of the learned in Baha and belittle not
the rank of such rulers as administer justice amidst you.

24.6 The men of God's House of Justice have been charged with
the affairs of the people. They, in truth, are the Trustees of
God among His servants and the daysprings of authority in
His countries.

24.7 None must contend with those who wield authority over the
people; leave unto them that which is theirs, and direct your
attention to men's hearts.

24.8 Respect ye the divines and learned amongst you, they whose
conduct accords with their professions, who transgress not
the bounds which God hath fixed, whose judgments are in
conformity with His behests as revealed in His Book. Know
ye that they are the lamps of guidance unto them that are in
the heavens and on the earth. They who disregard and neglect
the divines and learned that live amongst them—these have
truly changed the favor with which God hath favored them.

FROM THE WRITINGS AND
UTTERANCES OF 'ABDU'L-BAHÁ

24.9 The spiritually learned are lamps of guidance among the
nations, and stars of good fortune shining from the horizons
of humankind. They are fountains of life for such as lie in
the death of ignorance and unawareness, and clear springs of
perfections for those who thirst and wander in the wasteland
of their defects and errors.

24.10 For every thing, however, God has created a sign and symbol, and established standards and tests by which it may be known. The spiritually learned must be characterized by both inward and outward perfections; they must possess a good character, an enlightened nature, a pure intent, as well as intellectual power, brilliance and discernment, intuition, discretion and foresight, temperance, reverence, and a heartfelt fear of God. For an unlit candle, however great in diameter and tall, is no better than a barren palm tree or a pile of dead wood.

24.11 He has ordained and established the House of Justice, which is endowed with a political as well as a religious function, the consummate union and blending of church and state. This institution is under the protecting power of Bahá'u'lláh Himself. A universal, or international, House of Justice shall also be organized. Its rulings shall be in accordance with the commands and teachings of Bahá'u'lláh, and that which the Universal House of Justice ordains shall be obeyed by all mankind. This international House of Justice shall be appointed and organized from the Houses of Justice of the whole world, and all the world shall come under its administration.

24.12 As to the House of Justice: according to the explicit text of the Law of God, its membership is exclusively reserved to men. There is Divine wisdom in this which will presently be made manifest even as the mid-day sun.

24.13 ... the Universal House of Justice, if it be established under the necessary conditions—with members elected from all the people—that House of Justice will be under the protection and the unerring guidance of God. If that House of Justice shall decide unanimously, or by a majority, upon any question not mentioned in the Book, that decision and command will be guarded from mistake. Now the members of the House of Justice have not, individually, essential infallibility; but the body of the House of Justice is under the protection and the unerring guidance of God: this is called conferred infallibility.

FROM THE WRITINGS AND LETTERS WRITTEN BY, OR ON BEHALF OF, SHOGHI EFFENDI

24.14 Though loyal to their respective governments, though profoundly interested in anything that affects their security and welfare, though anxious to share in whatever promotes their best interests, the Faith with which the followers of Bahá'u'lláh stand identified is one which they firmly believe God has raised high above the storms, the divisions, and controversies of the political arena. Their Faith they conceive to be essentially non-political, supra-national in character, rigidly non-partisan, and entirely dissociated from nationalistic ambitions, pursuits, and purposes.

24.15 This Administrative Order, unlike the systems evolved after the death of the Founders of the various religions, is divine in origin, rests securely on the laws, the precepts, the ordinances and institutions which the Founder of the Faith has Himself specifically laid down and unequivocally established, and functions in strict accordance with the interpretations of the authorized Interpreters of its holy scriptures. Though fiercely assailed, ever since its inception, it has by virtue of its character, unique in the annals of the world's religious history, succeeded in maintaining unity of the diversified and far-flung body of its supporters, and enabled them to launch, unitedly and systematically, enterprises in both Hemispheres, designed to extend its limits and consolidate its administrative institutions.

The Faith which this order serves, safeguards and promotes, is, it should be noted in this connection, essentially supernatural, supranational, entirely non-political, non-partisan, and diametrically opposed to any policy or school of thought that seeks to exalt any particular race, class or nation. It is free from any form of ecclesiasticism, has neither priesthood nor rituals, and is supported exclusively by voluntary contributions made by its avowed adherents. Though loyal to their respective governments, though imbued with the love of their own country, and anxious to promote, at all times, its best interests, the followers of the Bahá'í Faith, nevertheless, viewing mankind as one entity, and profoundly attached to its vital interests, will not hesitate to subordinate every particular interest, be it personal, regional or national, to the over-riding interests of the generality of mankind, knowing full well that in a world of interdependent peoples and nations the advantage of the part is best to be reached by the advantage of the whole, and that no lasting result can be achieved by any of the component parts if the general interests of the entity itself are neglected.

24.16   On the election day the friends must whole-heartedly participate in the elections, in unity and amity, turning their hearts to God, detached from all things but Him, seeking His guidance and supplicating His aid and bounty.

24.17   If the Bahá'ís could evaluate their work properly they would see that whereas other forms of relief work are superficial in character, alleviating the sufferings and ills of men for a short time at best, the work they are doing is to lay the foundation of a new spiritual Order in the world founded on the Word of God, operating according to the laws He has laid down for this age. No one else can do this work except those who have fully realized the meaning of the Message of Bahá'u'lláh, whereas almost any courageous, sincere person can engage in relief work.

The believers are building a refuge for mankind. This their supreme sacred task and they should devote every moment they can to this task.

24.18   ... the elector... is called upon to vote for none but those whom prayer and reflection have inspired him to uphold.

24.19   ... in the time of election, the friends should be in the mood of prayer, disinterestedness and detachment from worldly motives. Then they will be inspired to elect the proper members to the assemblies.

24.20   Moreover, the practice of nomination, so detrimental to the atmosphere of a silent and prayerful election, is viewed with mistrust inasmuch as it gives the right to the majority of a body that, in itself under the present circumstances, often constitutes a minority of all the elected delegates, to deny that God-given right of every elector to vote only in favour of those who he is conscientiously convinced are the most worthy candidates. Should this simple system be provisionally adopted, it would safeguard the spiritual principle of the unfettered freedom of the voter, who will thus preserve intact the sanctity of the choice he first made. It would avoid the inconvenience of securing advance nominations from absent delegates and the impracticality of associating them with the assembled electors in the subsequent ballots that are often required to meet the exigencies of majority vote.

FROM THE WRITINGS AND LETTERS WRITTEN BY, OR ON BEHALF OF, THE UNIVERSAL HOUSE OF JUSTICE

24.21   In the years following the writing of the words quoted above, moreover, Shoghi Effendi not only accelerated the process of bringing the Universal House of Justice into being by appointing the International Bahá'í Council, but also, in accordance with the provisions of the Will of 'Abdu'l-Bahá, appointed the Hands of the Cause of God and began the development of the series of institutions comprising "eminent and devoted believers appointed for the specific purposes of protecting and propagating the Faith of Bahá'u'lláh under the guidance of the Head of that Faith", the vital importance of which can now be clearly seen in the functioning of the International Teaching Centre, the Continental Boards of Counsellors, the Auxiliary Board members and their assistants.

24.22   And since the primary purpose for which Local Spiritual Assemblies are established is to promote the teaching work, it is clear that every National Spiritual Assembly must give careful consideration to ways and means to encourage each Local Assembly under its jurisdiction to fulfil its principal obligation... it is important that Local Assemblies share with the local friends stories of successes achieved by some of them, descriptions of effective presentations found useful by them, examples of various ways that a Bahá'í subject could be introduced to inquirers, or illustrations of methods which would enable the believer to relate the needs of society to our teachings. Such information and suggestions should be offered to the friends at Nineteen Day Feasts, through a local newsletter, or by any means open to each Local Assembly. In all these contacts with the believers, each Local Spiritual Assembly should impress upon the friends the unique and irreplaceable role the individual plays in the prosecution of any Bahá'í undertaking...

24.23 As to your query about the Local Spiritual Assembly, it is indeed a divine institution, created by Bahá'u'lláh in His *Kitáb-i-Aqdas* as the Local House of Justice. 'Abdu'l-Bahá has clearly set out its provenance, authority and duties and has explained the differences between it and other administrative institutions, whether of the past or the present...

It is clear that while Local Spiritual Assemblies must supervise all Bahá'í matters in their areas, including arrangements for the Nineteen Day Feast, the observance of the Holy Days, the election of the members of the Assembly, promoting the teaching work, caring for the spiritual welfare and Bahá'í education of the friends and children, etc., they and the friends themselves must at the same time be good citizens and loyal to the civil government, whether it be a Tribal council, a Cacique or a municipal authority.

24.24 It is understandable that Bahá'ís who witness the miserable conditions under which so many human beings have to live, or who hear of a sudden disaster that has struck a certain area of the world, are moved to do something practical to ameliorate those conditions and to help their suffering fellow-mortals.

There are many ways in which help can be rendered. Every Bahá'í has the duty to acquire a trade or profession through which he will earn that wherewith he can support himself and his family; in the choice of such work he can seek those activities which are of benefit to his fellow-men and not merely those which promote his personal interests, still less those whose effects are actually harmful.

There are also the situations in which an individual Bahá'í or a Spiritual Assembly is confronted with an urgent need which neither justice nor compassion could allow to go unheeded and unhelped. How many are the stories told of 'Abdu'l-Bahá in such situations, when He would even take off a garment He was wearing and give it to a shivering man in rags.

But in our concern for such immediate obvious calls upon our succour we must not allow ourselves to forget the continuing, appalling burden of suffering under which millions of human beings are always groaning—a burden which they have bourne for century upon century and which it is the Mission of Bahá'u'lláh to lift at last. the principal cause of this suffering, which one can witness wherever one turns, is the corruption of human morals and the prevalence of prejudice, suspicion, hatred, untrustworthiness, selfishness and tyranny among men. It is not merely material well-being that people need. What they desperately need is to know how to live their lives—they need to know who they are', to what purpose they exist, and how they should act towards one another; and, once they know the answers to these questions they need to be helped to gradually apply these answers to every-day behavior. It is to the solution of this basic problem of mankind that the greater part of all our energy and resources should be directed...

CHAPTER 25

HARNESSING THE POWER OF BAHÁ'Í CONSULTATION

FROM THE WRITINGS OF BAHÁ'U'LLÁH

25.1 The Great Being saith: The heaven of divine wisdom is illumined with the two luminaries of consultation and compassion. Take ye counsel together in all matters, inasmuch as consultation is the lamp of guidance which leadeth the way, and is the bestower of understanding.

25.2 ... Say: No man can attain his true station except through his justice. No power can exist except through unity. No welfare and no well-being can be attained except through consultation.

25.3 Consultation bestoweth greater awareness and transmuteth conjecture into certitude. It is a shining light which, in a dark world, leadeth the way and guideth. For everything there is and will continue to be a station of perfection and maturity. The maturity of the gift of understanding is made manifest through consultation.

25.4 Such matters should be determined through consultation, and whatever emergeth from the consultation of those chosen, that indeed is the command of God, the Help in Peril, the Self-Subsisting.

25.5 In all things it is necessary to consult. This matter should be forcibly stressed by thee, so that consultation may be observed by all. The intent of what hath been revealed from the Pen of the Most High is that consultation may be fully carried out among the friends, inasmuch as it is and will always be a cause of awareness and of awakening and a source of good and well-being.

FROM THE WRITINGS AND UTTERANCES OF 'ABDU'L-BAHÁ

25.6 Look about thee at the world: here unity, mutual attraction, gathering together, engender life, but disunity and inharmony spell death. When thou dost consider all phenomena, thou wilt see that every created thing hath come into being through the mingling of many elements, and once this collectivity of elements is dissolved, and this harmony of components is dissevered, the life form is wiped out.

25.7 The shining spark of truth cometh forth only after the clash of differing opinions.

25.8 It is incumbent upon everyone not to take any step without consulting the Spiritual Assembly, and they must assuredly obey with heart and soul its bidding and be submissive unto it, that things may be properly ordered and well arranged. Otherwise every person will act independently and after his own judgment, will follow his own desire, and do harm to the Cause.

25.9 The prime requisites for them that take counsel together are purity of motive, radiance of spirit, detachment from all else save God, attraction to His Divine Fragrance, humility and lowliness amongst His loved ones, patience and long-suffering in difficulties, and servitude to His exalted Threshold. Should they be graciously aided to acquire these attributes, victory from the unseen Kingdom of Baha shall be vouchsafed to them. In this day, Assemblies of consultation are of the greatest importance and a vital necessity. Obedience unto them is essential and obligatory. The members thereof must take counsel together in such wise that no occasion for ill-feeling or discord may arise. This can be attained when every member expresseth with absolute freedom his own opinion and setteth forth his argument. Should any one oppose, he must on no account feel hurt for not until matters are fully discussed can the right way be revealed. The shining spark of truth cometh forth only after the clash of differing opinions. If, after discussion, a decision be carried unanimously, well and good; but if, the Lord forbid, differences of opinion should arise, a majority of voices must prevail.

25.10 The first condition is absolute love and harmony amongst the members of the Assembly. They must be wholly free from estrangement and must manifest in themselves the Unity of God, for they are the waves of one sea, the drops of one river, the stars of one heaven, the rays of one sun, the trees of one orchard, the flowers of one garden. Should harmony of thought and absolute unity be non-existent, that gathering shall be dispersed and that Assembly be brought to naught. The second condition: They must, when coming together, turn their faces to the Kingdom on High and ask aid from the Realm of Glory. They must then proceed with the utmost devotion, courtesy, dignity, care, and moderation to express their views. They must in every matter search out the truth and not insist upon their own opinion, for stubbornness and persistence in one's views will lead ultimately to discord and wrangling and the truth will remain hidden. The honoured members must with all freedom express their own thoughts, and it is in no wise permissible for one to belittle the thought of another, nay, he must with moderation set forth the truth, and should differences of opinion arise a majority of voices must prevail, and all must obey and submit to the majority. It is again not permitted that any one of the honoured members object to or censure, whether in or out of the meeting, any decision arrived at previously, though that decision be not right, for such criticism would prevent any decision from being enforced. In short, whatsoever thing is arranged in harmony and with love and purity of motive, its result is light, and should the least trace of estrangement prevail the result shall be darkness upon darkness.

25.11 Each bosom must be a telegraph station—one terminus of the wire attached to the soul, the other fixed in the Supreme Concourse—so that inspiration may descend from the Kingdom of Abha and questions of reality be discussed.

25.12 The purpose is to emphasize the statement that consultation must have for its object the investigation of truth. He who expresses an opinion should not voice it as correct and right but set it forth as a contribution to the consensus of opinion, for the light of reality becomes apparent when two opinions coincide. A spark is produced when flint and steel come together. Man should weigh his opinions with the utmost serenity, calmness and composure. Before expressing his own views he should carefully consider the views already advanced by others. If he finds that a previously expressed opinion is more true and worthy, he should accept it immediately and not willfully hold to an opinion of his own. By this excellent method he endeavors to arrive at unity and truth. Opposition and division are deplorable. It is better then to have the opinion of a wise, sagacious man; otherwise, contradiction and altercation, in which varied and divergent views are presented, will make it necessary for a judicial body to render decision upon the question. Even a majority opinion or consensus may be incorrect. A thousand people may hold to one view and be mistaken, whereas one sagacious person may be right. Therefore, true consultation is spiritual conference in the attitude and atmosphere of love. Members must love each other in the spirit of fellowship in order that good results may be forthcoming. Love and fellowship are the foundation.

25.13 We work and pray for the unity of mankind, that all the races of the earth may become one race, all the countries one country, and that all hearts may beat as one heart, working together for perfect unity and brotherhood.

25.14 Settle all things, both great and small, by consultation. Without prior consultation, take no important step in your own personal affairs. Concern yourselves with one another. Help along one another's projects and plans. Grieve over one another. Let none in the whole country go in need. Befriend one another until ye become as a single body, one and all ...

25.15 Man must consult in all things for this will lead him to the depths of each problem and enable him to find the right solution.

25.16 The purpose of consultation is to show that the views of several individuals are assuredly preferable to one man, even as the power of a number of men is of course greater than the power of one man.

FROM THE WRITINGS AND LETTERS WRITTEN BY, OR ON BEHALF OF, SHOGHI EFFENDI

25.17 Let us also bear in mind that the keynote of the Cause of god is not dictatorial authority but humble fellowship, not arbitrary power, but the spirit of frank and loving consultation. Nothing short of the spirit of a true Bahá'í can hope to reconcile the principles of mercy and justice, of freedom and submission, of the sanctity of the right of the individual and of self-surrender, of vigilance, discretion, and prudence on the one hand, and fellowship, candor, and courage on the other.

25.18 Let us also bear in mind that the keynote of the Cause of God is not dictatorial authority, but humble fellowship, not arbitrary power, but the spirit of frank and loving consultation. Nothing short of the spirit of a true Bahá'í can hope to reconcile the principles of mercy and justice, of freedom and submission, of the sanctity of the right of the individual and of self-surrender, of vigilance, discretion and prudence on the one hand and fellowship, candour and courage on the other. The duties of those whom the friends have freely and conscientiously elected as their representatives are no less vital and binding than the obligations of those who have chosen them. Their function is not to dictate, but to consult, and consult not only among themselves, but as much as possible with the friends whom they represent. They must regard themselves in no other light but that of chosen instruments for a more efficient and dignified presentation of the Cause of God. They should never be led to suppose that they are the central ornaments of the body of the Cause, intrinsically superior to others in capacity or merit, and sole promoters of its teachings and principles. They should approach their task with extreme humility, and endeavour by their open-mindedness, their high sense of justice and duty, their candour, their modesty, their entire devotion to the welfare and interests of the friends, the Cause, and humanity, to win not only the confidence and the genuine support and respect of those whom they should serve, but also their esteem and real affection.

They must at all times avoid the spirit of exclusiveness, the atmosphere of secrecy, free themselves from a domineering attitude, and banish all forms of prejudice and passion from their deliberations. They should, within the limits of wise discretion, take the friends into their confidence, acquaint them with their plans, share with them their problems and anxieties, and seek their advice and counsel. And when they are called upon to arrive at a certain decision, they should, after dispassionate, anxious, and cordial consultation, turn to God in prayer, and with earnestness and conviction and courage record their vote and abide by the voice of the majority, which we are told by our Master to be the voice of truth, never to be challenged, and always to be whole-heartedly enforced. To this voice the friends must heartily respond, and regard it as the only means that can ensure the protection and advancement of the Cause.

FROM THE WRITINGS AND LETTERS WRITTEN BY, OR ON BEHALF OF, THE UNIVERSAL HOUSE OF JUSTICE

25.19 Now, after all the years of constant teaching activity, the Community of the Greatest Name has grown to the stage at which the processes of this development must be incorporated into its regular pursuits; particularly its action compelled by the expansion of the Faith in Third World countries where the vast majority of its adherents reside. The steps to be taken must necessarily begin in the Bahá'í Community itself, with the friends endeavouring, through their application of spiritual principles, their rectitude of conduct and the practice of the art of consultation, to uplift themselves and thus become self-sufficient and self-reliant. Moreover, these exertions will conduce to the preservation of human honour, so desired by Bahá'u'lláh. In the process and as a consequence, the friends will undoubtedly extend the benefits of their efforts to society as a whole, until all mankind achieves the progress intended by the Lord of the Age.

25.20 The second principle is that of detachment in consultation. The members of an Assembly must learn to express their views frankly, calmly, without passion or rancour. They must also learn to listen to the opinions of their fellow members without taking offence or belittling the views of another. Bahá'í consultation is not an easy process. It requires love, kindliness, moral courage and humility. Thus no member should ever allow himself to be prevented from expressing frankly his view because it may offend a fellow member; and, realizing this, no member should take offence at another member's statements.

CHAPTER 26:

CONNECTING WITH THE STORY OF THE BAHÁ'Í FAITH

.

FROM THE WRITINGS OF BAHÁ'U'LLÁH

26.1 I swear by the Daystar of God's Testimony that hath shone from the horizon of certitude! This Wronged One, in the daytime and in the night-season, occupied Himself with that which would edify the souls of men, until the light of knowledge prevailed over the darkness of ignorance.

26.2 The Ancient Beauty hath consented to be bound with chains that mankind may be released from its bondage, and hath accepted to be made a prisoner within this most mighty Stronghold that the whole world may attain unto true liberty. He hath drained to its dregs the cup of sorrow, that all the peoples of the earth may attain unto abiding joy, and be filled with gladness. This is of the mercy of your Lord, the Compassionate, the Most Merciful. We have accepted to be abased, O believers in the Unity of God, that ye may be exalted, and have suffered manifold afflictions, that ye might prosper and flourish. He Who hath come to build anew the whole world, behold, how they that have joined partners with God have forced Him to dwell within the most desolate of cities!

26.3 Examine Our Cause, inquire into the things that have befallen Us, and decide justly between Us and Our enemies, and be ye of them that act equitably towards their neighbor. If ye stay not the hand of the oppressor, if ye fail to safeguard the rights of the down-trodden, what right have ye then to vaunt yourselves among men? What is it of which ye can rightly boast? Is it on your food and your drink that ye pride yourselves, on the riches ye lay up in your treasuries, on the diversity and the cost of the ornaments with which ye deck yourselves? If true glory were to consist in the possession of such perishable things, then the earth on which ye walk must needs vaunt itself over you, because it supplieth you, and bestoweth upon you, these very things, by the decree of the Almighty. In its bowels are contained, according to what God hath ordained, all that ye possess. From it, as a sign of His mercy, ye derive your riches. Behold then your state, the thing in which ye glory! Would that ye could perceive it!

26.4   We have made mention of certain martyrs of this Revelation, and have likewise cited some of the verses which were sent down concerning them from the kingdom of Our utterance. We fain would hope that, rid of all attachment to the world, thou wilt ponder the things which We have mentioned.

26.5   Amongst the proofs demonstrating the truth of this Revelation is this, that in every age and Dispensation, whenever the invisible Essence was revealed in the person of His Manifestation, certain souls, obscure and detached from all worldly entanglements, would seek illumination from the Sun of Prophethood and Moon of Divine guidance, and would attain unto the Divine Presence. For this reason, the divines of the age and those possessed of wealth, would scorn and scoff at these people. Even as He hath revealed concerning them that erred: "Then said the chiefs of His people who believed not, 'We see in Thee but a man like ourselves; and we see not any who have followed Thee except our meanest ones of hasty judgment, nor see we any excellence in you above ourselves: nay, we deem you liars.'" They caviled at those holy Manifestations, and protested saying: "None hath followed you except the abject amongst us, those who are worthy of no attention." Their aim was to show that no one amongst the learned, the wealthy, and the renowned believed in them. By this and similar proofs they sought to demonstrate the falsity of Him that speaketh naught but the truth.

        In this most resplendent Dispensation, however, this most mighty Sovereignty, a number of illumined divines, of men of consummate learning, of doctors of mature wisdom, have attained unto His Court, drunk the cup of His divine Presence, and been invested with the honour of His most excellent favour. They have renounced, for the sake of the Beloved, the world and all that is therein...

26.6   All these were guided by the light of that Sun of divine Revelation, confessed and acknowledged His truth. Such was their faith, that most of them renounced their substance and kindred, and cleaved to the good-pleasure of the All-Glorious. They laid down their lives for their Well-Beloved, and surrendered their all in His path. Their breasts were made targets for the darts of the enemy, and their heads adorned the spears of the infidel. No land remained which did not drink the blood of these embodiments of detachment, and no sword that did not bruise their necks. Their deeds, alone, testify to the truth of their words. Doth not the testimony of these holy souls, who have so gloriously risen to offer up their lives for their Beloved that the whole world marvelled at the manner of their sacrifice, suffice the people of this day? Is it not sufficient witness against the faithlessness of those who for a trifle betrayed their faith, who bartered away immortality for that which perisheth, who gave up the Kawthar of the divine Presence for salty springs, and whose one aim in life is to usurp the property of others? Even as thou dost witness how all of them have busied themselves with the vanities of the world, and have strayed far from Him Who is the Lord, the Most High.

Be fair: Is the testimony of those acceptable and worthy of attention whose deeds agree with their words, whose outward behaviour conforms with their inner life? The mind is bewildered at their deeds, and the soul marvelleth at their fortitude and bodily endurance. Or is the testimony of these faithless souls who breathe naught but the breath of selfish desire, and who lie imprisoned in the cage of their idle fancies, acceptable? Like the bats of darkness, they lift not their heads from their couch except to pursue the transient things of the world, and find no rest by night except as they labour to advance the aims of their sordid life. Immersed in their selfish schemes, they are oblivious of the divine Decree. In the day-time they strive with all their soul after worldly benefits, and in the night-season their sole occupation is to gratify their carnal desires. By what law or standard could men be justified in cleaving to the denials of such petty-minded souls, and in ignoring the faith of them that have renounced, for the sake of the good-pleasure of God, their life, and substance, their fame and renown, their reputation and honour?

26.7   Lauded be Thy name, O Thou Who beholdest all things and art hidden from all things! From every land Thou hearest the lamentations of them that love Thee, and from every direction Thou hearkenest unto the cries of such as have recognized Thy sovereignty. Were their oppressors to be asked: "Wherefore have ye oppressed them and held them in bondage in Baghdad and elsewhere? What injustice have they committed? Whom have they betrayed? Whose blood have they spilled, and whose property have they plundered?" they would know not what to answer.

Thou knowest full well, O my God, that their only crime is to have loved Thee. For this reason have their oppressors laid hold on them, and scattered them abroad. Aware as I am, O my God, that Thou wilt send down upon Thy servants only what is good for them, I nevertheless beseech Thee, by Thy name which overshadoweth all things, to raise up, for their assistance and as a sign of Thy grace and as an evidence of Thy power, those who will keep them safe from all their adversaries.

Potent art Thou to do Thy pleasure. Thou art, verily, the Supreme Ruler, the Almighty, the Help in Peril, the Self-Subsisting.

26.8   Consider these martyrs of unquestionable sincerity, to whose truthfulness testifieth the explicit text of the Book, and all of whom, as thou hast witnessed, have sacrificed their life, their substance, their wives, their children, their all, and ascended unto the loftiest chambers of Paradise. Is it fair to reject the testimony of these detached and exalted beings to the truth of this pre-eminent and Glorious Revelation, and to regard as acceptable the denunciations which have been uttered against this resplendent Light by this faithless people, who for gold have forsaken their faith, and who for the sake of leadership have repudiated Him Who is the First Leader of all mankind? This, although their character is now revealed unto all people who have recognized them as those who will in no wise relinquish one jot or one tittle of their temporal authority for the sake of God's holy Faith, how much less their life, their substance, and the like.

26.9   Say: O people! Let not this life and its deceits deceive you, for the world and all that is therein is held firmly in the grasp of His Will. He bestoweth His favor on whom He willeth, and from whom He willeth He taketh it away. He doth whatsoever He chooseth. Had the world been of any worth in His sight, He surely would never have allowed His enemies to possess it, even to the extent of a grain of mustard seed. He hath, however, caused you to be entangled with its affairs, in return for what your hands have wrought in His Cause. This, indeed, is a chastisement which ye, of your own will, have inflicted upon yourselves, could ye but perceive it. Are ye rejoicing in the things which, according to the estimate of God, are contemptible and worthless, things wherewith He proveth the hearts of the doubtful?

FROM THE WRITINGS AND UTTERANCES OF 'ABDU'L-BAHÁ

26.10 The Abha Beauty Himself—may the spirit of all existence be offered up for His loved ones—bore all manner of ordeals, and willingly accepted for Himself intense afflictions. No torment was there left that His sacred form was not subjected to, no suffering that did not descend upon Him. How many a night, when He was chained, did He go sleepless because of the weight of His iron collar; how many a day the burning pain of the stocks and fetters gave Him no moment's peace. From Niyavaran to Tihran they made Him run—He, that embodied spirit, He Who had been accustomed to repose against cushions of ornamented silk—chained, shoeless, His head bared; and down under the earth, in the thick darkness of that narrow dungeon, they shut Him up with murderers, rebels and thieves. Ever and again they assailed Him with a new torment, and all were certain that from one moment to the next He would suffer a martyr's death. After some time they banished Him from His native land, and sent Him to countries alien and far away. During many a year in Iraq, no moment passed but the arrow of a new anguish struck His holy heart; with every breath a sword came down upon that sacred body, and He could hope for no moment of security and rest. From every side His enemies mounted their attack with unrelenting hate; and singly and alone He withstood them all. After all these tribulations, these body blows, they flung Him out of Iraq in the continent of Asia, to the continent of Europe, and in that place of bitter exile, of wretched hardships, to the wrongs that were heaped upon Him by the people of the Qur'án were now added the virulent persecutions, the powerful attacks, the plottings, the slanders, the continual hostilities, the hate and malice, of the people of the Bayan. My pen is powerless to tell it all; but ye have surely been informed of it. Then, after twenty-four years in this, the Most Great Prison, in agony and sore affliction, His days drew to a close.

To sum it up, the Ancient Beauty was ever, during His sojourn in this transitory world, either a captive bound with chains, or living under a sword, or subjected to extreme suffering and torment, or held in the Most Great Prison. Because of His physical weakness, brought on by His afflictions, His blessed body was worn away to a breath; it was light as a cobweb from long grieving. And His reason for shouldering this heavy load and enduring all this anguish, which was even as an ocean that hurleth its waves to high heaven—His reason for putting on the heavy iron chains and for becoming the very embodiment of utter resignation and meekness, was to lead every soul on earth to concord, to fellow-feeling, to oneness; to make known amongst all peoples the sign of the singleness of God, so that at last the primal oneness deposited at the heart of all created things would bear its destined fruit, and the splendour of 'No difference canst thou see in the creation of the God of Mercy,'[1] would cast abroad its rays.
[1 Qur'án 67:3]

26.11 My purpose in all this is to show how unobservant are the people of the world and how ignorant, and on the day of the establishment of the Kingdom, they remain heedless and negligent.

Erelong the power of the Kingdom will encompass all the world and then they will be awakened and will cry and lament over those who were oppressed and martyred, and will sigh and moan. Such is the nature of people.

26.12 Sixty years ago Bahá'u'lláh rose up, even as the Day-Star, over Persia. He declared that the skies of the world were dark, that this darkness boded evil, and that terrible wars would come. From the prison at 'Akká, He addressed the German Emperor in the clearest of terms, telling him that a great war was on the way and that his city of Berlin would break forth in lamentation and wailing. Likewise did He write to the Turkish sovereign, although He was that Sultan's victim and a captive in his prison—that is, He was being held prisoner in the Fortress at 'Akká—and clearly stated that Constantinople would be overtaken by a sudden and radical change, so great that the women and children of that city would mourn and cry aloud. In brief, He addressed such words to all the monarchs and the presidents, and everything came to pass, exactly as He had foretold.

26.13 Praise be to God! The light of unity and love is shining in these faces. These spiritual susceptibilities are the real fruits of heaven. The Báb and Bahá'u'lláh over sixty years ago proclaimed the glad tidings of universal peace. The Báb was martyred in the Cause of God. Bahá'u'lláh suffered forty years as a prisoner and exile in order that the Kingdom of love might be established in the East and West. He has made it possible for us to meet here in love and unity. Because He suffered imprisonment, we are free to proclaim the oneness of the world of humanity for which He stood so long and faithfully. He was chained in dungeons, He was without food, His companions were thieves and criminals, He was subjected to every kind of abuse and infliction, but throughout it all He never ceased to proclaim the reality of the Word of God and the oneness of humanity. We have been brought together here by the power of His Word—you from America, I from Persia—all in love and unity of spirit. Was this possible in former centuries? If it is possible now after fifty years of sacrifice and teaching, what shall we expect in the wonderful centuries coming?

26.14 Fifty years ago Bahá'u'lláh sent Epistles to all the kings and nations of the world, at a time when there was no mention of international peace. One of these Epistles was sent by Him to the president of the American democracy. In these communications He summoned all to international peace and the oneness of the human world. He summoned mankind to the fundamentals of the teachings of all the Prophets. Some of the

European kings were arrogant. Among them was Napoleon III. Bahá'u'lláh wrote a second Epistle to him, which was published thirty years ago. The context is this: "O Napoleon! Thou hast become haughty indeed. Thou hast become proud. Thou hast forgotten God. Thou dost imagine that this majesty is permanent for thee, that this dominion is abiding for thee. A letter have we sent unto thee for acceptance with thy greatest love; but, instead, thou hast shown arrogance. Therefore, God shall uproot the edifice of thy sovereignty; thy country shall flee away from thee. Thou shalt find humiliation hastening after thee because thou didst not arise for that which was enjoined upon thee, whereas that which was a duty incumbent upon thee was the cause of life to the world. The punishment of God shall soon be dealt out to thee."

26.15 Sixty years ago Bahá'u'lláh was in Persia. Seventy years ago the Báb appeared there. These two Blessed Souls devoted Their lives to the foundation of international peace and love among mankind. They strove with heart and soul to establish the teachings by which divergent people might be brought together and no strife, rancor or hatred prevail. Bahá'u'lláh, addressing all humanity, said that Adam, the parent of mankind, may be likened to the tree of nativity upon which you are the leaves and blossoms. Inasmuch as your origin was one, you must now be united and agreed; you must consort with each other in joy and fragrance. He pronounced prejudice—whether religious, racial, patriotic, political—the destroyer of the body politic. He said that man must recognize the oneness of humanity, for all in origin belong to the same household, and all are servants of the same God. Therefore, mankind must continue in the state of fellowship and love, emulating the institutions of God and turning away from satanic promptings, for the divine bestowals bring forth unity and agreement, whereas satanic leadings induce hatred and war.

This remarkable Personage was able by these principles to establish a bond of unity among the differing sects and divergent people of Persia. Those who followed His teachings, no matter from what denomination or faction they came, were conjoined by the ties of love, until now they cooperate and live together in peace and agreement. They are real brothers and sisters. No distinctions of class are observed among them, and complete harmony prevails. Daily this bond of affinity is strengthening, and their spiritual fellowship continually develops. In order to ensure the progress of mankind and to establish these principles Bahá'u'lláh suffered every ordeal and difficulty. The Báb became a martyr, and over twenty thousand men and women sacrificed their lives for their faith. Bahá'u'lláh was imprisoned and subjected to severe persecutions. Finally, He was exiled from Persia to Mesopotamia; from Baghdad He was sent to Constantinople and Adrianople and from thence to the prison of 'Akká in Syria. Through all these ordeals He strove day and night to proclaim the oneness of humanity and promulgate the message of universal peace. From the prison of 'Akká He addressed the kings and rulers of the earth in lengthy letters, summoning them to international agreement and explicitly stating that the standard of the Most Great Peace would surely be upraised in the world.

FROM THE WRITINGS AND LETTERS WRITTEN BY, OR ON BEHALF OF, SHOGHI EFFENDI

26.16 The Bahá'í Faith revolves around three central Figures, the first of whom was a youth, a native of Shiraz, named Mirza Ali-Muhammad, known as the Báb (Gate), who in May, 1844, at the age of twenty-five, advanced the claim of being the Herald Who, according to the sacred Scriptures of previous Dispensations, must needs announce and prepare the way for the advent of One greater than Himself, Whose mission would be according to those same Scriptures, to inaugurate an era of righteousness and peace, an era that would be hailed as the consummation of all previous Dispensations, and initiate a new cycle in the religious history of mankind. Swift and severe persecution, launched by the organized forces of Church and State in His native land, precipitated successively His arrest, His exile to the mountains of Adhirbayjan, His imprisonment in the fortresses of Mah-Ku and Chihriq and His execution, in July, 1850, by a firing squad in the public square of Tabriz. No less than twenty thousand of his followers were put to death with such barbarous cruelty as to evoke the warm sympathy and the unqualified admiration of a number of Western writers, diplomats, travellers and scholars, some of whom were witnesses of these abominable outrages, and were moved to record them in their books and diaries.

Mirza Husayn-Ali, surnamed Bahá'u'lláh (the Glory of God), a native of Mazindaran, Whose advent the Báb had foretold, was assailed by those same forces of ignorance and fanaticism, was imprisoned in Tihran, was banished, in 1852, from His native land to Baghdad, and thence to Constantinople and Adrianople, and finally to the prison city of 'Akká, where He remained incarcerated for no less than twenty-four years, and in whose neighborhood He passed away in 1892. In the course of His banishment, and particularly in Adrianople and 'Akká, He formulated the laws and ordinances of His Dispensation, expounded, in over a hundred volumes, the principles of His Faith, proclaimed His Message to the kings and rulers of both the East and the West, both Christian and Muslim, addressed the Pope, the Caliph of Islam, the Chief Magistrates of the Republics of the American continent, the entire Christian sacerdotal order, the leaders of Shi'ih and Sunni Islam, and the high priests of the Zoroastrian religion. In these writings He proclaimed His Revelation, summoned those whom He addressed to heed His call and espouse His Faith, warned them of the consequences of their refusal, and denounced, in some cases, their arrogance and tyranny.

His eldest son, Abbas Effendi, known as 'Abdu'l-Bahá (the Servant of Baha), appointed by Him as the successor and the authorized interpreter of His teachings, who since early childhood had been closely associated with His Father, and shared His exile and tribulations, remained a prisoner until 1908, when as a result of the Young Turk Revolution, He was released from His confinement. Establishing His residence in Haifa, He embarked soon after on His three-year journey to Egypt, Europe and North America, in the course of which He expounded before vast audiences, the teachings of His Father and predicted the approach of that catastrophe that was soon to befall mankind. He returned to His home on the eve of

the first World War, in the course of which He was exposed
to constant danger, until liberation of Palestine by the forces
under the command of General Allenby, who extended the
utmost consideration to Him and the small band of His fel-
low-exiles in 'Akká and Haifa. In 1921 He passed away, and was
buried in a vault in the mausoleum erected on Mount Carmel,
at the express instruction of Bahá'u'lláh for the remains of the
Báb which had previously been transferred from Tabriz to the
Holy Land after having been preserved and concealed for no
less than sixty years.

The passing of 'Abdu'l-Bahá marked the termination of
the first and Heroic Age of the Bahá'í Faith and signalized the
opening of the Formative Age destined to witness the gradual
emergence of its Administrative Order, whose establishment
had been foretold by the Báb, whose laws were revealed by
Bahá'u'lláh, whose outlines were delineated by 'Abdu'l-Bahá in
His Will and Testament, and whose foundations are now being
laid by the national and local councils which are elected by the
professed adherents of the Faith, and which are paving the way
for the constitution of the World Council, to be designated as
the Universal House of Justice, which in conjunction with me,
as its appointed Head and authorized interpreter of the Bahá'í
teachings, must coordinate and direct the affairs of the Bahá'í
community, and whose seat will be permanently established in
the Holy Land, in close proximity to its world spiritual center,
the resting-places of its Founders.

26.17 A Revelation, hailed as the promise and crowning glory of past
ages and centuries, as the consummation of all the Dispensations
within the Adamic Cycle, inaugurating an era of at least a thousand years' duration, and a cycle destined to last no less than five
thousand centuries, signalizing the end of the Prophetic Era and
the beginning of the Era of Fulfillment, unsurpassed alike in the
duration of its Author's ministry and the fecundity and splendor
of His mission—such a Revelation was, as already noted, born
amidst the darkness of a subterranean dungeon in Tihran—an
abominable pit that had once served as a reservoir of water for
one of the public baths of the city.

26.18 The Shah's edict, equivalent to an order for the immediate expulsion of Bahá'u'lláh from Persian territory, opens a new and glorious chapter in the history of the first Bahá'í century. Viewed in its proper perspective it will be even recognized to have ushered in one of the most eventful and momentous epochs in the world's religious history. It coincides with the inauguration of a ministry extending over a period of almost forty years—a ministry which, by virtue of its creative power, its cleansing force, its healing influences, and the irresistible operation of the world-directing, world-shaping forces it released, stands unparalleled in the religious annals of the entire human race. It marks the opening phase in a series of banishments, ranging over a period of four decades, and terminating only with the death of Him Who was the Object of that cruel edict. The process which it set in motion, gradually progressing and unfolding, began by establishing His Cause for a time in the very midst of the jealously-guarded stronghold of Shí'ah Islam, and brought Him in personal contact with its highest and most illustrious exponents; then, at a later stage, it confronted Him, at the seat of the Caliphate, with the civil and ecclesiastical dignitaries of the realm and the representatives of the Sultan of Turkey, the most powerful potentate in the Islamic world; and finally carried Him as far as the shores of the Holy Land, thereby fulfilling the prophecies recorded in both the Old and the New Testaments, redeeming the pledge enshrined in various traditions attributed to the Apostle of God and the Imams who succeeded Him, and ushering in the long-awaited restoration of Israel to the ancient cradle of its Faith. With it, may be said to have begun the last and most fruitful of the four stages of a life, the first twenty-seven years of which were characterized by the care-free enjoyment of all the advantages conferred by high birth and riches, and by an unfailing solicitude for the interests of the poor, the sick and the down-trodden; followed by nine years of active and exemplary discipleship in the service of the Báb; and finally by an imprisonment of four months' duration, overshadowed throughout by mortal peril, embittered by agonizing sorrows, and immortalized, as it drew to a close, by the sudden eruption of the forces released by an overpowering, soul-revolutionizing Revelation.

FROM THE WRITINGS AND LETTERS WRITTEN BY, OR ON BEHALF OF, THE UNIVERSAL HOUSE OF JUSTICE

26.19 Bahá'u'lláh found the world in a "strange sleep". But what a disturbance His coming has unloosed! The peoples of the earth had been separated, many parts of the human race socially and spiritually isolated. But the world of humanity today bears little resemblance to that which Bahá'u'lláh left a century ago. Unbeknownst to the great majority, His influence permeates all living beings. Indeed, no domain of life remains unaffected. In the burgeoning energy, the magnified perspectives, the heightened global consciousness; in the social and political turbulence, the fall of kingdoms, the emancipation of nations, the intermixture of cultures, the clamour for development; in the agitation over the extremes of wealth and poverty, the acute concern over the abuse of the environment, the leap of consciousness regarding the rights of women; in the growing tendency towards ecumenism, the increasing call for a new world order; in the astounding advances in the realms of science, technology, literature and the arts—in all this tumult, with its paradoxical manifestations of chaos and order, integration and disintegration, are the signs of His power as World Reformer, the proof of His claim as Divine Physician, the truth of His Word as the All-Knowing Counsellor.

Bahá'u'lláh wrote voluminously about the purpose of this mysterious force and its transformative effects, but the essence can be drawn from these few perspicuous words: "Through the movement of Our Pen of Glory We have, at the bidding of the Omnipotent Ordainer, breathed a new life into every human frame, and instilled into every word a fresh potency. All created things proclaim the evidences of this worldwide regeneration." And again: "A new life is, in this age, stirring within all the peoples of the earth; and yet none hath discovered its cause or perceived its motive." And yet again: "He Who is the Unconditioned is come, in the clouds of light, that He may quicken all created things with the breezes of His Name, the Most Merciful, and unify the world, and gather all men around this Table which hath been sent down from heaven."

Let the denizens of the earth wake from their slumber at the resonances of His Name and arise from their confused dreams to embrace the clarity of the new Day: For "This is the King of Days, the Day that hath seen the coming of the Best-beloved, Him Who through all eternity hath been acclaimed the Desire of the World."

Our thoughts turn back to the mourning time in 1892 when a vast number of residents from the surrounding area came to join His bereaved followers in lamenting the departure of the immortal Beloved. These were not adherents of His Cause and had no real understanding of His station, but the effect of His presence among them was such as to fill them with a grave sense of loss. Today, a century later, it is we, who identify ourselves with His community, who have come in multitudinous array from the far corners of the earth to pay homage to the King of Glory. With us in spirit are the millions of His lovers scattered among tens of thousands of villages, towns and cities, themselves observing in their own localities this solemn anniversary, their hearts focused on the Primal Spot here at Bahji.

And among us at this Point of Adoration are a number of the heroic souls from the celebrated company who earned the accolade Knight of Bahá'u'lláh conferred upon them by Shoghi Effendi, Guardian of the Cause—this to signify their acts of daring and devotion as teachers of the Faith. It is they who were in the vanguard during the triumphant Ten Year World Crusade. Their exploits, built upon the dramatic feats of the Heroic Age and the sacrifices of countless martyrs and heroes of the past, and following the trail blazed by earlier teachers of the Faith, realized the actual establishment of the Cause of Bahá'u'lláh as a world religion.

CHAPTER 27:

LIVING THE CONCEPT OF WORLD CITIZENSHIP

FROM THE WRITINGS OF
BAHÁ'U'LLÁH

27.1   Let your vision be world-embracing, rather than confined to your own self.

27.2   The Great Being saith: Blessed and happy is he that ariseth to promote the best interests of the peoples and kindreds of the earth. In another passage He hath proclaimed: It is not for him to pride himself who loveth his own country, but rather for him who loveth the whole world. The earth is but one country, and mankind its citizens.

27.3   The word of God which the Supreme Pen hath recorded on the seventh leaf of the Most Exalted Paradise is this: O ye men of wisdom among nations! Shut your eyes to estrangement, then fix your gaze upon unity. Cleave tenaciously unto that which will lead to the well-being and tranquillity of all mankind. This span of earth is but one homeland and one habitation. It behoveth you to abandon vainglory which causeth alienation and to set your hearts on whatever will ensure harmony. In the estimation of the people of Baha man's glory lieth in his knowledge, his upright conduct, his praiseworthy character, his wisdom, and not in his nationality or rank. O people of the earth! Appreciate the value of this heavenly word. Indeed it may be likened unto a ship for the ocean of knowledge and a shining luminary for the realm of perception. The word of God which the Supreme Pen hath recorded on the eighth leaf of the Most Exalted Paradise is the following: Schools must first train the children in the principles of religion, so that the Promise and the Threat recorded in the Books of God may prevent them from the things forbidden and adorn them with the mantle of the commandments; but this in such a measure that it may not injure the children by resulting in ignorant fanaticism and bigotry.

27.4   Behold the disturbances which, for many a long year, have afflicted the earth, and the perturbation that hath seized its peoples. It hath either been ravaged by war, or tormented by sudden and unforeseen calamities. Though the world is encompassed with misery and distress, yet no man hath paused to reflect what the cause or source of that may be. Whenever the True Counsellor uttered a word in admonishment, lo, they all denounced Him as a mover of mischief and rejected His claim. How bewildering, how confusing is such behavior! No two men can be found who may be said to be outwardly and inwardly united. The evidences of discord and malice are apparent everywhere, though all were made for harmony and union. The Great Being saith: O well-beloved ones! The tabernacle of unity hath been raised; regard ye not one another as strangers. Ye are the fruits of one tree, and the leaves of one branch. We cherish the hope that the light of justice may shine upon the world and sanctify it from tyranny. If the rulers and kings of the earth, the symbols of the power of God, exalted be His glory, arise and resolve to dedicate themselves to whatever will promote the highest interests of the whole of humanity, the reign of justice will assuredly be established amongst the children of men, and the effulgence of its light will envelop the whole earth. The Great Being saith: The structure of world stability and order hath been reared upon, and will continue to be sustained by, the twin pillars of reward and punishment.... In another passage He hath written: Take heed, O concourse of the rulers of the world! There is no force on earth that can equal in its conquering power the force of justice and wisdom.... Blessed is the king who marcheth with the ensign of wisdom unfurled before him, and the battalions of justice massed in his rear. He verily is the ornament that adorneth the brow of peace and the countenance of security. There can be no doubt whatever that if the day star of justice, which the clouds of tyranny have obscured, were to shed its light upon men, the face of the earth would be completely transformed.

FROM THE WRITINGS AND UTTERANCES OF 'ABDU'L-BAHÁ

27.5 Religion, moreover, is not a series of beliefs, a set of customs; religion is the teachings of the Lord God, teachings which constitute the very life of humankind, which urge high thoughts upon the mind, refine the character, and lay the groundwork for man's everlasting honour.

Note thou: could these fevers in the world of the mind, these fires of war and hate, of resentment and malice among the nations, this aggression of peoples against peoples, which have destroyed the tranquillity of the whole world ever be made to abate, except through the living waters of the teachings of God? No, never!

And this is clear: a power above and beyond the powers of nature must needs be brought to bear, to change this black darkness into light, and these hatreds and resentments, grudges and spites, these endless wrangles and wars, into fellowship and love amongst all the peoples of the earth. This power is none other than the breathings of the Holy Spirit and the mighty inflow of the Word of God.

27.6 "One of the great events," affirms 'Abdu'l-Bahá, "which is to occur in the Day of the manifestation of that incomparable Branch is the hoisting of the Standard of God among all nations. By this is meant that all nations and kindreds will be gathered together under the shadow of this Divine Banner, which is no other than the Lordly Branch itself, and will become a single nation. Religious and sectarian antagonism, the hostility of races and peoples, and differences among nations, will be eliminated. All men will adhere to one religion, will have one common faith, will be blended into one race and become a single people. All will dwell in one common fatherland, which is the planet itself." "Now, in the world of being," He has more-over explained, "the Hand of Divine power hath firmly laid the foundations of this all-highest bounty, and this wondrous gift. Whatsoever is latent in the innermost of this holy Cycle shall gradually appear and be made manifest, for now is but the beginning of its growth, and the dayspring of the revelation of its signs. Ere the close of this century and of this age, it shall be made clear and evident how wondrous was that spring-tide, and how heavenly was that gift."

27.7 Bahá'u'lláh teaches that the world of humanity is in need of the breath of the Holy Spirit, for in spiritual quickening and enlightenment true oneness is attained with God and man. The Most Great Peace cannot be assured through racial force and effort; it cannot be established by patriotic devotion and sacrifice; for nations differ widely and local patriotism has limitations. Furthermore, it is evident that political power and diplomatic ability are not conducive to universal agreement, for the interests of governments are varied and selfish; nor will international harmony and reconciliation be an outcome of human opinions concentrated upon it, for opinions are faulty and intrinsically diverse. Universal peace is an impossibility through human and material agencies; it must be through spiritual power. There is need of a universal impelling force which will establish the oneness of humanity and destroy the foundations of war and strife. None other than the divine power can do this; therefore, it will be accomplished through the breath of the Holy Spirit.

27.8   The earth is one native land, one home; and all mankind are the children of one Father. God has created them, and they are the recipients of His compassion. Therefore, if anyone offends another, he offends God. It is the wish of our heavenly Father that every heart should rejoice and be filled with happiness, that we should live together in felicity and joy. The obstacle to human happiness is racial or religious prejudice, the competitive struggle for existence and inhumanity toward each other.

27.9   The people of the future will not say, 'I belong to the nation of England, France or Persia'; for all of them will be citizens of a universal nationality—the one family, the one country, the one world of humanity—and then these wars, hatreds and strifes will pass away.

27.10 As to you: Your efforts must be lofty. Exert yourselves with heart and soul so that, perchance, through your efforts the light of universal peace may shine and this darkness of estrangement and enmity may be dispelled from amongst men, that all men may become as one family and consort together in love and kindness, that the East may assist the West and the West give help to the East, for all are the inhabitants of one planet, the people of one original native land and the flocks of one Shepherd.

27.11 The body of the human world is sick. Its remedy and healing will be the oneness of the kingdom of humanity. Its life is the Most Great Peace. Its illumination and quickening is love. Its happiness is the attainment of spiritual perfections. It is my wish and hope that in the bounties and favors of the Blessed Perfection we may find a new life, acquire a new power and attain to a wonderful and supreme source of energy so that the Most Great Peace of divine intention shall be established upon the foundations of the unity of the world of men with God. May the love of God be spread from this city, from this meeting to all the surrounding countries. Nay, may America become the distributing center of spiritual enlightenment, and all the world receive this heavenly blessing! For America has developed powers and capacities greater and more wonderful than other nations. While it is true that its people have attained a marvelous material civilization, I hope that spiritual forces may animate this great body and a corresponding spiritual civilization be established. May the inhabitants of this country become like angels of heaven with faces turned continually toward God. May all of them become the servants of the Omnipotent One. May they rise from present material attainments to such a height that heavenly illumination may stream from this center to all the peoples of the world.

27.12 Erelong the darkness will pass away entirely, and the regions of the East will become completely illumined; enmity, hatred, ignorance and bigotry will no longer remain; the satanic powers which destroy human equality and religious unity will be dethroned, and the nations will dwell in peace and harmony under the overspreading banner of the oneness of humanity. Therefore, we supplicate the Lord our God with sincere and contrite hearts, asking aid and assistance in the accomplishment of this mighty end: that the nations shall be unified in the Word of God; that war, enmity and hatred between races, religions, native lands and denominations shall disappear and be forever unknown; and that peoples and nations shall spiritually embrace each other in the indissoluble bond and power of the love of God. Then will the world of humanity become radiant and the human race enjoy to the fullest capacity the graces of divine bestowal...

27.13   Prejudices of all kinds—whether religious, racial, patriotic or political—are destructive of divine foundations in man. All the warfare and bloodshed in human history have been the outcome of prejudice. This earth is one home and native land. God has created mankind with equal endowment and right to live upon the earth. As a city is the home of all its inhabitants although each may have his individual place of residence therein, so the earth's surface is one wide native land or home for all races of humankind. Racial prejudice or separation into nations such as French, German, American and so on is unnatural and proceeds from human motive and ignorance. All are the children and servants of God. Why should we be separated by artificial and imaginary boundaries? In the animal kingdom the doves flock together in harmony and agreement. They have no prejudices. We are human and superior in intelligence. Is it befitting that lower creatures should manifest virtues which lack expression in man?

FROM THE WRITINGS AND LETTERS WRITTEN BY, OR ON BEHALF OF, SHOGHI EFFENDI

27.14   No less enthralling is the vision of Isaiah, the greatest of the Hebrew Prophets, predicting, as far back as twenty five hundred years ago, the destiny which mankind must, at its stage of maturity, achieve: "And He (the Lord) shall judge among the nations, and shall rebuke many people: and they shall beat their swords into plowshares, and their spears into pruninghooks: nation shall not lift up sword against nation, neither shall they learn war any more ...And there shall come forth a rod out of the stem of Jesse, and a Branch shall grow out of his roots... And he shall smite the earth with the rod of his mouth, and with the breath of his lips shall he slay the wicked. And righteousness shall be the girdle of his loins, and faithfulness the girdle of his reins. The wolf also shall dwell with the lamb, and the leopard shall lie down with the kid; and the calf and the young lion and the fatling together... And the sucking child shall play on the hole of the asp, and the weaned child shall put his hand on the cockatrice's den. They shall not hurt nor destroy in all my holy mountain: for the earth shall be full of the knowledge of the Lord, as the waters cover the sea."

27.15 Who can doubt that such a consummation—the coming of age of the human race—must signalize, in its turn, the inauguration of a world civilization such as no mortal eye hath ever beheld or human mind conceived? Who is it that can imagine the lofty standard which such a civilization, as it unfolds itself, is destined to attain? Who can measure the heights to which human intelligence, liberated from its shackles, will soar? Who can visualize the realms which the human spirit, vitalized by the outpouring light of Bahá'u'lláh, shining in the plenitude of its glory, will discover?

27.16 From the Writings and Letters Written by, or on Behalf of, the Universal House of Justice Unbridled nationalism, as distinguished from a sane and legitimate patriotism, must give way to a wider loyalty, to the love of humanity as a whole. Bahá'u'lláh's statement is: "The earth is but one country, and mankind its citizens." The concept of world citizenship is a direct result of the contraction of the world into a single neighbourhood through scientific advances and of the indisputable interdependence of nations. Love of all the world's peoples does not exclude love of one's country. The advantage of the part in a world society is best served by promoting the advantage of the whole. Current international activities in various fields which nurture mutual affection and a sense of solidarity among peoples need greatly to be increased.

OTHER SOURCES

27.17   World citizenship begins with an acceptance of the oneness of the human family and the interconnectedness of the nations of 'the earth, our home.' While it encourages a sane and legitimate patriotism, it also insists upon a wider loyalty, a love of humanity as a whole. It does not, however, imply abandonment of legitimate loyalties, the suppression of cultural diversity, the abolition of national autonomy, nor the imposition of uniformity. Its hallmark is 'unity in diversity.' World citizenship encompasses the principles of social and economic justice, both within and between nations; non -adversarial decision making at all levels of society; equality of the sexes; racial, ethnic, national and religious harmony; and the willingness to sacrifice for the common good. Other facets of world citizenship—including the promotion of human honor and dignity, understanding, amity, cooperation, trustworthiness, compassion and the desire to serve—can be deduced from those already mentioned. (Bahá'í International Community in a concept paper shared at the 1st session of the United Nations Commission on Sustainable Development, New York, U.S.A. on 14-25 June 1993)

CONCLUSION

CHAPTER 28:

FACING DOUBTS WITH COURAGE

FROM THE WRITINGS OF BAHÁ'U'LLÁH

28.1   Beware lest the doubts of men debar you from the light of certitude.

28.2   Sow the seeds of My divine wisdom in the pure soil of thy heart, and water them with the water of certitude, that the hyacinths of My knowledge and wisdom may spring up fresh and green in the sacred city of thy heart.

28.3   Only when the lamp of search, of earnest striving, of longing desire, of passionate devotion, of fervid love, of rapture, and ecstasy, is kindled within the seeker's heart, and the breeze of His loving-kindness is wafted upon his soul, will the darkness of error be dispelled, the mists of doubts and misgivings be dissipated, and the lights of knowledge and certitude envelop his being.

28.4   Of these truths some can be disclosed only to the extent of the capacity of the repositories of the light of Our knowledge, and the recipients of Our hidden grace. We beseech God to strengthen thee with His power, and enable thee to recognize Him Who is the Source of all knowledge, that thou mayest detach thyself from all human learning, for, "what would it profit any man to strive after learning when he hath already found and recognized Him Who is the Object of all knowledge?" Cleave to the Root of Knowledge, and to Him Who is the Fountain thereof, that thou mayest find thyself independent of all who claim to be well versed in human learning, and whose claim no clear proof, nor the testimony of any enlightening book, can support.

28.5   Much hath been written in the books of old concerning the various stages in the development of the soul, such as concupiscence, irascibility, inspiration, benevolence, contentment, Divine good-pleasure, and the like; the Pen of the Most High, however, is disinclined to dwell upon them. Every soul that walketh humbly with its God, in this Day, and cleaveth unto Him, shall find itself invested with the honor and glory of all goodly names and stations

28.6   O FRIEND! In the garden of thy heart plant naught but the rose of love, and from the nightingale of affection and desire loosen not thy hold. Treasure the companionship of the righteous and eschew all fellowship with the ungodly.

28.7   O MY SON! The company of the ungodly increaseth sorrow, whilst fellowship with the righteous cleanseth the rust from off the heart. He that seeketh to commune with God, let him betake himself to the companionship of His loved ones; and he that desireth to hearken unto the word of God, let him give ear to the words of His chosen ones.

28.8   O SON OF DESIRE! The learned and the wise have for long years striven and failed to attain the presence of the All-Glorious; they have spent their lives in search of Him, yet did not behold the beauty of His countenance. Thou without the least effort didst attain thy goal, and without search hast obtained the object of thy quest. Yet, notwithstanding, thou didst remain so wrapt in the veil of self, that thine eyes beheld not the beauty of the Beloved, nor did thy hand touch the hem of His robe. Ye that have eyes, behold and wonder.

28.9   O SON OF SPIRIT! My claim on thee is great, it cannot be forgotten. My grace to thee is plenteous, it cannot be veiled. My love has made in thee its home, it cannot be concealed. My light is manifest to thee, it cannot be obscured.

28.10   People for the most part delight in superstitions. They regard a single drop of the sea of delusion as preferable to an ocean of certitude. By holding fast unto names they deprive themselves of the inner reality and by clinging to vain imaginings they are kept back from the Dayspring of heavenly signs. God grant you may be graciously aided under all conditions to shatter the idols of superstition and to tear away the veils of the imaginations of men. Authority lieth in the grasp of God, the Fountainhead of revelation and inspiration and the Lord of the Day of Resurrection.

28.11   Blessed art thou inasmuch as the darkness of vain imaginings hath been powerless to hinder thee from the light of certitude, and the onslaught of the people hath failed to deter thee from the Lord of mankind. Appreciate thou the value of this high station and beseech God—exalted is His glory—to graciously enable thee to safeguard it. Imperishable dominion hath exclusively pertained unto the One true God and His loved ones and will continue to pertain unto them everlastingly.

28.12 Therefore, O brother! kindle with the oil of wisdom the lamp of the spirit within the innermost chamber of thy heart, and guard it with the globe of understanding, that the breath of the infidel may extinguish not its flame nor dim its brightness. Thus have We illuminated the heavens of utterance with the splendours of the Sun of divine wisdom and understanding, that thy heart may find peace, that thou mayest be of those who, on the wings of certitude, have soared unto the heaven of the love of their Lord, the All-Merciful.

28.13 Wherefore, O my friend, it behooveth Us to exert the highest endeavour to attain unto that City, and, by the grace of God and His loving-kindness, rend asunder the "veils of glory"; so that, with inflexible steadfastness, we may sacrifice our drooping souls in the path of the New Beloved. We should with tearful eyes, fervently and repeatedly, implore Him to grant us the favour of that grace. That city is none other than the Word of God revealed in every age and dispensation. In the days of Moses it was the Pentateuch; in the days of Jesus the Gospel; in the days of Muhammad the Messenger of God the Qur'án; in this day the Bayán; and in the dispensation of Him Whom God will make manifest His own Book—the Book unto which all the Books of former Dispensations must needs be referred, the Book which standeth amongst them all transcendent and supreme. In these cities spiritual sustenance is bountifully provided, and incorruptible delights have been ordained. The food they bestow is the bread of heaven, and the Spirit they impart is God's imperishable blessing. Upon detached souls they bestow the gift of Unity, enrich the destitute, and offer the cup of knowledge unto them who wander in the wilderness of ignorance. All the guidance, the blessings, the learning, the understanding, the faith, and certitude, conferred upon all that is in heaven and on earth, are hidden and treasured within these Cities.

28.14 Know verily that the purpose underlying all these symbolic terms and abstruse allusions, which emanate from the Revealers of God's holy Cause, hath been to test and prove the peoples of the world; that thereby the earth of the pure and illuminated hearts may be known from the perishable and barren soil. From time immemorial such hath been the way of God amidst His creatures, and to this testify the records of the sacred books.

28.15 True loss is for him whose days have been spent in utter ignorance of his self.

28.16 It behoveth every man to blot out the trace of every idle word from the tablet of his heart, and to gaze, with an open and unbiased mind, on the signs of His Revelation, the proofs of His Mission, and the tokens of His glory.

28.17 Wherefore, be thankful to God, for having strengthened thee to aid His Cause, for having made the flowers of knowledge and understanding to spring forth in the garden of thine heart. Thus hath His grace encompassed thee, and encompassed the whole of creation. Beware, lest thou allow anything whatsoever to grieve thee. Rid thyself of all attachment to the vain allusions of men, and cast behind thy back the idle and subtle disputations of them that are veiled from God. Proclaim, then, that which the Most Great Spirit will inspire thee to utter in the service of the Cause of thy Lord, that thou mayest stir up the souls of all men and incline their hearts unto this most blessed and all-glorious Court....

    Know thou that We have annulled the rule of the sword, as an aid to Our Cause, and substituted for it the power born of the utterance of men. Thus have We irrevocably decreed, by virtue of Our grace. Say: O people! Sow not the seeds of discord among men,   and refrain from contending with your neighbor, for your Lord hath committed the world and the cities thereof to the care of the kings of the earth, and made them the emblems of His own power, by virtue of the sovereignty He hath chosen to bestow upon them. He hath refused to reserve for Himself any share whatever of this world's dominion. To this He Who is Himself the Eternal Truth will testify. The things He hath reserved for Himself are the cities of men's hearts, that He may cleanse them from all earthly defilements, and enable them to draw nigh unto the hallowed Spot which the hands of the infidel can never profane. Open, O people, the city of the human heart with the key of your utterance. Thus have We, according to a pre-ordained measure, prescribed unto you your duty.

28.18 By the righteousness of God! These are the days in which God hath proved the hearts of the entire company of His Messengers and Prophets, and beyond them those that stand guard over His sacred and inviolable Sanctuary, the inmates of the celestial Pavilion and dwellers of the Tabernacle of Glory. How severe, therefore, the test to which they who join partners with God must needs be subjected!

28.19 Tear asunder, in My Name, the veils that have grievously blinded your vision, and, through the power born of your belief in the unity of God, scatter the idols of vain imitation.

FROM THE WRITINGS AND UTTERANCES OF 'ABDU'L-BAHÁ

28.20 O ye roses in the garden of God's love! O ye bright lamps in the assemblage of His knowledge! May the soft breathings of God pass over you, may the Glory of God illumine the horizon of your hearts. Ye are the waves of the deep sea of knowledge, ye are the massed armies on the plains of certitude, ye are the stars in the skies of God's compassion, ye are the stones that put the people of perdition to flight, ye are clouds of divine pity over the gardens of life, ye are the abundant grace of God's oneness that is shed upon the essences of all created things.

28.21 Endeavour, therefore, that ye may scatter and disperse the army of doubt and of error with the power of the holy utterances. This is my exhortation and this is my counsel. Do not quarrel with anybody, and shun every form of dispute. Utter the Word of God. If he accepteth it the desired purpose is attained, and if he turneth away leave him to himself and trust to God.

28.22 Now some of the mischief-makers, with many stratagems, are seeking leadership, and in order to reach this position they instill doubts among the friends that they may cause differences, and that these differences may result in their drawing a party to themselves. But the friends of God must be awake and must know that the scattering of these doubts hath as its motive personal desires and the achievement of leadership.

Do not disrupt Bahá'í unity, and know that this unity cannot be maintained save through faith in the Covenant of God.

28.23 Doubt not that God is with us, on our right hand and on our left, that day by day He will cause our numbers to increase, and that our meetings will grow in strength and usefulness.

28.24 Today, men have grown into such adoring attachment to outward forms and ceremonies that they dispute over this point of ritual or that particular practice, until one hears on all sides of wearisome arguments and unrest. There are individuals who have weak intellects and their powers of reasoning have not developed, but the strength and power of religion must not be doubted because of the incapacity of these persons to understand.

28.25 To him who has the power of comprehension religion is like an open book, but how can it be possible for a man devoid of reason and intellectuality to understand the Divine Realities of God?

Put all your beliefs into harmony with science; there can be no opposition, for truth is one. When religion, shorn of its superstitions, traditions, and unintelligent dogmas, shows its conformity with science, then will there be a great unifying, cleansing force in the world which will sweep before it all wars, disagreements, discords and struggles—and then will mankind be united in the power of the Love of God.

28.26 When a soul has in it the life of the spirit, then does it bring forth good fruit and become a Divine tree. I wish you to try to understand this example. I hope that the unspeakable goodness of God will so strengthen you that the celestial quality of your soul, which relates it to the spirit, will for ever dominate the material side, so entirely ruling the senses that your soul will approach the perfections of the Heavenly Kingdom. May your faces, being steadfastly set towards the Divine Light, become so luminous that all your thoughts, words and actions will shine with the Spiritual Radiance dominating your souls, so that in the gatherings of the world you will show perfection in your life.

Some men's lives are solely occupied with the things of this world; their minds are so circumscribed by exterior manners and traditional interests that they are blind to any other realm of existence, to the spiritual significance of all things! They think and dream of earthly fame, of material progress. Sensuous delights and comfortable surroundings bound their horizon, their highest ambitions centre in successes of worldly conditions and circumstances! They curb not their lower propensities; they eat, drink, and sleep! Like the animal, they have no thought beyond their own physical well-being. It is true that these necessities must be despatched. Life is a load which must be carried on while we are on earth, but the cares of the lower things of life should not be allowed to monopolize all the thoughts and aspirations of a human being. The heart's ambitions should ascend to a more glorious goal, mental activity should rise to higher levels! Men should hold in their souls the vision of celestial perfection, and there prepare a dwelling-place for the inexhaustible bounty of the Divine Spirit.

Let your ambition be the achievement on earth of a Heavenly civilization! I ask for you the supreme blessing, that you may be so filled with the vitality of the Heavenly Spirit that you may be the cause of life to the world.

FROM THE WRITINGS AND LETTERS WRITTEN BY, OR ON BEHALF OF, SHOGHI EFFENDI

28.27 The Bahá'í Faith upholds the unity of God, recognizes the unity of His Prophets, and inculcates the principle of the oneness and wholeness of the entire human race. It proclaims the necessity and the inevitability of the unification of mankind, asserts that it is gradually approaching, and claims that nothing short of the transmuting spirit of God, working through His chosen Mouthpiece in this day, can ultimately succeed in bringing it about. It, moreover, enjoins upon its followers the primary duty of an unfettered search after truth, condemns all manner of prejudice and superstition, declares the purpose of religion to be the promotion of amity and concord, proclaims its essential harmony with science, and recognizes it as the foremost agency for the pacification and the orderly progress of human society....

28.28 The more we search for ourselves, the less likely we are to find ourselves; and the more we search for God, and to serve our fellow-men, the more profoundly will we become acquainted with ourselves, and the more inwardly assured. This is one of the great spiritual laws of life.

FROM THE WRITINGS AND LETTERS WRITTEN BY, OR ON BEHALF OF, THE UNIVERSAL HOUSE OF JUSTICE

28.29 Vision must be restored where hope is lost, confidence built where doubt and confusion are rife.

28.30 Have no fear or doubts. The power of the Covenant will assist you and invigorate you and remove every obstacle from your path.

CHAPTER 29:

TAKING THE NEXT STEPS

FROM THE WRITINGS OF BAHÁ'U'LLÁH

29.1 Be generous in prosperity, and thankful in adversity. Be worthy of the trust of thy neighbor, and look upon him with a bright and friendly face. Be a treasure to the poor, an admonisher to the rich, an answerer of the cry of the needy, a preserver of the sanctity of thy pledge. Be fair in thy judgment, and guarded in thy speech. Be unjust to no man, and show all meekness to all men. Be as a lamp unto them that walk in darkness, a joy to the sorrowful, a sea for the thirsty, a haven for the distressed, an upholder and defender of the victim of oppression. Let integrity and upright-ness distinguish all thine acts. Be a home for the stranger, a balm to the suffering, a tower of strength for the fugitive. Be eyes to the blind, and a guiding light unto the feet of the erring. Be an ornament to the countenance of truth, a crown to the brow of fidelity, a pillar of the temple of righteousness, a breath of life to the body of mankind, an ensign of the hosts of justice, a luminary above the horizon of virtue, a dew to the soil of the human heart, an ark on the ocean of knowledge, a sun in the heaven of bounty, a gem on the diadem of wisdom, a shining light in the firmament of thy generation, a fruit upon the tree of humility.

29.2 O friends! Be not careless of the virtues with which ye have been endowed, neither be neglectful of your high destiny. Suffer not your labors to be wasted through the vain imag-inations which certain hearts have devised. Ye are the stars of the heaven of understanding, the breeze that stirreth at the break of day, the soft-flowing waters upon which must depend the very life of all men, the letters inscribed upon His sacred scroll. With the utmost unity, and in a spirit of perfect fellowship, exert yourselves, that ye may be enabled to achieve that which beseemeth this Day of God. Verily I say, strife and dissension, and whatsoever the mind of man abhorreth are entirely unworthy of his station. Center your energies in the propagation of the Faith of God. Whoso is worthy of so high a calling, let him arise and promote it. Whoso is unable, it is his duty to appoint him who will, in his stead, proclaim this Revelation, whose power hath caused the foundations of the mightiest structures to quake, every mountain to be crushed into dust, and every soul to be dumbfounded. Should the greatness of this Day be revealed in its fullness, every man would forsake a myriad lives in his longing to partake, though it be for one moment, of its great glory—how much more this world and its corruptible treasures!

Be ye guided by wisdom in all your doings, and cleave ye tenaciously unto it. Please God ye may all be strengthened to carry out that which is the Will of God, and may be graciously assisted to appreciate the rank conferred upon such of His loved ones as have arisen to serve Him and magnify His name. Upon them be the glory of God, the glory of all that is in the heavens and all that is on the earth, and the glory of the inmates of the most exalted Paradise, the heaven of heavens.

29.3 The whole duty of man in this Day is to attain that share of the flood of grace which God poureth forth for him. Let none, therefore, consider the largeness or smallness of the receptacle. The portion of some might lie in the palm of a man's hand, the portion of others might fill a cup, and of others even a gallon-measure.

29.4 By My spirit and by My favor! By My mercy and by My beauty! All that I have revealed unto thee with the tongue of power, and have written for thee with the pen of might, hath been in accordance with thy capacity and understanding, not with My state and the melody of My voice.

29.5 Thou hast asked Me concerning the nature of the soul. Know, verily, that the soul is a sign of God, a heavenly gem whose reality the most learned of men hath failed to grasp, and whose mystery no mind, however acute, can ever hope to unravel. It is the first among all created things to declare the excellence of its Creator, the first to recognize His glory, to cleave to His truth, and to bow down in adoration before Him. If it be faithful to God, it will reflect His light, and will, eventually, return unto Him. If it fail, however, in its allegiance to its Creator, it will become a victim to self and passion, and will, in the end, sink in their depths.

FROM THE WRITINGS AND UTTERANCES OF 'ABDU'L-BAHÁ

29.6   Strive ye to receive your share of this eternal food, so that ye shall be loved and cherished in this world and the next.

29.7   O ye beloved of God! O ye children of His Kingdom! Verily, verily, the new heaven and the new earth are come. The holy City, new Jerusalem, hath come down from on high in the form of a maid of heaven, veiled, beauteous, and unique, and prepared for reunion with her lovers on earth. The angelic company of the Celestial Concourse hath joined in a call that hath run throughout the universe, all loudly and mightily acclaiming: 'This is the City of God and His abode, wherein shall dwell the pure and holy among His servants. He shall live with them, for they are His people and He is their Lord.'

He hath wiped away their tears, kindled their light, rejoiced their hearts and enraptured their souls. Death shall no more overtake them neither shall sorrow, weeping or tribulation afflict them. The Lord God Omnipotent hath been enthroned in His Kingdom and hath made all things new. This is the truth and what truth can be greater than that announced by the Revelation of St. John the Divine?

He is Alpha and Omega. He is the One that will give unto him that is athirst of the fountain of the water of life and bestow upon the sick the remedy of true salvation. He whom such grace aideth is verily he that receiveth the most glorious heritage from the Prophets of God and His holy ones. The Lord will be his God, and he His dearly-beloved son.

Rejoice, then, O ye beloved of the Lord and His chosen ones, and ye the children of God and His people, raise your voices to laud and magnify the Lord, the Most High; for His light hath beamed forth, His signs have appeared and the billows of His rising ocean have scattered on every shore many a precious pearl.

29.8   These few brief days shall pass away, this present life shall vanish from our sight; the roses of this world shall be fresh and fair no more, the garden of this earth's triumphs and delights shall droop and fade. The spring season of life shall turn into the autumn of death, the bright joy of palace halls give way to moonless dark within the tomb. And therefore is none of this worth loving at all, and to this the wise will not anchor his heart.

He who hath knowledge and power will rather seek out the glory of heaven, and spiritual distinction, and the life that dieth not. And such a one longeth to approach the sacred Threshold of God; for in the tavern of this swiftly-passing world the man of God will not lie drunken, nor will he even for a moment take his ease, nor stain himself with any fondness for this earthly life.

29.9   On the outspread tablet of this world, ye are the verses of His singleness; and atop lofty palace towers, ye are the banners of the Lord. In His bowers are ye the blossoms and sweet-smelling herbs, in the rose garden of the spirit the nightingales that utter plaintive cries. Ye are the birds that soar upward into the firmament of knowledge, the royal falcons on the wrist of God.

Why then are ye quenched, why silent, why leaden and dull? Ye must shine forth like the lightning, and raise up a clamouring like unto the great sea. Like a candle must ye shed your light, and even as the soft breezes of God must ye blow across the world. Even as sweet breaths from heavenly bowers, as musk-laden winds from the gardens of the Lord, must ye perfume the air for the people of knowledge, and even as the splendours shed by the true Sun, must ye illumine the hearts of humankind. For ye are the life-laden winds, ye are the jessamine-scents from the gardens of the saved. Bring then life to the dead, and awaken those who slumber. In the darkness of the world be ye radiant flames; in the sands of perdition, be ye well-springs of the water of life, be ye guidance from the Lord God. Now is the time to serve, now is the time to be on fire. Know ye the value of this chance, this favourable juncture that is limitless grace, ere it slip from your hands.

Soon will our handful of days, our vanishing life, be gone, and we shall pass, empty-handed, into the hollow that is dug for those who speak no more; wherefore must we bind our hearts to the manifest Beauty, and cling to the lifeline that faileth never. We must gird ourselves for service, kindle love's flame, and burn away in its heat. We must loose our tongues till we set the wide world's heart afire, and with bright rays of guidance blot out the armies of the night, and then, for His sake, on the field of sacrifice, fling down our lives.

Thus let us scatter over every people the treasured gems of the recognition of God, and with the decisive blade of the tongue, and the sure arrows of knowledge, let us defeat the hosts of self and passion, and hasten onward to the site of martyrdom, to the place where we die for the Lord. And then, with flying flags, and to the beat of drums, let us pass into the realm of the All-Glorious, and join the Company on high.

Well is it with the doers of great deeds.

29.10 ...Therefore, man should hear with attentive ear the call of the spiritual world, seeking first the Kingdom of God and its perfections. This is eternal life; this is everlasting remembrance.

29.11 Be not satisfied with words, but seek to understand the spiritual meanings hidden in the heart of the words.

29.12 Break all fetters and seek for spiritual joy and enlightenment; then, though you walk on this earth, you will perceive yourselves to be within the divine horizon.

APPENDIX:

SOURCES AND BIBLIOGRAPHY

SOURCES FOR MANIFEST YOUR POTENTIAL IN THE BAHÁ'Í FAITH

Chapter 1

1.1   Bahá'u'lláh, Gleanings from the Writings of Bahá'u'lláh, p. 67
1.2   Bahá'u'lláh, Gleanings from the Writings of Bahá'u'lláh, p. 261
1.3   Bahá'u'lláh, The Kitáb-i-Iqan, p. 120
1.4   Bahá'u'lláh, The Hidden Words, Arabic #64
1.5   Bahá'u'lláh, Gleanings from the Writings of Bahá'u'lláh, p. 205
1.6   Bahá'u'lláh, Gleanings from the Writings of Bahá'u'lláh, p. 206
1.7   'Abdu'l-Bahá, Selections from the Writings of 'Abdu'l-Bahá, p. 57
1.8   'Abdu'l-Bahá, Selections from the Writings of 'Abdu'l-Bahá, p. 75
1.9   'Abdu'l-Bahá, Some Answered Questions, p. 235
1.10   'Abdu'l-Bahá, The Promulgation of Universal Peace, p. 41
1.11   'Abdu'l-Bahá, The Promulgation of Universal Peace, p. 204
1.12   From a letter written on behalf of Shoghi Effendi to an individual believer on April 25, 1945. Lights of Guidance, p. 542
1.13   From a letter written on behalf of the Guardian to an individual believer, October 6, 1954: Living the Life, pp. 18-19. Lights of Guidance, p. 70
1.14   The Universal House of Justice, Ridvan 153, 1996 - Africa
1.15   The Universal House of Justice, Messages 1963 to 1986, p. 564
1.16   The Universal House of Justice, Messages 1963 to 1986, p. 686

Chapter 2

2.1   Bahá'u'lláh, Gleanings from the Writings of Bahá'u'lláh, p. 10
2.2   Bahá'u'lláh, The Proclamation of Bahá'u'lláh
2.3   Baha'u'llah, Epistle to the Son of the Wolf, p. 24
2.4   Baha'u'llah, The Kitab-i-Aqdas, p. 73
2.5   Baha'u'llah, Epistle to the Son of the Wolf, p. 11
2.6   Baha'u'llah, The Summons of the Lord of Hosts, p. 4
2.7   'Abdu'l-Bahá, Selections from the Writings of 'Abdu'l-Bahá, p. 100
2.8   'Abdu'l-Bahá, Selections from the Writings of 'Abdu'l-Bahá, p. 252
2.9   'Abdu'l-Bahá, The Promulgation of Universal Peace, p. 105
2.10   'Abdu'l-Bahá, The Promulgation of Universal Peace, p. 313
2.11   'Abdu'l-Bahá, The Promulgation of Universal Peace, p. 28
2.12   Shoghi Effendi, Summary Statement - 1947, Special UN Committee on Palestine
2.13   Shoghi Effendi, God Passes By, p. 281
2.14   The Universal House of Justice, 1985 Oct, The Promise of World Peace, p. 1
2.15   The Universal House of Justice, 1985 Oct, The Promise of World Peace, p. 1

Chapter 3

3.1   Bahá'u'lláh, The Hidden Words, Arabic #4
3.2   Bahá'u'lláh, The Hidden Words, Persian #29
3.3   Bahá'u'lláh, Gleanings from the Writings of Bahá'u'lláh, p. 199
3.4   Bahá'u'lláh, Gleanings from the Writings of Bahá'u'lláh, p. 150
3.5   Bahá'u'lláh, The Hidden Words, Arabic #40
3.6   Bahá'u'lláh, The Hidden Words, Persian #72
3.7   Bahá'u'lláh, Gleanings from the Writings of Bahá'u'lláh p. 1
3.8   Bahá'u'lláh, Gleanings from the Writings of Bahá'u'lláh, p. 49
3.9   Bahá'u'lláh, Gleanings from the Writings of Bahá'u'lláh, p. 47
3.10   Bahá'u'lláh, Gleanings from the Writings of Bahá'u'lláh, p. 80
3.11   'Abdu'l-Bahá, Some Answered Questions, p. 5
3.12   'Abdu'l-Bahá, Some Answered Questions, p. 5
3.13   'Abdu'l-Bahá, Some Answered Questions, p. 5
3.14   'Abdu'l-Bahá, Some Answered Questions, p. 6
3.15   'Abdu'l-Bahá, Some Answered Questions, p. 6

3.16   'Abdu'l-Bahá, Some Answered Questions, p. 7
3.17   'Abdu'l-Bahá, Some Answered Questions, p. 9
3.18   'Abdu'l-Bahá, Some Answered Questions, p. 10
3.19   Abdu'l-Baha, Some Answered Questions, p. 37
3.20   'Abdu'l-Bahá, The Promulgation of Universal Peace, p. 360
3.21   From a letter written on behalf of Shoghi Effendi to an individual believer, October
         26, 1932. Lights of Guidance, p. 479
3.22   The Universal House of Justice, Messages 1963 to 1986, p. 595

Chapter 4
4.1   Bahá'u'lláh, Tablets of Bahá'u'lláh, p. 129
4.2   Bahá'u'lláh, Tablets of Bahá'u'lláh, p. 125
4.3   Bahá'u'lláh, Gleanings from the Writings of Bahá'u'lláh, p. 81
4.4   Bahá'u'lláh, Tablets of Bahá'u'lláh, p. 155
4.5   Bahá'u'lláh, Tablets of Bahá'u'lláh, p. 168
4.6   Bahá'u'lláh, Tablets of Bahá'u'lláh, p. 220
4.7   Bahá'u'lláh, Tablets of Bahá'u'lláh, p.68
4.8   'Abdu'l-Bahá, The Secret of Divine Civilization, p. 79
4.9   'Abdu'l-Bahá, Foundations of World Unity, p. 15
4.10   'Abdu'l-Bahá, The Secret of Divine Civilization, p. 98
4.11   'Abdu'l-Bahá, The Secret of Divine Civilization, p. 70
4.12   'Abdu'l-Bahá, The Promulgation of Universal Peace, p. 128
4.13   'Abdu'l-Bahá, Paris Talks, p. 141
4.14   'Abdu'l-Bahá, The Promulgation of Universal Peace, p. 41
4.15   'Abdu'l-Bahá, The Promulgation of Universal Peace, p. 161
4.16   'Abdu'l-Bahá, The Promulgation of Universal Peace, p. 231
4.17   Shoghi Effendi, The Promised Day is Come, p. v
4.18   Shoghi Effendi, The World Order of Bahá'u'lláh, p. 180
4.19   From a letter written on behalf of the Guardian to the National Spiritual Assembly of
         the United States, July 19, 1956Lights of Guidance, p. 131
4.20   From a letter written on behalf of the Guardian to an individual believer, December 8,
         1935. Lights of Guidance, p. 134
4.21   The Universal House of Justice, Messages 1963 to 1986, p. 629
4.22   The Universal House of Justice, 1998 Feb 08, Materialistic Elements in Academic
         Scholarship, p. 5
4.23   The Universal House of Justice, Messages 1963 to 1986, p. 388
4.24   Commissioned by The Universal House of Justice, One Common Faith

Chapter 5
5.1   Bahá'u'lláh, The Proclamation of Bahá'u'lláh
5.2   Bahá'u'lláh, Gleanings from the Writings of Bahá'u'lláh, p. 9
5.3   Bahá'u'lláh, Gleanings from the Writings of Bahá'u'lláh, p. 319
5.4   Bahá'u'lláh, Gleanings from the Writings of Bahá'u'lláh, p. 10
5.5   Baha'u'llah, The Kitab-i-Iqan, p. 235
5.6   Bahá'u'lláh, Gleanings from the Writings of Bahá'u'lláh, p. 12
5.7   'Abdu'l-Bahá, Selections from the Writings of 'Abdu'l-Bahá, p. 286
5.8   'Abdu'l-Bahá, Selections from the Writings of 'Abdu'l-Bahá, p. 283
5.9   'Abdu'l-Bahá: Secret of Divine Civilization, pp. 2-3
5.10   'Abdu'l-Bahá, Selections from the Writings of 'Abdu'l-Bahá, p. 127
5.11   'Abdu'l-Bahá, Selections from the Writings of 'Abdu'l-Bahá, p. 92
5.12   'Abdu'l-Bahá, Paris Talks, p. 109
5.13   'Abdu'l-Bahá, Paris Talks, p. 72
5.14   'Abdu'l-Bahá, The Promulgation of Universal Peace, p. 452
5.15   'Abdu'l-Bahá: Promulgation of Universal Peace, 1982 ed., p. 204
5.16   'Abdu'l-Bahá, Paris Talks, p. 15
5.17   'Abdu'l-Bahá, The Promulgation of Universal Peace, p. 215
5.18   'Abdu'l-Bahá, The Promulgation of Universal Peace, p. 210

5.19	From a letter written on behalf of Shoghi Effendi to an individual believer, July 24, 1943. Lights of Guidance, p. 113
5.20	From a letter written on behalf of Shoghi Effendi to an individual believer, May 18, 1927. Lights of Guidance, p. 125
5.21	From a letter written on behalf of Shoghi Effendi to an individual believer, November 5, 1949. Lights of Guidance, p. 129
5.22	From a letter written on behalf of Shoghi Effendi to an individual believer, February 2, 1925. Lights of Guidance, p. 111
5.23	From a letter written on behalf of Shoghi Effendi to an individual believer, July 14, 1945 Compilations. Lights of Guidance, p. 115
5.24	From a letter written on behalf of the Universal House of Justice to an individual believer, August 30, 1984. Lights of Guidance, p. 520

Chapter 6

6.1	Bahá'u'lláh, The Hidden Words, Arabic #56
6.2	Bahá'u'lláh, Gleanings from the Writings of Bahá'u'lláh, p. 314
6.3	Bahá'u'lláh, The Compilation of Compilations vol. I, p. 154
6.4	Bahá'u'lláh, Gleanings from the Writings of Bahá'u'lláh, p. 205
6.5	Bahá'u'lláh, The Hidden Words, Persian #40
6.6	Bahá'u'lláh, Gleanings from the Writings of Bahá'u'lláh, p. 12
6.7	Bahá'u'lláh, Gleanings from the Writings of Bahá'u'lláh, p. 294
6.8	Bahá'u'lláh, Epistle to the Son of the Wolf, p. 56
6.9	'Abdu'l-Bahá, The Secret of Divine Civilization, p. 3
6.10	'Abdu'l-Bahá, Selections from the Writings of 'Abdu'l-Bahá, p. 25
6.11	'Abdu'l-Bahá, Selections from the Writings of 'Abdu'l-Bahá, p. 245
6.12	'Abdu'l-Bahá, Selections from the Writings of 'Abdu'l-Bahá, p. 178
6.13	'Abdu'l-Bahá, Selections from the Writings of 'Abdu'l-Bahá, p. 178
6.14	'Abdu'l-Bahá, Tablets of the Divine Plan, p. 44
6.15	'Abdu'l-Bahá, Tablets of the Divine Plan, p. 34
6.16	'Abdu'l-Bahá, Tablets of the Divine Plan, p. 95
6.17	'Abdu'l-Bahá, Paris Talks, p. 178
6.18	'Abdu'l-Bahá, Paris Talks, p. 111
6.19	'Abdu'l-Bahá, The Promulgation of Universal Peace, p. 336
6.20	'Abdu'l-Bahá, Paris Talks, p. 38
6.21	Shoghi Effendi: Citadel of Faith, p. 149. Lights of Guidance, p. 137
6.22	From a letter written on behalf of Shoghi Effendi to an individual believer, October 15, 1952. Lights of Guidance, p. 112
6.23	Letter from the Universal House of Justice to an individual believer, March 19, 1938: Bahá'í Journal of the United Kingdom, No. 217, p. 7, June 1973. Lights of Guidance, p. 112

Chapter 7

7.1	Bahá'u'lláh, The Hidden Words, Persian #63
7.2	Bahá'u'lláh, The Kitáb-i-Aqdas, p. 37
7.3	Bahá'u'lláh, Gleanings from the Writings of Bahá'u'lláh, p. 5
7.4	Bahá'u'lláh, Gleanings from the Writings of Bahá'u'lláh, p. 130
7.5	Bahá'u'lláh, Tablets of Bahá'u'lláh pg. 268
7.6	Bahá'u'lláh, Gleanings from the Writings of Bahá'u'lláh, p. 98
7.7	Bahá'u'lláh, The Hidden Words, Persian #2
7.8	Bahá'u'lláh, Epistle to the Son of the Wolf, p. 10
7.9	Bahá'u'lláh, Tablets of Bahá'u'lláh, p. 24
7.10	Bahá'u'lláh, The Hidden Words, Persian #44
7.11	Bahá'u'lláh, The Hidden Words, Persian #21
7.12	Bahá'u'lláh, Gleanings from the Writings of Bahá'u'lláh, p. 277
7.13	Bahá'u'lláh, Gleanings from the Writings of Bahá'u'lláh, p. 314
7.14	Bahá'u'lláh, Epistle to the Son of the Wolf, p. 27
7.15	Bahá'u'lláh, Gleanings from the Writings of Bahá'u'lláh, p. 125
7.16	Bahá'u'lláh, Gleanings from the Writings of Bahá'u'lláh, p. 310

8.32   From a letter written on behalf of Shoghi Effendi to an individual believer, January 8, 1949. Lights of Guidance, p. 114

8.33   From a letter written by Shoghi Effendi to the believers in Australia and New Zealand, 1923-1957, pp. 1-2. Lights of Guidance, p. 135

8.34   From a letter written on behalf of Shoghi Effendi to an individual believer, April 5, 1956. Lights of Guidance, p. 603

8.35   From a letter written on behalf of the Guardian to an individual believer, February 18, 1945; Living the Life, p. 12. Lights of Guidance, p. 601

8.36   From a letter written on behalf of Shoghi Effendi to an individual believer, October 4, 1950
. Lights of Guidance, p. 403

8.37   From a letter written on behalf of Shoghi Effendi to an individual believer, April 5, 1956. Lights of Guidance, p. 603

8.38   From a letter of the Universal House of Justice to the National Spiritual Assembly of the United States, September 7, 1965. Lights of Guidance, p. 341

8.39   From a letter written on behalf of the Universal House of Justice to an individual believer, January 9, 1977. Lights of Guidance, p. 366

8.40   From a letter written on behalf of the Universal House of Justice to an individual believer, January 9, 1977. Lights of Guidance, p. 366

8.41   From a letter written on behalf of the Universal House of Justice to an individual believer, March 19, 1981. Lights of Guidance, p. 127

8.42   From a letter written on behalf of the Universal House of Justice to an individual believer, April 15, 1976. Lights of Guidance, p. 127

8.43   From a letter of the Universal House of Justice to an individual believer, excerpts from letter to all National Spiritual Assemblies, February 6, 1973. Lights of Guidance, p. 359

Chapter 9

9.1   Bahá'u'lláh, Kitáb-i-Aqdas, Pg. 65

9.2   Bahá'u'lláh, The Hidden Words, Arabic #31

9.3   Bahá'u'lláh, The Hidden Words, Arabic #32

9.4   Bahá'u'lláh, The Hidden Words, Arabic #33

9.5   Bahá'u'lláh, The Hidden Words, Arabic #35

9.6   Bahá'u'lláh, Gleanings from the Writings of Bahá'u'lláh, p. 343

9.7   Bahá'u'lláh, Gleanings from the Writings of Bahá'u'lláh, p. 161

9.8   Bahá'u'lláh, Gleanings from the Writings of Bahá'u'lláh, p. 169

9.9   Bahá'u'lláh, Gleanings from the Writings of Bahá'u'lláh, p. 156

9.10   Bahá'u'lláh, Gleanings from the Writings of Bahá'u'lláh, p. 156

9.11   Bahá'u'lláh, Gleanings from the Writings of Bahá'u'lláh, p. 156

9.12   Bahá'u'lláh, Gleanings from the Writings of Bahá'u'lláh, p. 344

9.13   Bahá'u'lláh, Prayers and Meditations by Bahá'u'lláh, p. 278

9.14   Bahá'u'lláh, Prayers and Meditations by Bahá'u'lláh, p. 278

9.15   'Abdu'l-Bahá, Selections from the Writings of 'Abdu'l-Bahá, p. 201

9.16   'Abdu'l-Bahá, Selections from the Writings of 'Abdu'l-Bahá, p. 170

9.17   'Abdu'l-Bahá, Selections from the Writings of 'Abdu'l-Bahá, p. 27

9.18   'Abdu'l-Bahá, Selections from the Writings of 'Abdu'l-Bahá p. 177

9.19   'Abdu'l-Bahá, Selections from the Writings of 'Abdu'l-Bahá, p. 184

9.20   'Abdu'l-Bahá, Selections from the Writings of 'Abdu'l-Bahá, p. 199

9.21   'Abdu'l-Bahá, Some Answered Questions, p. 228

9.22   'Abdu'l-Bahá, Paris Talks, p. 179

9.23   'Abdu'l-Bahá, Ten Days in the Light of Akka, pg. 9

9.24   From a letter written on behalf of Shoghi Effendi to an individual believer, October 22, 1932. Lights of Guidance, p. 207

9.25   From a letter written on behalf of the Guardian to an individual believer, April 2, 1955. Lights of Guidance, p. 194

9.26   From a letter written on behalf Shoghi Effendi to an individual believer, July 6, 1935. Lights of Guidance, p. 196

9.27   From a letter written on behalf of Shoghi Effendi to an individual believer, January 12, 1957. Lights of Guidance, p. 209

9.28   From a letter written on behalf of the guardian to an individual believer, November 13, 1944. Lights of Guidance, p. 97

9.29   From a letter written on behalf of Shoghi Effendi to an individual believer, December 9, 1931. Lights of Guidance, p. 203

9.30   From a letter written on behalf of Shoghi Effendi to an individual believer, December 10, 1952. Lights of Guidance, p. 204

9.31   From a letter written on behalf of Shoghi Effendi to an individual believer, December 31, 1937. Lights of Guidance, p. 204

9.32   From a letter written on behalf of the Guardian to an individual believer, May 22, 1935. Lights of Guidance, p. 204

9.33   From a letter written on behalf of Shoghi Effendi to an individual believer, January 13, 1932. Lights of Guidance, p. 207

9.34   From a letter written on behalf of Shoghi Effendi to an individual believer, December 31, 1932. Lights of Guidance, p. 207

9.35   The Universal House of Justice, Synopsis and Codification of the Kitáb-i-Aqdas, pp.62-63. Lights of Guidance, p. 194

9.36   Letter written on behalf of the Universal House of Justice to the National Spiritual Assembly of Ecuador, December 3, 1975. Lights of Guidance, p. 194

9.37   From a letter written on behalf of the Universal House of Justice to a National Spiritual Assembly, December 31, 1972. Lights of Guidance, p. 196

9.38   From a letter written on behalf of the Universal House of Justice to an individual believer, June 7, 1979. Lights of Guidance, p. 203

Chapter 10

10.1   Bahá'u'lláh, Gleanings from the Writings of Bahá'u'lláh, p. 8

10.2   Bahá'u'lláh, Gleanings from the Writings of Bahá'u'lláh, p. 205

10.3   Bahá'u'lláh, The Hidden Words, Persian #44

10.4   Bahá'u'lláh, Tablets of Bahá'u'lláh, p. 156

10.5   Bahá'u'lláh, The Hidden Words, Persian #5

10.6   Bahá'u'lláh, The Hidden Words, Arabic #46

10.7   Bahá'u'lláh, Gleanings from the Writings of Bahá'u'lláh, p. 28

10.8   Bahá'u'lláh, Tablets of Bahá'u'lláh, p. 252

10.9   Bahá'u'lláh, The Hidden Words, Persian #75

10.10   'Abdu'l-Bahá, Selections from the Writings of 'Abdu'l-Bahá, p. 10

10.11   'Abdu'l-Bahá, Selections from the Writings of 'Abdu'l-Bahá, p. 10

10.12   'Abdu'l-Bahá, Selections from the Writings of 'Abdu'l-Bahá, p. 204

10.13   'Abdu'l-Bahá, Selections from the Writings of 'Abdu'l-Bahá, p. 204

10.14   'Abdu'l-Bahá, Selections from the Writings of 'Abdu'l-Bahá, p. 233

10.15   'Abdu'l-Bahá, Selections from the Writings of 'Abdu'l-Bahá, p. 22

10.16   'Abdu'l-Bahá, Selections from the Writings of 'Abdu'l-Bahá, p. 22

10.17   'Abdu'l-Bahá, Selections from the Writings of 'Abdu'l-Bahá, p. 186

10.18   'Abdu'l-Bahá, The Compilation of Compilations vol II, p. 346

10.19   'Abdu'l-Bahá, The Promulgation of Universal Peace, p. 148

10.20   'Abdu'l-Bahá, Paris Talks, p. 122

10.21   'Abdu'l-Bahá, The Promulgation of Universal Peace, p. 24

10.22   Shoghi Effendi, The World Order of Bahá'u'lláh, p. 190

10.23   Shoghi Effendi, The Advent of Divine Justice, p. 41

10.24   The Universal House of Justice, A Wider Horizon, Selected Letters 1983-1992, p. 96

Chapter 11

11.1   Bahá'u'lláh, Gleanings from the Writings of Bahá'u'lláh, p. 215

11.2   Bahá'u'lláh, Gleanings from the Writings of Bahá'u'lláh, p. 250

11.3   Bahá'u'lláh, Gleanings from the Writings of Bahá'u'lláh, p. 342

11.4   Bahá'u'lláh, Tablets of Bahá'u'lláh, p. 172

11.5   Bahá'u'lláh, Gleanings from the Writings of Bahá'u'lláh, p. 234

11.6   Bahá'u'lláh, Gleanings from the Writings of Bahá'u'lláh, p. 335

11.7   Bahá'u'lláh, The Hidden Words, Persian #53

11.8   Bahá'u'lláh, Gleanings from the Writings of Bahá'u'lláh, p. 138

11.9	Bahá'u'lláh, Tablets of Bahá'u'lláh, p. 138
11.10	Bahá'u'lláh, Tablets of Bahá'u'lláh, p. 138
11.11	Bahá'u'lláh, Gleanings from the Writings of Bahá'u'lláh, p. 210
11.12	Bahá'u'lláh, Gleanings from the Writings of Bahá'u'lláh, p. 214
11.13	Bahá'u'lláh, Gleanings from the Writings of Bahá'u'lláh, p. 288
11.14	Bahá'u'lláh, Gleanings from the Writings of Bahá'u'lláh, p. 38
11.15	Bahá'u'lláh:, The Compilation of Compilations vol. I, p. 459
11.16	'Abdu'l-Bahá, The Secret of Divine Civilization, p. 59
11.17	'Abdu'l-Bahá, Selections from the Writings of 'Abdu'l-Bahá, p. 233
11.18	'Abdu'l-Bahá, Selections from the Writings of 'Abdu'l-Bahá, p. 116
11.19	'Abdu'l-Bahá, Selections from the Writings of 'Abdu'l-Bahá, p. 150
11.20	'Abdu'l-Bahá: Selections from the Writings of 'Abdu'l-Bahá, pp. 152-153
11.21	'Abdu'l-Bahá, Some Answered Questions, p. 188
11.22	Shoghi Effendi, The Advent of Divine Justice, p. 30
11.23	From a letter written on behalf of Shoghi Effendi to an individual believer, November 22, 1936. Lights of Guidance, p. 533
11.24	From a letter dated 5 July 1947 written on behalf of the Guardian to an individual believer The Universal House of Justice, 1999 Dec 13, Two Compilations on Scholarship - 1979 and 1983
11.25	The Universal House of Justice, Messages 1963 to 1986, p. 437
11.26	The Universal House of Justice, Messages 1963 to 1986, p. 736
11.27	The Universal House of Justice, A Wider Horizon, Selected Letters 1983-1992, p. 219

Chapter 12

12.1	Bahá'u'lláh, Gleanings from the Writings of Bahá'u'lláh, p. 330
12.2	Bahá'u'lláh, The Seven Valleys, p. 39
12.3	Bahá'u'lláh, Gleanings from the Writings of Bahá'u'lláh, p. 332
12.4	Bahá'u'lláh, Gleanings from the Writings of Bahá'u'lláh, p. 279
12.5	Bahá'u'lláh, Gleanings from the Writings of Bahá'u'lláh, p. 299
12.6	Bahá'u'lláh, Gleanings from the Writings of Bahá'u'lláh, p. 213
12.7	Bahá'u'lláh, Gleanings from the Writings of Bahá'u'lláh, p. 214
12.8	Bahá'u'lláh, Gleanings from the Writings of Bahá'u'lláh, p. 147
12.9	Bahá'u'lláh, Gleanings from the Writings of Bahá'u'lláh, p. 332
12.10	Bahá'u'lláh, The Hidden Words, Arabic #27
12.11	Bahá'u'lláh, Gleanings from the Writings of Bahá'u'lláh, p. 265
12.12	Bahá'u'lláh, Gleanings from the Writings of Bahá'u'lláh, p. 265
12.13	'Abdu'l-Bahá, Selections from the Writings of 'Abdu'l-Bahá, p. 132
12.14	'Abdu'l-Bahá, Paris Talks, p. 141
12.15	'Abdu'l-Bahá, The Promulgation of Universal Peace, p. 9
12.16	'Abdu'l-Bahá, The Promulgation of Universal Peace, p. 17
12.17	'Abdu'l-Bahá. Lights of Guidance, p. 91
12.18	'Abdu'l-Bahá. Lights of Guidance, p. 349
12.19	'Abdu'l-Bahá. Lights of Guidance, p. 91
12.20	'Abdu'l-Bahá: Daily Lessons Received at 'Akká p. 35, 1979 ed. Lights of Guidance, p. 512
12.21	Shoghi Effendi, The Advent of Divine Justice, p. 29
12.22	Shoghi Effendi, Directives from the Guardian, p. 86
12.23	From a letter written on behalf of Shoghi Effendi to an individual believer, April 19, 1941. Lights of Guidance, p. 354
12.24	From a letter written on behalf of Shoghi Effendi to an individual believer, September 5, 1938: Messages from the Universal House of Justice, 1968-1973, p. 108. Lights of Guidance, p. 344
12.25	From a letter written on behalf of the Guardian to an individual believer, May 21, 1954. . Lights of Guidance, p. 364
12.26	From a letter written on behalf of the Guardian to an individual believer, March 26, 1950. Lights of Guidance, p. 364
12.27	From a letter written on behalf of Shoghi Effendi to an individual believer, February 15, 1926: . Lights of Guidance, p. 349

1945. Lights of Guidance, p. 115

13.22   From a letter written on behalf of Shoghi Effendi to an individual believer, July 24, 1946. Lights of Guidance, p. 456

13.23   From a letter written on behalf of Shoghi Effendi to the National Spiritual Assembly of India, April 27, 1937: Dawn of a New Day, p.67. Lights of Guidance, p. 457

13.24   From a letter written on behalf of the Guardian to an individual believer, October 14, 1937. Lights of Guidance, p. 457

13.25   From a letter written on behalf of Shoghi Effendi to an individual believer, November 10, 1946. Lights of Guidance, p. 200

13.26   Letter from the Guardian to an individual believer, December 8, 1935; Bahá'í Youth, p. 10. Lights of Guidance, p. 543

13.27   From a letter written on behalf of the Universal House of Justice to an individual believer, July 23, 1984. Lights of Guidance, p. 282

13.28   The Universal House of Justice, Messages 1963 to 1986, p. 384

Chapter 14
14.1   Bahá'u'lláh, Tablets of Bahá'u'lláh, p. 143
14.2   Bahá'u'lláh, Gleanings from the Writings of Bahá'u'lláh, p. 69
14.3   Bahá'u'lláh, Gleanings from the Writings of Bahá'u'lláh, p. 185
14.4   Bahá'u'lláh, Gleanings from the Writings of Bahá'u'lláh, p. 215
14.5   Bahá'u'lláh, Epistle to the Son of the Wolf, p. 55
14.6   Bahá'u'lláh, Tablets of Bahá'u'lláh, p. 162
14.7   Bahá'u'lláh, Tablets of Bahá'u'lláh, p. 72
14.8   Bahá'u'lláh, The Kitáb-i-Iqan, p. 237
14.9   Bahá'u'lláh, The Kitáb-i-Iqan, p. 8
14.10   Bahá'u'lláh, The Kitáb-i-Iqan, p. 216
14.11   Bahá'u'lláh, The Proclamation of Bahá'u'lláh, p. 107
14.12   Bahá'u'lláh, Tablets of Bahá'u'lláh, p. 143
14.13   Bahá'u'lláh: Tablets of Bahá'u'lláh, p. 200
14.14   Bahá'u'lláh, Gleanings from the Writings of Bahá'u'lláh, p. 149
14.15   Bahá'u'lláh, Prayers and Meditations by Bahá'u'lláh, p. 197
14.16   'Abdu'l-Bahá, Selections from the Writings of 'Abdu'l-Bahá, p. 240
14.17   'Abdu'l-Bahá, Paris Talks, p. 174
14.18   From a letter written of behalf of Shoghi Effendi to an individual believer, November 19, 1945. Lights of Guidance, p. 456
14.19   From a letter written on behalf of Shoghi Effendi to an individual believer, January 25, 1943: Spiritual Foundations: Prayer, Meditation, and the Devotional Attitude. Lights of Guidance, p. 455
14.20   From a letter written on behalf of Shoghi Effendi to an individual believer, January 19, 1942Lights of Guidance, p. 208
14.21   From a letter written of behalf of Shoghi Effendi to an individual believer, May 15, 1944: . Lights of Guidance, p. 456
14.22   From a letter written on behalf of the Universal House of Justice to a National Spiritual Assembly, September 1, 1983. Lights of Guidance, p. 540
14.23   From a letter written on behalf of the Universal House of Justice to an individual believer, June 7, 1974 . Lights of Guidance, p. 456

Chapter 15
15.1   Bahá'u'lláh, The Importance of Obligatory Prayer and Fasting
15.2   Bahá'u'lláh, The Importance of Obligatory Prayer and Fasting
15.3   Bahá'u'lláh, The Importance of Obligatory Prayer and Fasting
15.4   Bahá'u'lláh, The Importance of Obligatory Prayer and Fasting
15.5   Bahá'u'lláh, The Importance of Obligatory Prayer and Fasting
15.6   Bahá'u'lláh, The Importance of Obligatory Prayer and Fasting
15.7   Bahá'u'lláh, The Importance of Obligatory Prayer and Fasting
15.8   Bahá'u'lláh, The Importance of Obligatory Prayer and Fasting
15.9   Bahá'u'lláh, The Importance of Obligatory Prayer and Fasting
15.10   Bahá'u'lláh, The Importance of Obligatory Prayer and Fasting

17.8   'Abdu'l-Bahá, Selections from the Writings of 'Abdu'l-Bahá, p. 219
17.9   'Abdu'l-Bahá, Some Answered Questions, p. 65
17.10   'Abdu'l-Bahá, The Promulgation of Universal Peace, p. 27
17.11   Shoghi Effendi, God Passes By, p. 183
17.12   Shoghi Effendi, Citadel of Faith, p. 95
17.13   Shoghi Effendi, God Passes By, p. 257
17.14   The Universal House of Justice, Messages from the Universal House of Justice 1968-1973, p. 23
17.15   The Universal House of Justice, 2001 May 24, To Believers Gathered for Terrace Events, p. 1
17.16   Bahá'í World Center, Notes on The Kitáb-i-Aqdas, p. 191
17.17   Bahá'í World Center, Notes on The Kitáb-i-Aqdas, p. 191
17.18   Isaiah 35:2, KJV

Chapter 18
18.1   Bahá'u'lláh, The Kitáb-i-Aqdas, p. 41
18.2   Bahá'u'lláh, The Kitáb-i-Aqdas, p. 74
18.3   Bahá'u'lláh, The Kitáb-i-Aqdas, p. 43
18.4   Bahá'u'lláh. Lights of Guidance, p. 228
18.5   Bahá'u'lláh, The Kitáb-i-Aqdas, p. 37
18.6   'Abdu'l-Bahá, Selections from the Writings of 'Abdu'l-Bahá, p. 120
18.7   'Abdu'l-Bahá, Selections from the Writings of 'Abdu'l-Bahá, p. 118
18.8   'Abdu'l-Bahá, Selections from the Writings of 'Abdu'l-Bahá, p. 278
18.9   'Abdu'l-Bahá, Selections from the Writings of 'Abdu'l-Bahá, p. 118
18.10   'Abdu'l-Bahá, The Secret of Divine Civilization, p. 115
18.11   'Abdu'l-Bahá, Selections from the Writings of 'Abdu'l-Bahá, p. 142
18.12   'Abdu'l-Bahá, Selections from the Writings of 'Abdu'l-Bahá, p. 127
18.13   'Abdu'l-Bahá, Selections from the Writings of 'Abdu'l-Bahá, p. 122
18.14   'Abdu'l-Bahá, Selections from the Writings of 'Abdu'l-Bahá, p. 134
18.15   'Abdu'l-Bahá, Selections from the Writings of 'Abdu'l-Bahá, p. 159
18.16   'Abdu'l-Bahá, Selections from the Writings of 'Abdu'l-Bahá, p. 136
18.17   'Abdu'l-Bahá, Selections from the Writings of 'Abdu'l-Bahá, p. 139
18.18   'Abdu'l-Bahá, Selections from the Writings of 'Abdu'l-Bahá, p. 126
18.19   'Abdu'l-Bahá, Selections from the Writings of 'Abdu'l-Bahá, p. 124
18.20   'Abdu'l-Bahá, Selections from the Writings of 'Abdu'l-Bahá, p. 123
18.21   'Abdu'l-Bahá, The Compilation of Compilations vol II, p. 443
18.22   'Abdu'l-Bahá. Lights of Guidance, p. 219
18.23   'Abdu'l-Bahá, Bahá'í Prayers, p. 34
18.24   'Abdu'l-Bahá. Lights of Guidance, p. 146
18.25   Talks of 'Abdu'l-Bahá. Lights of Guidance, p. 146
18.26   'Abdu'l-Bahá. Lights of Guidance, p. 152
18.27   Shoghi Effendi, The Light of Divine Guidance v II, p. 69
18.28   From a letter written on behalf of the Guardian to an individual believer, December 19, 1947. Lights of Guidance, p. 392
18.29   From a letter written on behalf of the Guardian to an individual believer, April 5, 1952: Extracts from the Bahá'í Teachings Discouraging Divorce, pp. 5-6. Lights of Guidance, p. 392
18.30   From a letter written on behalf of the Guardian to an individual believer, April 17, 1947. Lights of Guidance, p. 393
18.31   From a letter written on behalf of the Guardian to an individual believer in India, November 16, 1939: Dawn of a New Day, p. 202. Lights of Guidance, p. 148
18.32   From a letter written on behalf of Shoghi Effendi to an individual believer, June 20, 1931. Lights of Guidance, p. 140
18.33   From a letter written on behalf of Shoghi Effendi to the Bahá'í children of Kenosha, Wisconsin, December 28, 1956. Lights of Guidance, p. 156
18.34   The Universal House of Justice, Messages 1963 to 1986, p. 550
18.35   From letter of the Universal House of Justice December 28, 1980 to the National Spiritual Assembly of New Zealand. Lights of Guidance, p. 219

20.5	Bahá'u'lláh, Gleanings from the Writings of Bahá'u'lláh, p. 143
20.6	Bahá'u'lláh, Gleanings from the Writings of Bahá'u'lláh, p. 176
20.7	Bahá'u'lláh, Gleanings from the Writings of Bahá'u'lláh, p. 266
20.8	Bahá'u'lláh, Gleanings from the Writings of Bahá'u'lláh, p. 266
20.9	Bahá'u'lláh, Gleanings from the Writings of Bahá'u'lláh, p. 290
20.10	Bahá'u'lláh, Gleanings from the Writings of Bahá'u'lláh, p. 326
20.11	Bahá'u'lláh, The Hidden Words, Persian #12
20.12	Bahá'u'lláh, The Hidden Words, Persian #33
20.13	Bahá'u'lláh, The Hidden Words, Persian #34
20.14	Bahá'u'lláh, Gleanings from the Writings of Bahá'u'lláh, p. 316
20.15	Bahá'u'lláh, Gleanings from the Writings of Bahá'u'lláh, p. 97
20.16	Bahá'u'lláh, Gleanings from the Writings of Bahá'u'lláh, p. 175
20.17	'Abdu'l-Bahá, Selections from the Writings of 'Abdu'l-Bahá, p. 186
20.18	'Abdu'l-Bahá, The Secret of Divine Civilization", pp. 109-110
20.19	'Abdu'l-Bahá, The Secret of Divine Civilization, p. 3
20.20	'Abdu'l-Bahá, The Secret of Divine Civilization, p. 18
20.21	'Abdu'l-Bahá, Selections from the Writings of 'Abdu'l-Bahá, p. 36
20.22	'Abdu'l-Bahá, Selections from the Writings of 'Abdu'l-Bahá, p. 294
20.23	'Abdu'l-Bahá, The Promulgation of Universal Peace, p. 154
20.24	'Abdu'l-Bahá, The Promulgation of Universal Peace, p. 460
20.25	'Abdu'l-Bahá, Paris Talks, p. 165
20.26	From a letter written on behalf of the Guardian to an individual believer, March 13, 1932: Lights of Guidance, p. 566
20.27	From a letter written on behalf of the Guardian to the Spiritual Assembly of Eliot, Maine, March 27, 1933 Lights of Guidance, p. 584
20.28	The Universal House of Justice, A Wider Horizon, Selected Letters 1983-1992, p. 142
20.29	From a letter of the Universal House of Justice to an individual believer October 17, 1968: Lights of Guidance, p. 359
20.30	From the Message of the Universal House of Justice to the Bahá'ís of the World, Ridvan 1967: Wellspring of Guidance, pp. 114-115
20.31	From a letter of the Universal House of Justice to an individual believer, May 27, 1966. Lights of Guidance, p. 311

Chapter 21

21.1	Bahá'u'lláh, Gleanings from the Writings of Bahá'u'lláh, p. 288
21.2	Bahá'u'lláh, Gleanings from the Writings of Bahá'u'lláh, p. 277
21.3	Bahá'u'lláh, The Individual and Teaching - Raising the Divine Call
21.4	Bahá'u'lláh, Gleanings from the Writings of Bahá'u'lláh, p. 278
21.5	Bahá'u'lláh, Gleanings from the Writings of Bahá'u'lláh, p. 278
21.6	Bahá'u'lláh, Gleanings from the Writings of Bahá'u'lláh, p. 278
21.7	Bahá'u'lláh, Tablets of Bahá'u'lláh, p. 143
21.8	Bahá'u'lláh, Gleanings from the Writings of Bahá'u'lláh, p. 139
21.9	Bahá'u'lláh, The Hidden Words, Persian #76
21.10	Bahá'u'lláh, The Advent of Divine Justice, p. 20
21.11	Bahá'u'lláh, Tablets of Bahá'u'lláh, p. 200
21.12	Bahá'u'lláh, Gleanings from the Writings of Bahá'u'lláh, p. 277
21.13	Abdu'l-Bahá, Selections from the Writings of 'Abdu'l-Bahá, p. 175
21.14	'Abdu'l-Bahá, Selections from the Writings of 'Abdu'l-Bahá, p. 22
21.15	'Abdu'l-Bahá, Selections from the Writings of 'Abdu'l-Bahá, p. 264
21.16	'Abdu'l-Bahá, Selections from the Writings of 'Abdu'l-Bahá, p. 268
21.17	'Abdu'l-Bahá, The Individual and Teaching - Raising the Divine Call, p. 11
21.18	'Abdu'l-Bahá, The Individual and Teaching - Raising the Divine Call, p. 10
21.19	'Abdu'l-Bahá , The Individual and Teaching - Raising the Divine Call, p. 10
21.20	'Abdu'l-Bahá, The Individual and Teaching - Raising the Divine Call, p. 11
21.21	'Abdu'l-Bahá, The Individual and Teaching - Raising the Divine Call, p. 12
21.22	'Abdu'l-Bahá, The Individual and Teaching - Raising the Divine Call, p. 9
21.23	'Abdu'l-Bahá, The Individual and Teaching - Raising the Divine Call, p. 8
21.24	Shoghi Effendi: Advent of Divine Justice, p. 52

22.18   'Abdu'l-Bahá, The Promulgation of Universal Peace, p. 11
22.19   'Abdu'l-Bahá, The Promulgation of Universal Peace, p. 143
22.20   Shoghi Effendi, The Promised Day is Come, p. 17
22.21   Shoghi Effendi, The World Order of Bahá'u'lláh, p. 202
22.22   Shoghi Effendi, The World Order of Bahá'u'lláh, p. 48
22.23   Shoghi Effendi: Dawn of a New Day, p. 200
22.24   From a letter written on behalf of Shoghi Effendi to an individual believer, March 19,
         1945. Lights of Guidance, p. 542
22.25   From a letter written on behalf of the Guardian to an individual believer, April 16,
         1950: Living the Life, p. 16 Compilations. Lights of Guidance, p. 77
22.26   From a letter written on behalf of the Guardian to an individual believer, November
         14, 1935. Lights of Guidance, p. 473
22.27   The Universal House of Justice, A Wider Horizon, Selected Letters 1983-1992, p. 37
22.28   The Universal House of Justice, A Wider Horizon, Selected Letters 1983-1992, p. 148
22.29   The Universal House of Justice, , A Wider Horizon, Messages 1963 to 1986, p. 27

Chapter 23
23.1   Bahá'u'lláh, Gleanings from the Writings of Bahá'u'lláh, p. 315
23.2   Bahá'u'lláh, Gleanings from the Writings of Bahá'u'lláh, p. 270
23.3   Bahá'u'lláh, The Hidden Words, Persian #56
23.4   Baha'u'llah, The Kitab-i-Iqan, p. 193
23.5   Baha'u'llah, The Hidden Words, Arabic #27
23.6   'Abdu'l-Bahá, Selections from the Writings of 'Abdu'l-Bahá, p. 80
23.7   'Abdu'l-Bahá, Tablets of the Divine Plan, p. 56
23.8   'Abdu'l-Bahá, Selections from the Writings of 'Abdu'l-Bahá, p. 291
23.9   'Abdu'l-Bahá, Selections from the Writings of 'Abdu'l-Bahá, p. 243
23.10   'Abdu'l-Bahá, Selections from the Writings of 'Abdu'l-Bahá, p. 112
23.11   Abdu'l-Baha, Selections from the Writings of Abdu'l-Baha, p. 231
23.12   'Abdu'l-Bahá, Bahá'u'lláh and the New Era, p. 82
23.13   'Abdu'l-Bahá, The Promulgation of Universal Peace, p. 286
23.14   'Abdu'l-Bahá, The Promulgation of Universal Peace, p. 452
23.15   Shoghi Effendi: Messages to America, p. 14
23.16   From a letter written on behalf of the Universal House of Justice to an individual
         believer, September 23, 1975. Lights of Guidance, p. 91
23.17   Message from the Universal House of Justice to the Bahá'ís of the World, September,
         1964: Wellsprings of Guidance, pp. 37-38. Lights of Guidance, p. 79

Chapter 24
24.1   Bahá'u'lláh, Gleanings from the Writings of Bahá'u'lláh, p. 7
24.2   Baha'u'llah, The Kitab-i-Aqdas, p. 29
24.3   Bahá'u'lláh, Gleanings from the Writings of Bahá'u'lláh, p. 215
24.4   Bahá'u'lláh, Tablets of Bahá'u'lláh, p. 221
24.5   Bahá'u'lláh, Tablets of Bahá'u'lláh, p. 138
24.6   Bahá'u'lláh, The Kitáb-i-Aqdas, p. 91
24.7   Bahá'u'lláh, The Kitáb-i-Aqdas, p. 54
24.8   Bahá'u'lláh, Gleanings from the Writings of Bahá'u'lláh, p. 128
24.9   'Abdu'l-Bahá, The Secret of Divine Civilization, p. 33
24.10   'Abdu'l-Bahá, The Secret of Divine Civilization, p. 33
24.11   'Abdu'l-Bahá, The Promulgation of Universal Peace, p. 455
24.12   'Abdu'l-Bahá. Lights of Guidance, p. 612
24.13   'Abdu'l-Bahá. Lights of Guidance, p. 316
24.14   Shoghi Effendi, The World Order of Bahá'u'lláh, p. 198
24.15   Shoghi Effendi, Summary Statement - 1947, Special UN Committee on Palestine
24.16   Letter from the Guardian to the friends in Persia, January 30, 1923: . Lights of
         Guidance, p. 11
24.17   Letter written on behalf of the Guardian to individual believer. . Lights of Guidance, p.
         423
24.18   From a letter written on behalf of Shoghi Effendi to the National Spiritual Assembly

of the United States and Canada, May 27, 1927: Bahá'í Administration, p. 136

24.19   From a letter written on behalf of Shoghi Effendi to an individual believer, June 7, 1924. Lights of Guidance, p. 11

24.20   Shoghi Effendi, Principles of Baha'i Administration, p. 66

24.21   The Universal House of Justice, 1995 Dec 02, Email Discussion Group Concerns

24.22   From a letter of the Universal House of Justice to all National Spiritual Assemblies, March 3, 1977. Lights of Guidance, p. 4

24.23   From a letter written on behalf of the Universal House of Justice to the National Spiritual Assembly of Brazil, April 13, 1983. Lights of Guidance, p. 4

24.24   From a letter written on behalf of the Universal House of Justice to the National Spiritual Assembly of Italy, November 19, 1974. Lights of Guidance, p. 122

Chapter 25

25.1   Bahá'u'lláh, Tablets of Bahá'u'lláh, p. 168

25.2   Bahá'u'lláh: Consultation: Compiled by the Research Department of the Universal House of Justice

25.3   Bahá'u'lláh: Consultation: Compiled by the Research Department of the Universal House of Justice

25.4   Bahá'u'lláh: Consultation: Compiled by the Research Department of the Universal House of Justice

25.5   Bahá'u'lláh: Consultation: Compiled by the Research Department of the Universal House of Justice

25.6   'Abdu'l-Bahá, Selections from the Writings of 'Abdu'l-Bahá, p. 31

25.7   'Abdu'l-Bahá, Selections from the Writings of 'Abdu'l-Bahá, p. 87

25.8   'Abdu'l-Bahá, The Compilation of Compilations vol II, p. 54

25.9   'Abdu'l-Bahá, The Compilation of Compilations vol. I, p. 94

25.10   'Abdu'l-Bahá, The Compilation of Compilations vol. I, p. 94

25.11   'Abdu'l-Bahá, The Promulgation of Universal Peace, p. 183

25.12   'Abdu'l-Bahá, The Promulgation of Universal Peace, p. 72

25.13   'Abdu'l-Bahá, Paris Talks, p. 99

25.14   'Abdu'l-Bahá. Lights of Guidance, p. 178

25.15   'Abdu'l-Bahá. Lights of Guidance, p. 228

25.16   'Abdu'l-Bahá. Lights of Guidance, p. 176

25.17   Shoghi Effendi, Bahá'í Administration, pp. 63-64

25.18   From a letter dated 23 February 1924 written by Shoghi Effendi to the Bahá'ís of America, The Compilation of Compilations vol II, p. 107

25.19   From a letter of the Universal House of Justice to the Bahá'ís of the World, October 20, 1983. Lights of Guidance, p. 544

25.20   Letter from the Universal House of Justice, dated August 26, 1965, to a National Spiritual Assembly. Lights of Guidance, p. 179

Chapter 26

26.1   Bahá'u'lláh, Epistle to the Son of the Wolf, p. 70

26.2   Baha'u'llah, Gleanings from the Writings of Baha'u'llah, p. 99

26.3   Baha'u'llah, Gleanings from the Writings of Baha'u'llah, p. 252

26.4   Bahá'u'lláh, Epistle to the Son of the Wolf, p. 86

26.5   Baha'u'llah, The Kitab-i-Iqan, p. 221

26.6   Baha'u'llah, The Kitab-i-Iqan, p. 224

26.7   Bahá'u'lláh, Prayers and Meditations by Bahá'u'lláh, p. 22

26.8   Bahá'u'lláh, Gleanings from the Writings of Bahá'u'lláh, p. 182

26.9   Baha'u'llah, Gleanings from the Writings of Baha'u'llah, p. 208

26.10   'Abdu'l-Bahá, Selections from the Writings of 'Abdu'l-Bahá, p. 262

26.11   'Abdu'l-Bahá, Selections from the Writings of 'Abdu'l-Bahá, p. 310

26.12   'Abdu'l-Bahá, Selections from the Writings of 'Abdu'l-Bahá, p. 248

26.13   'Abdu'l-Bahá, The Promulgation of Universal Peace, p. 6

26.14   'Abdu'l-Bahá, The Promulgation of Universal Peace, p. 222

26.15   'Abdu'l-Bahá, The Promulgation of Universal Peace, p. 124

26.16   Shoghi Effendi, Summary Statement - 1947, Special UN Committee on Palestine

26.17   Shoghi Effendi, God Passes By, p. 100
26.18   Shoghi Effendi, God Passes By, p. 106
26.19   The Universal House of Justice, 1992 May 29, Centenary Tribute to Bahá'u'lláh, p. 3

Chapter 27
27.1   Bahá'u'lláh, Tablets of Bahá'u'lláh, p. 86
27.2   Bahá'u'lláh, Gleanings from the Writings of Bahá'u'lláh, p. 249
27.3   Bahá'u'lláh, Tablets of Bahá'u'lláh, p. 67
27.4   Baha'u'llah, Gleanings from the Writings of Baha'u'llah, p. 218
27.5   'Abdu'l-Bahá, Selections from the Writings of 'Abdu'l-Bahá, p. 52
27.6   'Abdu'l-Bahá, The World Order of Bahá'u'lláh, p. 204
27.7   'Abdu'l-Bahá, The Promulgation of Universal Peace, p. 108
27.8   'Abdu'l-Bahá, The Promulgation of Universal Peace, p. 468
27.9   'Abdu'l-Bahá, The Promulgation of Universal Peace, p. 19
27.10   'Abdu'l-Bahá, The Promulgation of Universal Peace, p. 469
27.11   'Abdu'l-Bahá, The Promulgation of Universal Peace, p. 19
27.12   'Abdu'l-Bahá, The Promulgation of Universal Peace, p. 440
27.13   'Abdu'l-Bahá, The Promulgation of Universal Peace, p. 287
27.14   Shoghi Effendi, The World Order of Bahá'u'lláh, p. 205
27.15   Shoghi Effendi, The World Order of Bahá'u'lláh, p. 205
27.16   The Universal House of Justice, 1985 Oct, The Promise of World Peace, p. 3
27.17   Bahá'í International Community in a concept paper shared at the 1st session of the
         United Nations Commission on Sustainable Development, New York, U.S.A. on
         14-25 June 1993

Chapter 28
28.1   Bahá'u'lláh, Tablets of Bahá'u'lláh, p. 78
28.2   Bahá'u'lláh, The Hidden Words, Persian #33
28.3   Bahá'u'lláh, The Kitáb-i-Iqan, p. 195
28.4   Bahá'u'lláh, Gleanings from the Writings of Bahá'u'lláh, p. 176
28.5   Bahá'u'lláh, Gleanings from the Writings of Bahá'u'lláh, p. 159
28.6   Bahá'u'lláh, The Hidden Words, Persian #3
28.7   Bahá'u'lláh, The Hidden Words, Persian #56
28.8   Bahá'u'lláh, The Hidden Words, Persian #22
28.9   Bahá'u'lláh, The Hidden Words, Arabic #20
28.10   Bahá'u'lláh, Tablets of Bahá'u'lláh, p. 57
28.11   Bahá'u'lláh, Tablets of Bahá'u'lláh, p. 259
28.12   Bahá'u'lláh, The Kitáb-i-Iqan, p. 60
28.13   Bahá'u'lláh, The Kitáb-i-Iqan, p. 195
28.14   Baha'u'llah, The Kitab-i-Iqan, p. 49
28.15   Bahá'u'lláh, Tablets of Bahá'u'lláh, p. 156
28.16   Bahá'u'lláh, Gleanings from the Writings of Bahá'u'lláh, p. 10
28.17   Bahá'u'lláh, Gleanings from the Writings of Bahá'u'lláh, p. 303
28.18   Baha'u'llah, Gleanings from the Writings of Baha'u'llah, p. 11
28.19   Bahá'u'lláh, Gleanings from the Writings of Baha'u'llah, p. 142
28.20   'Abdu'l-Bahá, Selections from the Writings of 'Abdu'l-Bahá, p. 266
28.21   'Abdu'l-Bahá, Selections from the Writings of 'Abdu'l-Bahá, p. 209
28.22   'Abdu'l-Bahá, Selections from the Writings of 'Abdu'l-Bahá, p. 214
28.23   'Abdu'l-Bahá, Paris Talks, p. 100
28.24   'Abdu'l-Bahá, Paris Talks, p. 145
28.25   'Abdu'l-Bahá, Paris Talks, p. 145
28.26   'Abdu'l-Bahá, Paris Talks, p. 97
28.27   Shoghi Effendi, The Promised Day is Come, p. v
28.28   From a letter written on behalf of Shoghi Effendi to an individual believer, February
         18, 1954. Lights of Guidance, p. 114
28.29   The Universal House of Justice, A Wider Horizon, Selected Letters 1983-1992, p. 200
28.30   The Universal House of Justice, A Wider Horizon, Selected Letters 1983-1992, p. 202

Chapter 29
29.1   Bahá'u'lláh, Gleanings from the Writings of Bahá'u'lláh, p. 284
29.2   Bahá'u'lláh, Gleanings from the Writings of Bahá'u'lláh, p. 196
29.3   Bahá'u'lláh, Gleanings from the Writings of Bahá'u'lláh, p. 8
29.4   Bahá'u'lláh, The Hidden Words, Arabic #67
29.5   Bahá'u'lláh, Gleanings from the Writings of Bahá'u'lláh, p. 158
29.6   'Abdu'l-Bahá, Selections from the Writings of 'Abdu'l-Bahá, p. 77
29.7   'Abdu'l-Bahá, Selections from the Writings of 'Abdu'l-Bahá, p. 12
29.8   'Abdu'l-Bahá, Selections from the Writings of 'Abdu'l-Bahá, p. 220
29.9   'Abdu'l-Bahá, Selections from the Writings of 'Abdu'l-Bahá, p. 266
29.10   'Abdu'l-Bahá, The Promulgation of Universal Peace, p. 210
29.11   'Abdu'l-Bahá, The Promulgation of Universal Peace, p. 458
29.12   'Abdu'l-Bahá, 'Abdu'l-Bahá in London, p. 87

BIBLIOGRAPHY

Bahá'u'lláh. *The Seven Valleys*. Wilmette, Illinois, Bahá'í Publishing Trust: 1986 Edition
Bahá'u'lláh. *The Kitáb-i-Iqan*. Wilmette, Illinois, Bahá'í Publishing Trust: 1983 Edition
Bahá'u'lláh. *The Hidden Words*. Wilmette, Illinois, Bahá'í Publishing Trust: 2002 Edition
Bahá'u'lláh. *Tablets of Bahá'u'lláh*. Wilmette, Illinois: Bahá'í Publishing Trust,1983 Edition
Bahá'u'lláh. *Gleanings from the Writings of Bahá'u'lláh*. Wilmette, Illinois: Bahá'í Publishing Trust,1983
     Edition
Bahá'u'lláh. *Prayers and Meditations by Bahá'u'lláh*. Wilmette, Illinois, Bahá'í Publishing Trust: 1987
     Edition
Bahá'u'lláh. *The Proclamation of Bahá'u'lláh*. Wilmette, Illinois: Bahá'í Publishing Trust,1967 Edition
Bahá'u'lláh, *Epistle to the Son of the Wolf*. Wilmette, Illinois: Bahá'í Publishing Trust, 1988 Edition
Bahá'u'lláh. *The Kitab-i-Aqdas*. Wilmette, Illinois: Bahá'í Publishing Trust, 1992 Edition
Bahá'u'lláh. *The Summons of the Lord of Hosts*. Haifa, Bahá'í World Centre, 2002 Edition

'Abdu'l-Bahá. *Selections from the Writings of 'Abdu'l-Bahá*. Haifa: Bahá'í World Centre, 1982 Edition
'Abdu'l-Bahá. *Tablets of the Divine Plan*. Wilmette, Illinois: Bahá'í Publishing Trust, 1993 Edition
'Abdu'l-Bahá. *The Promulgation of Universal Peace*. Wilmette, Illinois: Bahá'í Publishing Trust, 1982
     Edition
'Abdu'l-Bahá. *Some Answered Questions*. Wilmette, Illinois: Bahá'í Publishing Trust, 1987 Edition
'Abdu'l-Bahá. *Paris Talks*. London: Bahá'í Publishing Trust, 1995
'Abdu'l-Bahá. *'Abdu'l-Bahá in London*. London: Bahá'í Publishing Trust, 1983
'Abdu'l-Bahá. *Secret of Divine Civilization*. London: Bahá'í Publishing Trust, 2007
'Abdu'l-Bahá. *Foundations of World Unity*. Wilmette, Illinois: Bahá'í Publishing Trust, 1968 Edition

Shoghi Effendi. *The Promised Day is Come*. Wilmette, Illinois: Bahá'í Publishing Trust, 1996 Edition
Shoghi Effendi. *The Advent of Divine Justice*. Wilmette, Illinois: Bahá'í Publishing Trust, 2003
     Edition
Shoghi Effendi. *The World Order of Bahá'u'lláh*. Wilmette, Illinois: Bahá'í Publishing Trust, 1993
     Edition
Shoghi Effendi. *Citadel of Faith*. Wilmette, Illinois: Bahá'í Publishing Trust, 2000 Edition
Shoghi Effendi. *God Passes By*. Wilmette, Illinois: Bahá'í Publishing Trust, 1974 Edition
Shoghi Effendi. *Dawn of a New Day*. New Delhi. Bahá'í Publishing Trust, 1974 Edition
Shoghi Effendi. *Directives from the Guardian,* New Delhi. Bahá'í Publishing Trust, 1955 Edition
Shoghi Effendi. *Summary Statement - 1947, Special UN Committee on Palestine*. Haifa, Bahá'í World Centre
Shoghi Effendi, *The Light of Divine Guidance*, Baha'i-Verlag Deutschland (Baha'i Publishing Trust
     Germany, 1985
Shoghi Effendi, *Baha'i Administration: Selected Messages 1922 - 1932*, Wilmette, Illinois: Bahá'í Publishing

Trust, 2000 Edition

The Universal House of Justice, *Wellspring of Guidance, Messages 1963 to 1986*. Wilmette, Illinois: Bahá'í
    Publishing Trust, 1970 Edition
The Universal House of Justice, *Ridvan 153, 1996 - Africa*
The Universal House of Justice, 1998 Feb 08, *Materialistic Elements in Academic Scholarship*
The Universal House of Justice, 1999 Dec 13, *Two Compilations on Scholarship - 1979 and 1983*
The Universal House of Justice, 1995 Dec 02, *Email Discussion Group Concerns*
The Universal House of Justice, 2001 May 24, *To Believers Gathered for Terrace Events*
The Universal House of Justice, *One Common Faith,* Haifa. 2005
The Universal House of Justice, 1992 May 29, *Centenary Tribute to Bahá'u'lláh*

The Compilation of Compilations vol. I & vol II. Prepared by the Research Department of the Universal
    House of Justice. Maryborough, Victoria: Bahá'í Publications Australia, 1991
Fire and Light. Prepared by the Research Department of the Universal House of Justice. Haifa
Lights of Guidance. Compiled by Helen Hornby. New Delhi. Bahá'í Publishing Trust, 1994 Edition
Consultation: Compiled by the Research Department of the Universal House of Justice
The Importance of Obligatory Prayer and Fasting, Compiled by the Research Department of the
    Universal House of Justice: Haifa, 2000
The Individual and Teaching - Raising the Divine Call, Compiled by the Research Department of the
    Universal House of Justice: Haifa, 1977
Bahá'í Prayers, Wilmette, Illinois: Bahá'í Publishing Trust, 1991 Edition

Julia M. Grundy. *Ten Days in the Light of 'Akká*. Wilmette, Illinois: Bahá'í Publishing Trust, 1979
    Edition

J.E. Esslemont, *Bahá'u'lláh and the New Era*, Wilmette, Illinois: Bahá'í Publishing Trust, 1980 Edition

WhyUnite?

because your journey matters to the world.

We hope you have enjoyed this WhyUnite? book. We are committed to providing quality introductory materials for the Bahá'í Faith across all mediums. To learn more about our products, find recommendations for further reading, and connect with more Bahá'ís, please visit: http://www.whyunite.com

www.ingramcontent.com/pod-product-compliance
Lightning Source LLC
Chambersburg PA
CBHW020846090426
42736CB00008B/251